Political and Social Economy Series
Edited by C. Addison Hickman and Michael P. Shields

Daniel R. Fusfeld
Timothy Bates

The
Political Economy
of the
Urban Ghetto

Southern Illinois University Press
Carbondale and Edwardsville

Library of Congress Cataloging in Publication Data

Fusfeld, Daniel Roland, 1922–
    The political economy of the urban ghetto.

    (Political and social economy series)
    Includes index.
    1. Afro-Americans—Economic conditions. 2. Afro-
Americans—Segregation. 3. Afro-Americans—Employment—
History—20th century. 4. Cities and towns—
United States—History—20th century. 5. United States—
Economic conditions. 6. United States—Race relations.
I. Bates, Timothy Mason. II. Title. III. Series.
E185.8.F87 1984   330.973′00899607301732   83-20424
ISBN 0-8093-1157-7
ISBN 0-8093-1158-5 (pbk.)

87 86 85 84   4 3 2 1

    Portions of this material, now revised and updated, originally
    appeared in *The Basic Economics of the Urban Racial Crisis*
    (New York: Holt, Rinehart & Winston, 1973).

Contents

Tables

Figures

xi

Preview: What This Book
Is About

THERE IS SOMETHING TERRIBLY WRONG IN THE WAY AMERICAN society deals with the interrelated problems of race and poverty. An affluent society that professes to believe in the inherent equality of all has created an underclass excluded from the mainstream of American life. Public policies ostensibly addressed to this problem serve largely to perpetuate and even to extend it, treating symptoms rather than causes and diverting attention to peripheral rather than central issues.

One reason for this state of affairs is that affluent America needs and benefits from the excluded underclass. Urban racial ghettos provide a source of low-wage labor, and the steady drain of income and resources out of the ghettos provides economic benefits to specific groups in affluent America. This relationship is sustained by a flow of income from the government into the urban ghettos, financed by the average taxpayer.

These economic relationships are the product of a complex pattern of historical development and change in which black–white economic relationships play a major part, along with patterns of industrial, agricultural, and technological change and urban development. Today's urban racial ghettos are the result of the same forces that created modern America, and one of the byproducts of American affluence is a ghettoized racial underclass.

These two themes—the economic basis of the urban ghetto and its roots in the forces out of which modern America emerged—are essential for an understanding of the problem and for the formulation of policy. Racism is more than a psychological problem of whites; it has roots in white–black economic relationships. Poverty is not simply the result of poor education, skills, and work habits of the poor. It is one outcome of the structure and functioning of the economy. Solutions require more than policies that seek to change people: they await the recognition that basic economic relationships need to be changed. That is what this book is about.

Chapter 1 sets the stage by examining some of the characteristics of American cities, with emphasis on changes that take place as the economic base of urban areas develops and shifts, and on the underlying sources of conflict—racial, cultural, and economic. These themes are developed further in the next five chapters, which examine the development of the black racial ghetto. Chapter 2 looks at the economic roots of urban racial segregation and discrimination to the 1920s. Segregation in the labor market was paralleled by the emergence of black racial ghettos, which is examined in chapter 3. Chapter 4 deals with the disastrous effects of the Great Depression on black urban life, and chapter 5 with advances made during World War II. Two economic factors that had profound effects on the urban racial ghettos, the collapse of traditional southern agriculture and the relationship between organized labor and black workers, are dealt with in chapters 6 and 7, respectively.

These chapters on the historical background are followed by two that document the current situation. Chapter 8 examines recent changes in urban areas in the United States, particularly the contrast between the cities that grew up around the great manufacturing industries of the "snowbelt," and those that developed in recent decades around the high technology and information processing industries of the "sunbelt." Chapter 9 traces the changes in black economic well-being during this period of change in the urban context. One of its important points is that increased opportunities for blacks in the primary sector of the labor market have not significantly improved the plight of ghettoized blacks in the secondary sector.

The next three chapters present a theoretic analysis of the urban ghettos: its economic dynamics in chapter 10, the pattern of work and wages in chapter 11, and labor market discrimination and job competition in chapter 12. In these chapters, the urban racial ghetto is seen as an exploited subsystem within a larger economy—its chief function is to supply low-wage labor to the more affluent, progressive sector. It is kept poor by an economic process that continuously drains resources from the ghetto. It is sustained by a constant flow of government transfer payments into the ghetto. Chapter 13 examines the most important of those transfer payments, the welfare system, in more detail. Chapter 14 discusses ghetto business enterprises.

Conclusions are presented in chapter 15. Most public policies serve to sustain the existing relationships between the ghetto and the larger economy in which it functions, treating symptoms rather than causes. One possible way out of the present impasse is for the blacks and Hispanics of the ghettos to build an economic base for political power which could then be used to build a stronger and more independent pattern of economic development. Some policy suggestions along these lines are presented. Such a program will inevitably conflict with the powerful economic interests that benefit from the status quo, however. Another possible solution may come through traumatic changes in the larger society that fundamentally transform the relationships between the ghetto and the surrounding economy—revolutionary changes during a time of troubles. In any case, change will not come easily or without conflict.

The two authors are jointly responsible for the entire book. Nevertheless, primary responsibility for individual chapters was divided. Chapters 1, 10 through 13, and 15 were written largely by Fusfeld with suggestions and modifications by Bates, who was primarily responsible for chapters 2 through 9 and 14, with modifications and suggestions by Fusfeld. Beth Bates co-authored Chapter 7. Portions of the theoretic analysis in chapters 10 through 12 were developed by Fusfeld in a series of papers published in the late 1960s and early 1970s, and in a short book, *The Basic Economics of the Urban Racial Crisis* (New York: Holt, 1973), but all have been thoroughly reworked in the light of developments in the last decade. Several recent papers by Bates form the basis for parts of chapters 2, 3, 8, 9, and 14.

The
Political Economy
of the
Urban Ghetto

1

The Ghetto and the City

American cities present a series of paradoxes. Urban areas are growing larger and contain an increasing portion of the population; yet,
at the same time, their density is diminishing, and urban sprawl is
growing. On the one hand, cities are the dynamic center of the economy and support thriving cultural activities, on the other, the central
cores are disintegrating and deteriorating. Cities are economic units
in which the various parts are highly articulated and closely integrated
with each other; but, in other respects, cities are full of conflict, animosity, and hatred. These paradoxes are the outward aspect of the
malaise that grips American urban life. They are manifestations of
the urban problem of our time.

American urban areas have serious problems that remain unre-
solved, not because the means for their solution are unavailable, but
because the social and economic conflicts that are built into American
society prevent us from taking effective action. At the heart of that
conflict are extremes of wealth and poverty exacerbated by the fact
that racial differences and economic differences overlap. The inner
portions of the central cities are poor, black, and Hispanic (with other
minority groups also represented), while the suburbs are affluent and
largely white. The result is continuing warfare between central city
and suburb, rich and poor, white and black; a warfare that is usually

muted but sometimes overt. The urban problem is an urban and racial problem with deep roots in economic relationships as well as racial attitudes.

The Ghetto

In the heart of the central cities are the ghettos. They are peopled largely by blacks, Puerto Ricans, Spanish-speaking Americans, and other minority groups—and by some whites, mostly older people. It is here that poverty reigns. It is here that despair brings drug addiction and crime and where anger leads to militancy and violence.

The ghetto has three chief characteristics. Its people are clearly recognizable as racial or national minorities. It is poor. And there are cultural differences which are far less obvious and much more difficult to define. For example, black cultural patterns and values—which include such intangibles as world view as well as attitudes and family structure—differ from those of the dominant white Protestant and white Catholic groups or the white Jewish minority. They also differ from the Latin Catholic, racially-mixed culture of Spanish-speaking Americans. Conflicts between cultural patterns are as much a part of the urban racial crisis as conflicts between races and conflicts between the affluent and the poor.

Race and income are the chief distinguishing characteristics of urban ghettos, but the geographic boundaries defined by race and income do not coincide. In the typical, racially segregated urban region, as we move outward from the inner core of the central city, the density of population decreases and the income, wealth, and educational level of the people rise. Unemployment rates decline as we move outward, and racial segregation diminishes. On the outlying edges of the ghetto, the social and economic characteristics of the black and Hispanic population are hardly distinguishable from those of the surrounding white population. The mix of blue-collar, white-collar, and professional employment is approximately the same, and unemployment rates are similar. Geographical segregation of minority groups is reduced. The outlying edge of the ghetto differs greatly from the teeming population, racial segregation, and intense poverty that characterize the core of both ghetto and city.[1]

Poverty, on the other hand, is broader than the boundaries of the racial ghetto in the inner city. The congested residential areas of inner cities include the poor of all ages, races, and nationalities. Overcrowded and deteriorating housing, high incidence of disease and high infant mortality rates, high crime rates, family disorganization, a high proportion of poorly educated, and high unemployment rates—all of the social pathology of poverty—are prevalent.

The racial ghetto and the poverty ghetto overlap, but they do not coincide. The American inner city is segregated by race and by income. But there are largely black and Hispanic middle-and upper-income areas that are not poor, and poor areas that are largely white. There are, however, very large areas where people are both poor and black or Hispanic. These patterns are shown conceptually in figure 1.1.

Long-term Trends

Today's urban and racial crisis has its roots in three long-range problems: the changing nature of American cities, the persistence of poverty, and the failure of the American social system to make an equal place for black people. These three problems have been with us for a long time, and they will remain indefinitely into the future. Together

FIGURE 1.1. A model of the urban ghetto: race and income.

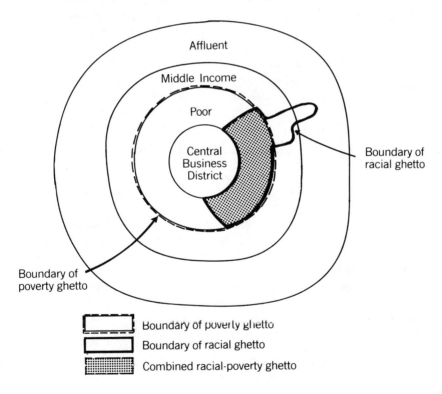

Affluent

Middle Income

Poor

Central Business District

Boundary of racial ghetto

Boundary of poverty ghetto

- - - Boundary of poverty ghetto

—— Boundary of racial ghetto

▓▓▓ Combined racial-poverty ghetto

they would have brought an urban and racial problem of major proportion even if other events had not accelerated the situation into a crisis.

The Changing City

Modern technology has fundamentally changed American cities. Decentralization of both manufacturing and population has been a long-term trend, clearly evident for the last sixty years. Before World War I, cities developed chiefly around railroad and port facilities. The development of mass rail transit, which brought both people and goods into the industrial core, gave further impetus to the growth of cities. But after World War I, motor transportation set into motion a countermovement. It made decentralization possible for both manufacturing and wholesale distribution. In addition, mass production industries using one-story plants for continuous-flow processes required large tracts, which were difficult and expensive to assemble in downtown areas. The availability of cheap land and cheap transportation enabled goods production to move from the central-city core into the suburbs.[2] The automobile enabled people to move, too.

Urban decentralization was slowed by the depression of the 1930s and the outbreak of World War II. For a time the war tended to lock urban growth into traditional central locations. After World War II, however, decentralization trends reasserted themselves more strongly than ever. A backlog of technological change that had piled up for fifteen years from 1930 through 1945 began to be rapidly applied, and industry expanded at unprecedented rates. People, much manufacturing and wholesaling, and a great deal of retail trade were suburbanized far from the central cities.

As industry moved to less crowded areas, central cities increasingly became centers of administration, finance, recreation, and other types of services. Except for the most efficient or the most backward of the old plants, generally only the low-wage industries such as clothing manufacture remained, drawn by the surplus labor of overcrowded slums. For the most part, high-wage industrial jobs deserted the cities for the suburbs.

These changes in the cities brought important changes in employment opportunities for the low-income residents of the central-city areas. Women found jobs to be relatively easily available in the administrative and service industries of downtown areas, in places served by public transportation facilities. Men seeking industrial jobs for the most part, however, had to rely on automobiles or inadequate public transportation to the outlying industrial areas.

A substantial portion of the decentralization of cities was subsidized by the federal government. Movement of people was assisted by subsidies to housing, particularly by mortgage guarantees under the GI Bill and by the FHA (Federal Housing Administration), while the Federal National Mortgage Association assured the housing industry of an adequate flow of capital. Federal highway programs also promoted suburbanization of both people and industry. After World War II, the automobile became an essential item for those not living in the central cities, regardless of their incomes. As a result, urban and suburban mass transit systems were allowed to deteriorate; much of the public now no longer needed or wanted them.

Decentralization also had the effect of reducing the financial resources of central cities. Two initial advantages of moving to the suburbs were low property taxes and relatively cheap land. Low tax rates, in turn, meant meager urban services—volunteer rather than professional fire departments, for example, or weak public library systems. As people and industry located in the suburbs, the smaller tax base had to provide for the expanding normal needs of the central cities. Furthermore, as we shall see, the migration and growth of the black population were putting additional strains on city budgets in some entirely new ways.

These economic trends were exacerbated by an archaic political structure. City boundaries were not exended to include the growing suburbs, and a multiplicity of political jurisdictions made metropolitan problem solving extremely difficult. Inadequate aid to the cities came from state governments, for domination of state legislatures by rural interests was the general rule. Even the redistricting of legislatures in the 1960s has not helped cities significantly: the balance of power has been placed in the suburbs, and people there originally fled the cities and look upon them with suspicion and fear. Even at the national level the influence of the suburbs and rural areas has been dominant. Most federal programs ignored the cities and provided aid to the suburbs instead until the central-city upheavals of the mid- and late 1960s.

The Persistence of Poverty

American cities have always had contrasts of wealth and poverty. Slums, present from the very beginning, served two functions. They were temporary stopping places for immigrants from abroad and from rural areas who were starting the journey upward in American society. But they have also been the end of the line for failures, for those who were society's dropouts and rejects.

American slums, or "urban poverty areas," have consistently had bad housing, crowded living conditions, poor education, bad health conditions, high death rates, inadequate public facilities, high crime rates, and police brutality. Present conditions are nothing new, although they may be both more widespread and concentrated more heavily for a single racial group.

The economy of urban poverty areas has always featured high rates of unemployment, low wage rates, and an "irregular" economy partially inside and partially outside the law. Labor is the major economic resource of the slums, and it has always been relatively unskilled and uneducated when compared with the labor resources of the economy as a whole. Permanent depression and economic underdevelopment have been characteristic of slum areas through the years.

The conditions of life in a poor community tend to reinforce and preserve poverty. Low incomes are the result of low productivity, which is promoted, in turn, by poor diet and poor health, two of the chief hallmarks of poverty. Low incomes mean crowded and unsanitary housing, which leads to bad health and low productivity. Poverty breeds crime, and a police record makes it difficult to get a decent job, which reinforces the poverty that may have led to the criminal behavior in the first place. Poverty leads to difficulties with the credit system, which, in turn, leads to difficulties in holding jobs (many employers fire workers for repeated wage garnishments by creditors). A poor neighborhood often has little political strength, which leads to inadequate public facilities: poor schools, libraries, hospitals, and other public services. Lack of public services reinforces the poor health and education which are basic causes of low productivity. The circular causation of poverty—"the poor are poor because they are poor"—is one of the reasons for its persistence.

Nevertheless, the urban poverty areas of earlier times differed in two important ways from those of today. First, the European nationality groups were not segregated. Although nationality groups tended to cluster together, the clusters were usually not large. The more common pattern was for nationality groups to be intermingled with each other in the same city block and even within the same tenement house. Second, most ethnic groups (other than blacks) have in part bypassed the slums. For example, although some Irish immigrants moved first into urban slum areas, others did not. They moved directly into higher-income and more respectable parts of the cities. As a result, when the slum Irish moved up and out of the slums, economically and physically, they found themselves moving into urban areas where others like themselves had already broken the ground. The older residents knew what the Irish were like because they already had some as neighbors. Other groups followed similar patterns and some, like the Germans, largely bypassed the big city slums altogether.

Neither of these two patterns applied to blacks. The black parts of slum areas tended to be segregated from the earliest days, and as the black population of cities rose, the black sector of the slums became more crowded and expanded into nearby white-occupied areas. As the blacks moved in, the whites moved out. New York's Harlem of the 1920s and 1930s is perhaps the classic example of this development. Furthermore, blacks seldom bypassed the black areas of cities even when their economic status might have permitted it. By the 1960s, the black ghetto comprised both slum and nonslum areas. As a result, today's problems of urban poverty and racial ghettos, although not synonymous, are inextricably intertwined.

White Racism

Some racial and nationality groups have escaped the vicious circle of slum life by pulling themselves out into the progressive, higher-income sectors of the economy. Blacks have been less successful because of the racial attitudes of whites. Blacks have always been at the bottom of the economic ladder. Low-wage, unskilled jobs with little opportunity for advancement, limited and inadequate educational opportunities, and restricted entry into skilled trades reduced economic opportunities in the blue-collar occupations. Administrative positions and white-collar jobs were unavailable because of the generally WASPish nature of business leadership and its attitudes (which discriminated against Catholics, Jews, and recent immigrants as well, although to a lesser extent). Only during periods of severe labor shortages, such as during the two world wars, were blacks able to make significant progress in the labor market.

Jobs for blacks in the federal government were limited to those at the bottom level, first by the alliance of conservative southern congressmen with conservative northern Republicans (first hammered out in 1876), and later in Democratic administrations by the strength of the southern wing of the party. For example, the Supreme Court decisions that validated the "separate but equal" doctrine came from courts dominated by conservative Republican justices after the so-called Compromise of 1876, which gave the presidency to Rutherford B. Hayes in exchange for the return of state government control in the South to white conservatives. Most of the official segregation in Washington, D.C. and the federal government was introduced in the Democratic administration of Woodrow Wilson.

The history of white racism in the United States has yet to be written, but the general outlines can be sketched.[3] Racist attitudes grew in intensity and breadth from the 1880s into the 1920s. This development coincided with the overseas imperialism of both the United States and Europe. In the United States, it led to passage of Jim Crow laws, lynchings in the South, violence against blacks in the North, and discrimination against blacks in employment and labor unions. Some historians place the peak of this development in the mid-1920s. It was supported by the appearance of an ideology and pseudoscience which held that the white European races were superior to others. Philosophers like Nietzsche, scholars like William Z. Ripley and the early physical anthropologists, while not overtly racist like Gobineau, H. S. Chamberlain, and Homer Lea, helped create the intellectual environment which enabled racial discrimination to go largely unquestioned even by the intellectual community.

A reaction to racism began in the years before World War I, marked perhaps by the founding of the NAACP (National Association for the Advancement of Colored People) in 1909 and the National Urban League in 1911. It has proceeded unevenly ever since, picking up speed after World War II with the civil rights movement, groundbreaking Supreme Court decisions, and congressional civil rights legislation. With all of its false starts, steps backward, and explosive social tensions, the United States has taken a path away from the racism of the years before World War I. At the very least, the old attitudes and practices are no longer respectable. Nevertheless, the entrenched economic patterns of the past have persisted, particularly discrimination in employment, housing, and some labor unions. The attack on these economic aspects of racial discrimination has been late in coming and has had only mixed results. Perhaps a beginning has been made.

Sources of Urban Conflict

Racial animosities are the most obvious and troubling sources of conflict in American cities at the present time. But there are other sources of the antagonisms that divide urban America.

One is the wide economic disparity that divides metropolitan areas into three different communities of the poor and near-poor, the affluent middle-income majority, and the rich. Cities are divided geographically by income levels, with the three income goups living separately, working separately, and spending their leisure time separately. An informal economic apartheid has developed in American urban areas. In fact, early analyses of 1980 census data suggest that urban racial segregation has diminished somewhat since the 1970 census, but economic apartheid increased.

The central-city ghettos and the surrounding areas, which contain between 20 and 25 percent of a city's population, are where the poor and near-poor live. These parts of the urban area are close to the older industrial districts and downtown commercial areas, although most metropolitan areas also have a few scattered islands of poverty and near-poverty in the suburbs.

One very significant aspect of urban development in recent years has been the spread of ghettoization into the suburbs. In some instances a nucleus was provided by the remnants of a black ghetto that had formed around suburban World War II industrial plants. But the chief reason for growth of suburban ghettos has been the process of urban decentralization itself. As economic activity moved into the suburbs, some of the low-wage, menial labor force moved with it. These workers found places to settle nearby, and ghettoization began. The suburban ghettos are proof that ghettos are one outcome of the present economic organization, that ghettos have deep roots in the pattern of income distribution, and that ghettos appear wherever American urban society spreads.

The middle-income majority live in the suburbs and in the central-city areas surrounding the central core of poverty. They make up some 70 to 75 percent of the urban population. These are the Americans whose well-scrubbed life is celebrated on television as the American Way. They live in single-family homes or in neat garden apartment developments, filled with electrical appliances and surrounded by lawns on tree-shaded streets, with late-model cars in the driveway. Their children typically go to college and thereby gain a ticket of admittance to the race for economic success, in which few fail to achieve the incomes that enable them to at least replicate their parents' middle-income way of life.

The wealthy are relatively few in number. Only some 5 to 10 percent of urban families fall in the affluent category. They live in either the silk stocking downtown areas of the city in luxury apartment houses or in the country club suburbs in large homes. Here are those who manage the American economy and make the decisions, who have income from accumulated wealth, and who dominate the economy's business and financial structure.

These economic distinctions create separate ways of life. American economic classes live apart, have different forms of recreation in different places, and seldom come into contact with each other on the job. The corporation executive does not eat lunch with a bookkeeper, nor does he invite the janitor to his home for dinner. The plant manager does not sit down with an assembly-line worker at his coffee break or go bowling with a sweeper. Separation based on economic disparity is the rule.

Economic differences are supplemented by cultural differences. The old view of American cities as melting pots in which people of greatly different national and cultural backgrounds were transformed into Americans similar to each other is now considered to be inadequate. Instead, cities are viewed as places in which successive waves of immigrants strengthened their own national and cultural values while they were also becoming Americans. The result was the development of a society of multicultural diversity. Several different patterns of attitudes and value systems emerged, which social psychologists now can identify as white Protestant, white Catholic, and white Jewish.[4]

The white Protestant culture was brought with the first English settlers. The other two developed during the great era of immigration from 1840 to 1910. The immigrants came into the urban slums of those days, where, surrounded by a hostile world and living in unfamiliar surroundings, they reacted by sticking together and trying to preserve their common heritage. They formed their own religious and fraternal organizations, emphasized family solidarity, published newspapers in their native language, and developed a political awareness that led to bloc voting. Crowded into low-wage occupations and discriminated against by white Protestant America, they came together and reasserted their identity. Many of these earlier immigrant groups retained that solidarity even after they escaped the ghettos by developing their own communities or neighborhoods within the larger city, maintaining separate parochial school systems in whole or in part and establishing organizations that preserved their cultural patterns. By the third quarter of the twentieth century, these cultural patterns began to intermingle geographically in the rapidly spreading suburbs, but they retained their identity nevertheless.

Blacks and Hispanics are now following the same path, and for essentially the same reasons. Crowded into slums and segregated from the main stream of American life, they are developing a fuller awareness of their own cultures and are developing political strength. A fivefold pattern of diverse cultures is emerging in urban America, with a black Protestant and a Hispanic Catholic culture supplementing the three earlier ones. But there is one difference. The earlier cultural differences were variations among racially homogeneous whites. The two emerging cultural patterns are racially differentiated from the other three. Blacks have always been subjected to racial segregation in this country, and one characteristic feature of the Hispanic Catholic culture is its background of liberal attitudes toward racial mixtures. The black and Latin cultures bring the new element of racial differences to the multicultural pattern of present-day urban metropolitan regions.

A strong foundation for social and economic conflict has been built in urban America. Economic disparities strengthened by an informal economic apartheid are supplemented by substantial cultural differnces. To these must be added racial differences and antagonisms. Under the surface of the apparently smooth functioning of the daily life of the city lies a potentially explosive conflict. Sometimes it emerges as individual acts of violence, sometimes as riots. But it is always there in the less obvious form of suspicion, hostility, and hatred.

2

The Evolution of Urban Racial Segregation and Discrimination

THE CREATION AND PERSISTENCE OF BLACK URBAN GHETTOS ARE NOT random outcomes of nearly a century of black migration from rural southern to urban areas. Rather, they are the products of specific economic and historical circumstances. Black crowding together in ghetto districts has not, by and large, been caused by the desire of ghetto residents to share common cultural, linguistic, and religious traditions. The shape and form of the ghetto reflect, instead, a systematic pattern of discrimination imposed upon urban blacks by the dominant white society. Blacks are indeed loosely bound together by a common cultural heritage; they are tightly bound together by a common set of grievances.

Unable to remember a time when black ghettos were not the norm in U.S. cities, many Americans assume that "things have always been like that." Few people realize that black ghettos are a relatively recent urban phenomenon, and even fewer have accurate notions of how or why the system arose. Urban ghettos throughout this country have been shaped along lines that originated largely in northern cities during the early twentieth century. Extreme racial segregation in housing has not always been characteristic of urban black residential patterns;

it is, in fact, a northern, post–World War I phenomenon. The common trait—severe disparities in black-white unemployment rates—has typified ghetto populations only since the 1930s. Before the depression decade, black-white differentials in unemployment rates were not common in either urban or rural areas.

Widespread black ghettoization emerged in its present form during the World War I years. Indeed, black urbanites were a small group, numerically, prior to the choking off of immigration from Europe after 1914. As recently as 1910, about nine out of every ten blacks lived in the southern states and eight out of every ten southern blacks lived in rural areas.[1] Nevertheless, the circumstances under which urban blacks lived and worked before World War I highlight the black worker's heritage as he moved into twentieth-century urban-industrial America on a large scale.

As country after country entered into the First World War, the United States was gradually transforming its industry into an arsenal in support of the war effort. Factories expanded production to meet wartime demand, but European immigration, the traditional source of unskilled labor for industry, was virtually halted by the conflict in Europe. In this time of great production demand, U.S. manufacturing experienced severe labor shortages. Black workers from rural southern states migrated to northern industrial cities by the hundreds of thousands to seek jobs in manufacturing during World War I. When the war ended, almost all of the recent black migrants elected to remain in the urban North. Blacks were segregated from whites by an involuntary spatial separation in housing, which was imposed on older black settlers as well as recent arrivals. Blacks were forced to live in segregated areas regardless of their ability to pay for housing.

The sheer size of the wartime black migration—over one million people—created animosity in the industrial cities as blacks and whites competed for scarce housing. The World War I black arrivals, however, also encountered an urban heritage of black-white animosity in the labor market. To explain the rise of urban racism in this period, it is necessary to understand pre-war black-white relations, especially as they relate to job competition. The roots of twentieth-century black ghettos and the nature of twentieth-century racism were shaped by patterns of job competition that developed during the nineteenth century.

The Status of Urban Blacks before World War I

Blacks residing in northern cities in the late nineteenth century typically were employed as waiters, domestics, pullman car porters, and in a variety of other low-paying service occupations. Black males often worked as common laborers, but they were rarely employed in the region's rapidly growing manufacturing industries.[2] Black city dwellers preferred northern cities located in close proximity to the South, such as Baltimore, St. Louis, Washington, D.C., and Philadelphia. Blacks in 1890 made up 1.3 percent and 1.5 percent, respectively, of the population in Chicago and New York City. Philadelphia was known for its large nineteenth-century black population, which constituted 3.8 percent of the city's total inhabitants in 1890.[3]

Social relations between blacks and whites rooted in years of slavery were often still dominant in the 1890s. While blacks were, generally, considered the racial and social inferior of whites, the affluent northerner tempered this attitude with condescending missionary zeal. The southern white gentleman class maintained its traditional paternalistic attitude toward blacks even after slavery had been abolished. After the overthrow of Reconstruction and the establishment of "home rule" in the South, blacks in that region were often highly reliant upon the southern gentleman for protection of their rights and liberties.[4] Virulent racism was found predominantly among lower-income whites. Blacks were well aware of class differences among whites concerning race prejudice, and in northern cities they naturally viewed prosperous whites (who were often employers) as their most likely allies and protectors.

Black-white working-class antagonism was initially shaped by the circumstances of the dual labor market fostered by slavery. In agriculture, the black and white worker were conditioned by the economic relations of the slave economy. For the black, this meant that he never faced the direct competition inherent in a free, unprotected market economy since the slave was an asset owned and cared for by the slavemaster. Thus, the economic position of many slaves was better than that of the poor white who operated in a totally free, unprotected market. While the poor white envied the greater economic security of the slave, the black envied the greater freedom of the white.

Similar relationships characterized the conditions under which black and white artisans worked and competed in the towns. Rather than depending upon white labor, slavemasters often relied upon their own slaves trained in carpentry, blacksmithing, and other skilled trades. Many masters sent their skilled slave artisans to the cities, where their services were either hired by master craftsmen or offered to the general public. Slave mechanics were often allowed to hire out on their own in return for a fixed sum of money or a percentage of the slave's earnings. White mechanics resented the competition that slave labor offered. Actually, the white workers were competing frequently against slave owners who could control the skilled trades market by utilizing their large financial resources and political power, as well as their skilled slave labor. Skilled white workers appealed to government, demanding that blacks be legally restricted to menial jobs. Aside from certain municipalities (and the state of Georgia), these efforts were largely unsuccessful. Planter-dominated legislatures saw limitations on slave labor use as a threat to the value of their property. At the end of the Civil War, an estimated 100,000 out of a total of 120,000 artisans in southern states were black.[5]

Emancipation and post-Reconstruction basically reversed the economic positions of black and white artisans so that blacks had to sell their labor in a free, unprotected market while whites were often protected by craft unions and Jim Crow institutions. No longer protected by slavery, skilled black workers lost ground in the southern cities to white workers. South Carolina, for example, required after 1865 that blacks purchase licenses before working as artisans, mechanics, or shopkeepers. The license for black artisans was ten dollars annually; white artisans were not required to pay license fees.[6] Craft unionism with its apprenticeship system was particularly effective in diminishing the ranks of black artisans. Relative to the South, craft union exclusion of blacks was often more effective in the heavily unionized northern cities; blacks typically maintained dominant positions in the building trade crafts in nonunion southern areas. In 1890, black artisans still accounted for over 16.1 percent of all carpenters in the South, as well as over 25 percent of all southern masons and plasterers.[7] Widely prevalent antiunion attitudes among blacks were rooted in black exclusion from most craft unions, and this attitude greatly facilitated use of blacks as strikebreakers in the late nineteenth and early twentieth centuries.

Thus, the nineteenth century produced a heritage of race relations that included widespread black-white working-class antagonism, strong antilabor union attitudes among black workers and community leaders, and a tendency in black communities to view prosperous whites as their protectors and allies. As black migration to the cities increased in the 1890s, the new urban dwellers brought along views of race relations that were deeply rooted in this heritage.

A combination of circumstances forced many rural southern blacks off the land in the 1890s in spite of the hold that sharecropping and debt tenure had previously maintained. The economic depression in the mid-1890s hit southern agriculture particularly hard, and cotton prices fell sharply. Floods ravaged the lower Mississippi River repeatedly in the early 1890s, and the flood years were followed by drought. Drought in 1896 caused an almost total loss of crops in the hill country of Louisiana, Mississippi, Arkansas, and Texas. And in 1892 a new and terrifying enemy, the boll weevil, moved northward into Texas, beginning an invasion that would shortly overrun the entire cotton kingdom. Blacks forced out of agriculture often migrated to southern cities were they were met by an upsurge of Jim Crow legislation, imposing rigid segregation and a virtual elimination of their right to vote. In addition, some traditional black occupations became white during the 1890s in southern cities, as unemployed whites "skidded" into these jobs, becoming longshoremen, teamsters, and barbers. The effectiveness of disenfranchisement is reflected in the number of registered black voters in Louisiana, which fell from 130,334 in 1896 to 1,342 in 1904.[8]

Economic depression and political oppression combined to produce an increase in black migration to many northern cities during the 1890s. The rapidly growing city of Chicago experienced a tripling in the number of black residents (from 14,271 to 44,103) between 1890 and 1910. Since the overall population of Chicago increased substantially during this period, the proportion of the city's population that was black rose less impressively, from 1.3 percent in 1890 to 2.0 percent in 1910. New York City was home for over 90,000 blacks (1.9 percent of the city's population) by 1910. Harlem was rapidly developing into the nation's largest black city within a city. A majority of the late nineteenth- and early twentieth-century black migrants to northern cities came from towns and mines rather than farms. Jobs vacated by these migrants were, in turn, filled by southerners who were abandoning agriculture.

Severe housing segregation was not the norm faced by the growing black population of northern cities prior to World War I. The emergence of Harlem as a dominant black residential area was very much the exception in northern black housing patterns. A more typical pattern was found in Pittsburgh, where blacks lived in six sections of the city. Although not segregated, these districts were racially distinct. In Columbus, Ohio, black housing was scattered throughout the city in a pattern that reflected economic rather than racial segregation in the housing market. Because of their economic position, blacks frequently resided in low-income districts located in the older parts of northern cities. These neighborhoods were often being voluntarily vacated gradually by upwardly mobile white families, and cheap housing was readily available. As long as there was no severe shortage of inexpensive housing, the expansion of urban black populations caused little friction.

Thus, on the eve of the great migration generated by World War I, most northern blacks lived in clusters of racially mixed neighborhoods. Since residence and employment patterns are interdependent, these clusters were often located at the periphery of wealthy white residential areas, where many of the blacks worked as servants. The few affluent blacks were the group most likely to experience discrimination in the housing market, because prosperous residential areas were least tolerant of racially integrated housing. Within the racially integrated neighborhood clusters, black community institutions such as churches were formed. Around these institutions well-defined black districts arose during World War I that represented embryonic ghettos. Yet even in Chicago, where the black ghetto was well defined by 1920, more than two-thirds of the black inhabitants resided in 1910 in areas that were more than 50 percent white. A third of Chicago's black residents in 1910 lived in districts that were more than 90 percent white.[9] Most blacks indeed resided in substandard housing, but the quality of shelter was rather like that of low-income urban dwellers in general.

Racial Antagonism in the Labor Market

Most black workers have traditionally been employed in jobs that white workers have shunned, thus minimizing black–white job competition in normal times. Blacks, however, were brought into many industries initially as strikebreakers or as instruments to divide and weaken white workers. Two disinct types of strikebreaking activity were common: staying on the job while other workers were on strike, and bringing in workers from outside to replace workers on strike. The latter was initially most common regarding the use of blacks, and the former became increasingly common after World War I.

Before the Civil War, black strikebreakers were used in New York City to defeat a longshoremen's strike. These activities generated bitter resentment towards blacks and the result was often riot and bloodshed, as occurred along the New York waterfront in 1855. In the Civil War days, unskilled laborers were commonly Irish, and they resented competition from black workers. Longshoremen's work was overwhelmingly an Irish occupation in northern ports and a black occupation in the southern ports. A pattern of violence occurred in city after city (Buffalo, New York, Boston, Chicago, etc.) when blacks were brought in to break the strikes and generally to undermine the unionization efforts of Irish dockworkers. In June 1863, 3,000 Irish longshoremen in New York lost a strike largely because black strikebreakers were introduced with police protection. A month later, Irish longshoremen led the New York draft riots, resisting military service for a war that they viewed as being on the behalf of blacks, their hated industrial rivals. Thus did racial antagonism spread between the few northern blacks and unskilled white workers, particularly those recent European immigrant groups who were at the bottom of the economic ladder. Blacks, in fact, were eventually accepted into the longshoremen's union, but not by choice. Blacks were accepted by the dockworkers (and by certain other unions) solely for the protection of the white workers' interests. Exclusion of blacks simply encouraged them to break the strikes of the unions from which they were denied membership.

One of the important origins of twentieth-century racism is the historic use of blacks for strikebreaking. Use of blacks to weaken organized labor was one of the most effective divide and conquer strategies ever utilized by employers to limit the bargaining power of their unionized employees. In the process, a certain amount of employer-employee antagonism is diverted into intra-employee conflict, and friction between the races is increased. Union exclusion served as the initial justification for black strikebreaking but it also had the effect of intensifying antiblack feelings among white workers. Since black workers undermined the union, many whites felt that discriminatory union activity was justified, but these discriminatory union policies were precisely those that encouraged blacks to oppose organized labor. It was this vicious circle of growing, self-reinforcing racial antagonism that characterized most union–black worker interactions in the late nineteenth and early twentieth centuries.

To understand the consequence of utilizing blacks to undermine unions, periods of unionization efforts marred by racial conflict are examined for the steel, meatpacking, and ladies garment industries. The steel industry discussion is drawn primarily from the book, *The Black Worker: The Negro and the Labor Movement* by Sterling Spero and Abram Harris.[10]

Steel

Many steel industry jobs are precisely the type of work—hot, dirty, often dangerous—that white workers prefer to avoid when alternative employment is available. The rapidly growing steel industry of the late nineteenth century relied in the North upon European immigrants to fulfill its manpower requirements. Southern steel mills in areas such as Alabama could not obtain an adequate supply of immigrant workers to perform their unskilled and less desirable jobs, so they relied upon blacks to fill the role that foreigners held in the North. In 1907, blacks made up 39.1 percent of the steel industry's work force in the South, as opposed to 0.5 percent in the Midwest.

Black workers entered the northern steel industry initially as strike-breakers in 1875. The most important craft union in the steel industry, the Sons of Vulcan, barred all blacks from membership by constitutional provision. In an 1875 Pittsburgh strike, black skilled steelworkers from southern states were induced to take the places of striking white workers who were members of the Sons of Vulcan. The Amalgamated Association of Iron and Steel Workers was formed in 1876, by combining the existing steel unions, for the declared purpose of "embracing every iron and steel worker in the country." Nonetheless, this union did not admit blacks to membership. Contrary to union expectations, its discriminatory policies simply accelerated introduction of black workers into the northern steel industry. Repeatedly from 1878 to the mid-1880s, black steelworkers were brought in from southern mills to replace striking whites. The lure of higher wages was sufficient to draw the black steelworkers northward, and discriminatory union policies served to unite these workers against the Amalgamated Association of Iron and Steel Workers. Use of blacks as strikebreakers in 1884 precipitated a serious riot at the Elba Works near Pittsburgh when white strikers attempted to resist introduction of black workers.

After learning the hard way that black workers could not be ignored, Amalgamated offered to admit blacks into their ranks under certain terms. Like many other labor unions that admitted blacks during the 1880s, Amalgamated placed black workers, wherever possible, into separate, racially segregated union locals. In 1887, the union established a separate black local in Pittsburgh. Black workers were duly cynical about the union membership offer, and black support for Amalgamated was not strong. When a strike against Carnegie Steel Company took place in 1892, blacks willingly served as strikebreakers. Local black Pittsburgh residents as well as black strikebreakers from the South helped Carnegie defeat the strike and eliminate unions completely from the giant Homestead Works. Black strikebreakers were typically retained by their Pittsburgh employers, particularly Carnegie Steel, as permanent employees. Many other industries in the late nineteenth century would utilize blacks as strikebreakers, but they would fire most black workers when the strike ended, displacing blacks by rehiring whites who had been on strike.

Steel unions declined in strength after 1892, but Amalgamated did manage to organize a strike against U.S. Steel in 1901. Black workers, including those who were union members, largely remained on the job during the 1901 strike. During World War I, blacks capitalized upon the wartime labor shortages to become a major part of the northern steel industry's permanent labor force. On the eve of the great steel strike in 1919, blacks typically made up 10 to 20 percent of the work force in the major Chicago and Pittsburgh steel districts, and they constituted up to 40 percent in some of the smaller Pittsburgh mills. Many of the black workers who entered the steel mills during the war were fresh from the southern fields. They tended to be grateful for their jobs and they felt that the pay was good. Many of these new workers were largely ignorant of organized labor's goals, and their more sophisticated black co-workers did not encourage them to embrace the unions. Black community leaders typically opposed the 1919 strike, and many feared that the union would try to eliminate blacks from the steel mills after the strike was won.

When the giant strike began on 22 September 1919, only a few blacks joined the 25,000 whites who walked off the job in the Pittsburgh region. The Homestead Works of U.S. Steel employed 1,737 blacks among its 14,687 employees, and only eight of these blacks were union members. Among white unskilled workers, 75 percent joined the union and 90 percent struck; among blacks, exactly one worker walked out when the strike commenced. Black workers in steel mills throughout the nation were similarly apathetic in their response to the strike call. In addition to the black workers who stayed on their jobs, thousands more entered the mills as strikebreakers. Unemployed black local residents were often sufficiently numerous to fill the demand for strikebreakers, but Pittsburgh imported numerous blacks from other regions of the country. Whites also served as strikebreakers, but union resentment focused upon the 30,000 to 40,000 black workers who were believed to be responsible for destroying the strike effort. From long experience, many blacks believed that strikebreaking offered the best chance for entrance into the steel industry. While this had been true historically, blacks had by 1919 already established themselves as a permanent and important part of the steel industry's workforce. In fact, nearly all of the blacks who came into the mills from the outside during the 1919 strike lost their jobs when the walkout ended. Striking employees returned to their old jobs after the strike had been defeated, and black workers retained basically the same position in steel that they held before the strike. Unionization would not again seriously threaten the big steel companies until the 1930s.

Meatpacking

Before the strike in 1894, a few blacks were employed in the giant stockyards and packing plants of Chicago, Omaha, and Kansas City. Their presence generated no apparent opposition from the foreign-born white workers who dominated the industry's labor force. During the 1894 walkout, large numbers of Polish workers served as strikebreakers, along with much smaller numbers of blacks. After the strike, the small numbers of blacks employed in the stockyards were seen as a threat to labor unions, even though their role as strikebreakers had been insignificant. A much greater influx of black workers into the industry occurred during the strike of 1904. Blacks from the South filled many of the unskilled jobs during the strike and black workers overall, being the easiest to obtain, were the largest strikebreaking element. The 1904 strike demonstrated that management could tap a vast supply of cheap labor in the South, simultaneously securing a labor force that was extremely resistant to unionization. For these reasons, the black strikebreakers caused intense resentment among the striking meatpacking workers. To prevent white attacks on the black workers in Chicago, the blacks had to be housed within the stockyard compounds during the strike. During this era, many industries in addition to meatpacking would attempt to restrain union demands by threatening to "bring in Negroes."

When the 1904 meatpacking strike was settled, some blacks retained their jobs, but most were discharged and replaced with returning union workers. Blacks would not constitute a major portion of this industry's labor force until World War I labor shortages forced the meatpackers to employ tens of thousands of blacks, primarily migrants from agricultural regions in the deep South. In fact, the companies sent agents into the South during the war to recruit blacks for unskilled packinghouse jobs. The Stock Yards Labor Council was formed in 1917 by the stockyards craft unions, and the Council immediately addressed the problem of forming a coherent union policy toward blacks. Due to the growing industry reliance on black workers, the Council realized that any unionization effort was unlikely to succeed without black cooperation. The meatpacking unions, like the steelworkers before them, realized that black workers could no longer be ignored. Of the various craft unions that made up the Stock Yards Labor Council, at least ten followed sharply discriminatory policies. Realizing their dilemma, many union leaders urged that blacks be admitted to all unions, but union constitutional provisions prohibited this in several instances. Although a coherent policy towards black workers was not forthcoming, the Council began its 1917 campaign to unionize the meatpackers' labor force. Blacks were eligible for membership in a number of the stockyards unions, but their overall response to the unionization campaign was weak. Among northern-born blacks, roughly 90 percent joined unions, but the more numerous southern-born blacks showed little interest.[11] Overall, only about one-third of the black packinghouse workers affiliated with unions, a figure much lower than the incidence of white union membership. Management exploited this situation by accelerating employment of southern blacks. Lack of a consistent racial policy made the unions vulnerable to management efforts of portraying unions as the black man's enemy. Large Chicago packinghouses hired a colorful black promoter, Richard Parker, to organize an all-black union, the American Unity Labor Union. Parker's well-financed effort to generate racial discord further confused the unionization issue. The packing companies also, according to the Chicago Federation of Labor, "subsidized Negro preachers and Negro politicians and sent them out among the colored people to induce them not to join unions."[12] Two black Chicago aldermen were charged with working for packinghouse management to discourage union membership in the black community.

Unions tried to counter these efforts by using black organizers, and the Chicago Meatcutters and Butcher Workmen's Union in particular succeeded in attracting several thousand black members. By contrast, the steelworker unions had made little direct effort to recruit black members prior to the 1919 strike, and no black organizers were employed during their unionization campaign. Meatpacking unions, furthermore, paid particular attention to the demands and grievances of their black members. These unusual efforts by the meatpacking unions were, however, probably nullified by strong opposition of black community leaders to the union drive for members.

Unionization of black packinghouse workers was still not substantial in the early 1920s, and blacks played a major role in breaking the strike that was called in December 1921. The strike followed a now-familiar pattern: many employed blacks did not heed the strike call, thousands of others were employed as strikebreakers, and continuing violence between strikers and scabs, between picketers and police, and between blacks and whites characterized the strike. After two months the strike collapsed completely, and the unions were not able to mount another serious organizing campaign until the 1930s. Many striking workers were never rehired, and blacks who served as strikebreakers generally retained their positions permanently. Despite the fact that thousands of blacks had walked off the job with their fellow unionized white workers, the 1921 strike in meatpacking revealed the continuing vulnerability of organized labor to the black strikebreaker.

Ladies Garments

Steel, meatpacking, and ladies garment workers unions pursued distinctly different approaches to the special problems of organizing black workers. The Amalgamated Association of Iron and Steel Workers was initially an association of skilled workers only. Although it did seek to attract unskilled workers to its ranks, it made no particular effort to unionize blacks. In contrast, many participating unions in the Stock Yards Labor Council made special efforts to recruit blacks, including use of black labor organizers and the adoption of internal union policies that were clearly nondiscriminatory. Nonetheless, these policies were compromised by the continuing racist activities of some meatpacking unions and the Council's failure to adopt a consistently nondiscriminatory racial policy. The International Ladies Garment Workers Union (ILGWU) did not pursue discriminatory practices. Yet the ILGWU encountered problems in organizing black workers that were typical of the woes facing those few unions which accepted blacks as equals.

After the labor shortages of World War I eased and unemployment increased generally, unionized employers began to open nonunion shops staffed by poorly paid black women. Despite ILGWU's non-discriminatory policies, black women served as strikebreakers. When the ILGWU did succeed in organizing blacks, many employers would refuse to hire them. A common employer policy in times of labor surplus was to employ blacks only if they could pay them below union wages or utilize them as strikebreakers. When employers had to meet union wage scales, they preferred to employ white workers. Since unionization threatened to bring unemployment, many blacks in the ladies garment industry preferred to work at nonunion shops for less than union scale wages. ILGWU efforts to unionize garment producing firms were thus at times undermined by lack of black worker support for union representation. Overall union bargaining power in the garment industry suffered accordingly.

Overview

Chapter 7 provides a more detailed analysis of twentieth-century labor union–black worker interactions. American Federation of Labor (AFL) craft union policies that were commonly discriminatory were the main influence shaping black worker perceptions of organized labor until the 1930s. The rise of industrial unionism in the form of the Congress of Industrial Organizations (CIO) produced a strong challenge to union racism during the late years of the Great Depression. Before the CIO era, however, relations between blacks and unions were notoriously bad, and this reality contributed to general black-white antagonism throughout the United States. Blacks were willing to break strikes for a variety of reasons, but their resentment towards discriminatory union policies was always a major justification for strikebreaking. A distrust of white workers that was rooted in the slavery heritage did not endear blacks to labor organizations dominated by working-class whites. Strikebreaking, along with a frequent willingness to work for less than the prevailing wage scale, was often viewed by blacks as their most viable strategy for entering certain industries. Once at work, many black employees were grateful for their jobs and they tended to identify with management rather than their co-workers as potential protectors and allies. Blacks moving directly from southern agriculture into industrial employment (which was widespread during World War I) knew little of factories, much less unions, and they often lacked knowledge of union tactics and goals. Frequently existing near the edge of poverty, many black workers feared that job loss and replacement by whites would be the consequences of participating in union activities. Certain large corporations in fields ranging from automobile assembly to meatpacking viewed the antiunion tendencies of black workers as a major justification for increasing black employment, thereby weakening union strength. According to former Secretary of Labor Ray Marshall, "employers like Henry Ford were willing to hire Negroes in many job categories, doubtless for altruistic reasons, but also to keep unions out of their plants."[13] White worker antagonism toward blacks, in turn, was frequently rooted in fears that black willingness to work for lower wages would displace whites. The striking white worker feared that his job would be lost permanently to the black strikebreaker. Finally, many whites saw blacks as an obstacle to their efforts via unionization to increase wages, shorten the workday, and improve working conditions. Since black-white antagonism lessened the unity and hence the bargaining power of labor, management often had a vested interest in its perpetuation. Thus, the meatpacking companies did not initiate or invent racism in the early twentieth century, but they did their best to exacerbate it for selfish corporate purposes.

3

The Emergence of Black
Ghettos

Ghetto Building During World War I and Its Aftermath

The events of World War I permanently altered the pace and character
of life for blacks in northern cities. The unprecedented economic
expansion that resulted from industries geared up to supply the war
effort created an enormous demand for labor. The lure of city jobs
was enhanced by the vacuum created when the door to European
immigration was closed. Total immigration fell from an all-time high
of 1,218,480 in 1914, to 110,618 in 1918.[1] Deprived of its abundant
foreign labor supply, industry was forced to seek workers from the
domestic agricultural hinterlands. From the deep southern states of
Mississippi, Alabama, Louisiana, Georgia, and South Carolina came
thousands of blacks. The lure is clear when one examines the northern
cities to which blacks were migrating (table 3.1). The newcomers were
concentrated quite heavily in the large, predominantly industrial cities
of the East and Midwest. Simultaneously, these cities were struggling
to absorb growing white populations, and housing construction had
nearly halted during the war years. Detroit, the most rapidly growing
large city, experienced a 611.3 percent increase in black population
between 1910 and 1920, along with more than a doubling in the

Table 3.1. Black and White Population Increase in Selected Northern Cities, 1910–1920

	Black Population		Percentage Black Increase	Percentage White Increase
	1910	*1920*	*1910–1920*	*1910–1920*
Large Cities				
Detroit	5,741	40,838	611.3	106.9
Cleveland	8,448	34,451	307.8	38.1
Chicago	44,103	109,458	148.2	21.0
New York	91,709	152,467	66.3	16.9
Philadelphia	84,459	134,229	58.9	15.4
St. Louis	43,960	69,854	58.9	9.4
Smaller Cities				
Gary	383	5,299	1,283.6	205.1
Canton	291	1,349	363.6	71.7
Toledo	1,877	5,690	203.1	42.5
Fort Wayne	572	1,476	158.0	34.3
Dayton	4,842	9,029	86.5	28.0

Source: Chicago Commission on Race Relations, *The Negro in Chicago: A Study of Race Relations and a Race Riot* (Chicago: Univ. of Chicago Pr., 1922) p. 80.

number of white inhabitants.[2] Table 3.1 reveals that black population growth was typically greatest in precisely those cities experiencing the most rapid overall growth during decade between 1910 and 1920. The six large cities in table 3.1 accounted for a majority of all South to North black migration during the war decade, but smaller industrial cities, such as Gary, often registered the largest relative gains in black population. The largest part of this phenomenal rural to urban migration occurred between 1916 and 1919, and it was followed in the 1920s by a similar in-migration of even greater magnitude.

Northern mills, foundries, and assembly plants sent recruiting agents to the deep South inviting, even urging, blacks to come to the great industrial cities. They spoke glowingly of northern job prospects, sometimes offering free transportation to likely candidates. Some southern areas feared that the magnitude of the northward migration would create local labor shortages. Montgomery, Alabama, enacted a law forbidding firms and their recruiters from "enticing, persuading, or influencing" labor to leave the area. The Macon, Georgia city council demanded a recruiting license fee of $25,000 from northern corporate recruiters.[3] In Mississippi, agents were arrested, trains were stopped, and ticket agents were intimidated, but nonetheless the northbound migration continued. Certain southern areas, though, welcomed the great migration because agricultural changes were making thousands of black workers obsolete. By 1915, the boll weevil had ravaged cotton crops in Mississippi and Alabama, and the pest was beginning to attack western Georgia. Many farmers responded by switching to food crops and livestock, requiring fewer laborers and forcing black tenants to seek their livelihood elsewhere. Thousands of additional blacks moved northward at the end of World War I when many returning veterans felt the South, with its widespread poverty and all-pervasive political segregation, was no longer a viable place to live.

When black workers arrived in the cities, most males entered unskilled jobs in the steel mills, foundries, auto plants, and packing houses; also common were jobs in highway construction and railroad maintenance. Black females entered the garment factories and worked as domestics.[4] Black workers were critical to this phase of American economic expansion because they served as a reserve army that could be called upon in periods of labor shortage. They were willing to take the lowest paying, least attractive jobs at a time when foreign-born whites were vacating them for better opportunities. Because large-scale European immigration did not resume after World War I, black workers continued to be a crucial component of the industrial labor force during the rapid growth years of the 1920s.

Before World War I, black migrants to northern cities had typically been southern urban dwellers, and they were acclimated to the ways of city life. Relative to all southern blacks, these early migrants had above-average education and training, and they had come largely from states in the upper South, such as Kentucky and Virginia. In contrast, most of the World War I migrants came directly from a life of subsistence agriculture in the deep South. They were peasants abandoning a form of feudal existence; their lives had been akin to that of European peasants of the Middle Ages. The transition to urban living was often a trying experience. Their slow southern black dialect and folk expressions were often difficult for northerners to understand. Because most had been brought up in isolation from white people and were accustomed to Jim Crow laws, the migrants hastened to northern black communities. Older black residents often viewed the newcomers as "country bumpkins" and expressed their disapproval of the new arrivals. This rejection complicated the process of urbanization. As migrants continued to flow in from the South, older blacks feared that the unsophisticated ways of the new arrivals would disturb relationships between the black and white communities. To established city residents, the newcomers seemed dirty, noisy, unintelligible, and too numerous. On the job, manufacturers had to cope with the fact that new black migrants were not accustomed to working a fixed number of hours each day and week; they were often tardy, they were unfamiliar with machinery, they exhibited the traits that peasants throughout the centuries have displayed when first exposed to urban existence. "The Negro migrant was strange; soon he became the object of ridicule. Ultimately he was feared."[5]

Housing

The increased black population was accompanied by a concentration of blacks in constricted sections of the northern cities. Perhaps like the European migrants before them, blacks from the agrarian deep South initially preferred residential segregation in order to ease the transition from a primitive rural existence to an urban way of life. Wartime migrants initially gravitated toward the poorest districts that were being abandoned by former residents who could afford to live elsewhere. The clusters of racially mixed neighborhoods where black community life had been centered rapidly lost their white populations. Residences of departing whites were filled either by upwardly mobile blacks or by new migrant families arriving from the South. In the process, racially mixed black neighborhoods became racially homogeneous. The demand for housing was still unfulfilled. The existing black sections filled up, and rents for all kinds of accommodations skyrocketed due to the tremendous demand for housing. Large profits could be made by those who could supply the housing units, and black residential areas started to spread.

As whites began to flee before the vast influx of black migrants, white communities increasingly spoke in such military terms as black "invasion" of the neighborhoods. Realtors sometimes profited by creating panic in white neighborhoods by crying "the Negroes are coming" and then buying up cheaply the properties of fleeing whites. Housing acquired in this manner was quickly rented or sold to blacks at inflated prices. The rapidity with which neighborhoods changed racially and the magnitude of the black population expansion frightened many whites. As housing shortages increasingly impacted white as well as black city residents, battle lines were drawn to prevent neighborhood "loss" to black invasion. That blacks would not be welcomed in white residential areas was made quite clear by acts of violence and terrorism.

Blacks moving into white neighborhoods as well as real estate agents who sold or rented to blacks occasionally had bombs hurled at their homes. In Chicago alone, fifty-eight such bombings occurred between mid-1917 and March 1921.[6] Periodic bombings and attacks on blacks venturing into white communities were merely a prelude to the great 1919 Chicago race riot. Five days of violence caused mainly by white gangs invading black neighborhoods took at least thirty-eight lives, caused over 500 injuries, destroyed much property, and left over 1000 people homeless. Blacks fought back, particularly along the boundary between Irish neighborhoods and Chicago's black belt. Although most of the fighting was done in black areas, black reprisals sometimes caused the violence to spill over into white communities. The 1919 riot dramatized the alteration of black-white relations in Chicago more than any other single event. In November 1919, a large and influential white property owners' association called for "segregation by mutual consent" and asked blacks to keep out of white neighborhoods for the sake of racial harmony.

The Chicago riot was caused by the black migration and housing conflicts, interacting with previously discussed labor market antagonisms. The return of soldiers seeking jobs in 1919 coincided with the fading of war-induced prosperity. As unemployment rose among blacks and whites alike, the two races viewed each other as competitors for scarce jobs in dominant sectors such as manufacturing. In the eyes of many working class whites, black migrants were competitors not only for housing and jobs, but they were cheap labor that threatened wage scales and complicated efforts to unionize the manufacturing sector. Among the antagonisms contributing to the 1919 Chicago riot was the meatpacking industry's two-year campaign to weaken a union membership drive by alienating blacks from the union movement. Because these factors relating to jobs and housing were intensifying black-white antagonisms in many urban areas, it was no coincidence that 1919 produced at least twenty-six race riots in U.S. cities. Many of these race riots were in the South, reflecting the unwillingness of returning black soldiers—their horizons expanded by wartime experiences—to accept the South's discriminatory status quo. Many other riots took place in northern cities, amounting to the greatest outbreak of racial violence that had occurred even in the North.

Once the color line had been drawn around existing black neighborhoods, the ghetto had been defined and blacks would have to fight block by block for additional housing. Although World War I's events had created a very tight housing market, wartime prosperity had at least created abundant jobs. In 1919, while the housing situation was not improving, the job market was getting worse. As industries retrenched after the war, thousands of blacks lost their jobs outright, while others were forced to accept lower wages. Meanwhile, migrants from the South continued to arrive in the northern cities, further increasing the competition for jobs and housing. After the ghetto boundaries had been drawn, it was inevitable that blacks would pay rents higher than those charged for comparable housing in other parts of the city. The average rent increase in Harlem from 1920 to 1924 was 32.2 percent, which greatly exceeded rent increases in other parts of New York City.[7] Higher rents encouraged the cutting up of large apartments into smaller units.

Nevertheless, northern ghettos expanded during the 1920s to accommodate hundreds of thousands of new arrivals from the South. Table 3.2 shows that large northern cities experienced black population growth in the 1920s decade that vastly exceeded the increases of the previous decade. Ghetto boundaries expanded, spurred on by the greed of the realtors and landlords and the growing demand for housing on the part of blacks. General economic conditions in the 1920s produced a great boom in new home construction. Influenced by the greater mobility that the automobile offered, middle-class families increasingly chose to occupy new housing being built in outlying city areas and suburbs. New subdivisions sprang up on the periphery of all large cities, and home construction reached all-time high levels of activity. Blacks were not welcome in these housing divisions, nor were most able to afford new homes. Instead, blacks were part of a filtering process whereby lower-income households moved into the inner-city homes that were being vacated by the middle-class new

Table 3.2. Black Population Increase in Selected Northern Cities, 1920–1930

	Black Population		Percentage Black Increase	Percentage Blacks in City Population	
	1920	1930	1920–1930	1920	1930
New York	152,467	327,706	114.9	2.7	4.7
Chicago	109,458	233,903	113.7	4.1	6.9
Philadelphia	134,229	219,599	63.6	7.4	11.3
Detroit	40,838	120,066	194.0	4.1	7.7
St. Louis	69,854	93,580	34.0	9.0	11.4
Cleveland	34,451	71,899	108.7	4.3	8.0

Source: U.S. Bureau of the Census, *Negroes in the United States, 1920–1932* (Washington, D.C.: Government Printing Office, 1935), p. 55.

home buyers. In white neighborhoods directly adjacent to ghettos, homes for sale often found few interested white buyers. Vacancies appeared increasingly in rental housing, and rent levels began to fall. Several short blocks away in the ghetto, rents were high and the demand for additional housing was great. Inner-city landlords in white residential districts often sought higher paying tenants by opening up their properties to blacks. Similarly, speculators would buy up property cheaply in the depressed housing area that stood adjacent to the ghetto, raise the rents, and then admit black tenants. Although such landlords were viewed as "disloyal" by neighborhood whites, their activities were apt to be very profitable. Once the neighborhood had been occupied by blacks, white residents would move out and the area would quickly become predominantly black. Thus, vacancies in the inner city caused by new construction on the urban periphery enabled ghettos to expand, block by block, during the 1920s.

Meanwhile, white neighborhoods developed new methods of keeping out blacks. In 1921, the Chicago Real Estate Board adopted a policy of expelling any realtor who sold property to blacks in areas that were all white. The profit potential of selling to blacks, though, was sufficiently strong to undermine this deterrent. Many cities discussed adoption of laws that would restrict blacks to certain residential zones, or bar them from moving into white neighborhoods. This strategy for maintaining segregation, however, was crippled by a 1917 Supreme Court decision that had declared unconstitutional a residential segregation law in Louisville, Kentucky. A more effective tool for enforcing segregated housing was the racially restrictive housing covenant, which was enthusiastically embraced by financial institutions, real estate firms, and developers after its introduction in 1925. Effective use of covenants entailed getting the mutual agreement of property owners in a given area not to sell or lease property to certain groups (blacks). Racial covenants were the offspring of neighborhood improvement associations, whose main reason for existence was to block ghetto expansion. Each new wave of black migration and the resulting pressure for more space acted to spur these associations into inventing additional obstacles to achieve ghetto containment. Covenants were legally enforceable and they helped to maintain racial segregation until they were overturned in 1948 by Supreme Court decision in *Shelley v. Kramer*.[8] Covenant use was particularly popular in new subdivisions, less so in neighborhoods adjoining ghettos. The covenant was merely one of a variety of factors that reduced the residential mobility of blacks in northern cities. Unlike earlier immigrant communities that had become less concentrated with the passage of time, black neighborhoods grew increasingly concentrated.

Rise of Racial Consciousness

Post–World War I race riots, bombings, and other aspects of the ghetto boundary hardening process aroused urban blacks to a high state of racial consciousness. Coming together for mutual help and protection, blacks quickly grasped the notion of building and supporting their own institutions. As growing spatial separation reduced contacts between the races, black institutions expanded and flourished. Partly by choice and partly as a means to avoid white rejection and possible conflict, blacks increasingly patronized their own churches, stores, and places of amusement. A conspicuous example of rising racial consciousness was the development of black community newspapers. A black-owned printing industry arose as black publications multiplied. Capitalizing upon racial sentiment and financing from high wartime incomes, black businesses formed in most lines of commerce and industry.[9] A "buy black" sentiment was prevalent, and many enterprises were financed by churches and fraternal lodges whose members would become loyal patrons of the newly formed firms. Black professionals, often moving northward along with their clients, saw their practices and incomes rise as segregation increased. The decline of normal and spontaneous black-white interactions tended to lessen racial tolerance and mutual understanding, causing reinforcement of ghetto existence in peoples' minds.

For most black migrants in northern cities during the 1920s, living in racially homogeneous, overcrowded ghettos and working in unskilled jobs were superior to their previous lifestyles in the South. Aside from some recession years in the early 1920s, jobs in this prosperous decade were readily available and unemployment was no higher than among whites.[10] Segregation's restrictions on housing and better job opportunities were not as severe as the more rigid and confining color line that existed in the South. In addition to the lure of economic opportunity, the greater freedom of northern life was attractive to the migrants. Representative comments solicited from migrants by Chicago's Commission on Race Relations in 1920 describe their perceptions of northern life:

1. "The schools are much better here."
2. "I live better, save more, and feel more like a man."
3. "My wife can have her clothes fitted here, she can try on a hat and if she doesn't want it, she doesn't have to keep it; go anywhere I please on the cars after I pay my fare."
4. "Not afraid to get on cars and sit where I please."
5. "Live in a better house and can go places denied at home."

6. "Don't have to look up to the white man."
7. "Don't have to go to the buzzard roost [Colloquial name for the Jim Crow balcony in southern theaters] at shows."

Such statements consistently showed a feeling of relief over the release from subordination and fear. The sense of freedom was more explicitly expressed in response to the question, "What do you like about the North?":

1. "Freedom in voting and conditions of colored people here."
2. "Liberty, better schools."
3. "Like the privileges."
4. "Freedom of speech and action."
5. "No discrimination; can express opinions and vote."
6. "The schools for the children, the better wages, the privileges for colored people."
7. "Work, can work anyplace; freedom."[11]

All of the above responses were collected in the year following Chicago's great 1919 race riot.

In the rural South, blacks always had their "place," a well-defined subordinate role that limited their freedom of action. In agriculture, the white landowner told them what to plant and how to plant it. Shopping was often confined to stores where the landowner had arranged credit for his tenant farmers. In the North, one's employer had no control over what one chose to do after work. Blacks could spend their money as they saw fit, support community newspapers, even participate in political organizations headed by black politicians. Life was indeed freer, more open in the North, especially when prosperity prevailed and jobs were readily available.

The Evolution of Black Urban Existence

Before World War I, blacks residing in northern cities were distinctly outside of the mainstream of economic life. Employed predominantly in such traditional black service jobs as porters and domestics, most had no contact with the great manufacturing industries that were spurring the growth of Chicago, Cleveland, and similar cities. The few employed in manufacturing had often been introduced to industry through strikebreaking.

In contrast to this pre-war situation, factories were the largest employers of northern black males during the 1920s, and manual labor in manufacturing exceeded service employment by a wide margin. In addition, many thousands of black males were employed as manual laborers in coal yards, garages, laundries, stores and warehouses, railroad yards, and construction sites. Service employment still counted for at least one-quarter of all jobs, with blacks being most prevalent as railroad porters, domestics, waiters, janitors, and elevator operators. By far the largest number of black females were still employed as domestics, but over one-fourth of their jobs were found in manual labor categories. Work in clothing manufacturing and employment as laundry operatives were particularly widespread; the rapidly growing clerical occupations were barely open to blacks. Black women with high school and college degrees were often forced to work as domestics because employers refused to hire them for white-collar occupations.[12] Thus, women had made small advances into the economic mainstream, while black men had become a crucial component of the labor force in manufacturing.

During the 1920s, it was the white-collar professions that grew most rapidly—clerical, managerial, and professional—in the northern cities. Black progress in these areas was largely confined to work within the ghetto. Small but growing numbers of males worked as physicians, clergy, owners of small businesses, actors, and musicians serving a ghetto clientele. Small numbers of females were similarly employed as teachers, actors, and musicians. Actually, black professionals in the entertainment categories acquired great fame in the 1920s, luring large numbers of whites to nightclubs in areas such as Harlem. In the clerical trades, female employment was rare, but many males worked as messengers, office boys and Post Office clerks. Since admission to Post Office employment was by nondiscriminatory competitive examination, this line of work became increasingly popular among blacks.

The growing number of white-collar jobs were filled by upwardly mobile and younger whites, and the significance for blacks lay in the fact that white workers were not available in sufficient numbers to fill manual occupations during the 1920s. To fill this shortage, blacks were employed in manual labor jobs that had been the domain of whites, particularly foreign-born immigrants, prior to World War I. Transformation of the ghetto labor force from service to manual work was rooted both in the decline of European immigration and in the nature of urban economic growth. Northern cities that had collected most of the black migrants were still vigorous, growing industrial centers during the 1920s.

Major technological advances after the Civil War were responsible for the continuing growth and vitality of giant eastern and midwestern cities. A well-developed railroad network in the region lowered the cost of transit and increased the flexibility of heavy cargo shipment. Rail transit combined advantages of water transit (cheap but inflexible) and horse-drawn wagon transit (flexible but expensive). Rail freight-yard and terminal cities offered choice locations for manufacturing and distribution activities. Enormous steel mills, refineries, packing plants, and warehouse complexes sprang up near these rail terminals. As the agricultural hinterland increasingly delivered its crops to these cities, great food processing complexes such as flour mills and brew-eries clustered near the rail yards. Perfection of electricity freed man-ufacturers from dependence upon steam and water power, giving them the flexibility to locate factories near the best transportation, sales, and labor sites rather than near sites of cheap power. The giant cities, Chicago, Philadelphia, and New York, were the greatest centers of manufacturing activity, and they were also the greatest terminal cities for the railroads. Similarly, two cheap modes of transit, rail and water, were available at each of the megalopolises. The region's large volume of rail traffic, along with the presence of competing rail sys-tems, kept rates low and service high. A vast regional market, con-nected to the rest of the nation by rail, was created and industrial development snowballed.[13] Proximity to other manufacturers in ad-dition to low rail rates often created external economies for industries. The automobile industry grew up within this region to capitalize upon good rail service and the large regional market. The auto producers were able to hold down transit and inventory costs by locating close to major suppliers such as steel mills.

Great manufacturing complexes required vast numbers of blue-collar workers, and blacks after 1915 accounted for a growing share of this industrial labor force. In contrast to their nineteenth-century status as southern agricultural workers and service employees, blacks were moving into twentieth-century urban-industrial America on a large scale. As long as the demand for their labor remained strong in these northern industrial centers, blacks continued en masse to abandon southern agricultural life in favor of northern factory work.

In addition to the shifting occupational structure, World War I was an important line of demarcation regarding black residential patterns. Black ghettos became the norm in northern cities, and white intol-erance toward integrated housing was nearly universal. Mere black presence in cities was not responsible for the segregated housing pat-terns that white communities now demanded. Integrated housing had been quite common in cities throughout the United States, and it was still widespread after World War I in many southern cities.[14] Accep-tance of integrated neighborhoods by whites was most common when blacks were predominantly service workers rather than factory proletarians. In southern communities where blacks continued to work primarily in racially stereotyped service jobs, integrated housing persisted; in the emerging southern industrial cities such as Birmingham, segregated residential patterns developed along northern lines.

Blacks who had resided in northern cities before the war overwhelmingly blamed the wartime southern migrants for the deterioration in race relations. The new residents, they felt, had disturbed the balance that had existed between the black and white communities. A common theme in the denunciations was that the new migrants "didn't know how to act" or that they "spoiled things."[15] Relative to the previous black residents, the migrants were distinctly less sophisticated, less educated, and ignorant of urban ways. Part of the white community's reaction to the migrants was undoubtedly rooted in considerations of class: these southern agrarians were deemed undesirable because they were lower class. But class considerations alone cannot explain the creation of the ghetto and the general decline in race relations. The very rapidity of the black influx and the wartime shortage of housing contributed to racial antagonism. But a new feature of the northern black population was their widespread employment in manufacturing where they were competitors for the jobs of whites. Black acceptance of lower wages, their frequent rejection of unions, and their willingness to break strikes were particularly threatening to whites during recession from 1919 to 1920. When blacks were few in number and working mainly in service jobs that most whites shunned, they were not threatening to many white workers. When blacks posed a genuine threat to the economic livelihood of blue-collar whites, racism flourished. Racial antagonism in the job market contributed mightily to the creation of the black ghetto.

4

Ghetto Life During the Great Depression

Unemployment

The phrase, "last hired, first fired," is a devastatingly accurate portrayal of economic well-being among black ghetto residents during the 1930s. Northern industrial cities in general were harder hit by the depression than other areas of the United States. By 1930, no substantial increase had occurred in unemployment rates of southern black males and females (which were in the 3 to 4 percent range), and differentials in black—white unemployment levels were virtually nonexistent. In contrast, 14.3 percent and 8.2 percent of northern black males and females, respectively, were unemployed by April 1930, while unemployment rates among white males and females were 8.2 and 4.9 percent. Northern manufacturing industries most quickly felt the impact of the depression, and it was quite common for manufacturers to have laid off or fired over one-half of their black employees by 1931. Areas of the economy that had accounted for the greatest gains in black employment since World War I were precisely those areas where black job loss was greatest.[1] Detroit provided the most vivid example of rapid industrial decline; by January 1931 nearly one-third of the white males and roughly 60 percent of the black male workers were unemployed in this industrial city.[2]

A new phenomenon, wide differentials in black–white unemployment rates, emerged in northern cities during the early 1930s. Black employment gains had occurred largely in prosperous periods when white workers were often unavailable to fill manual labor jobs. During the depression, though, abundant numbers of white workers were willing to accept the lower-paying manual labor jobs that they had shunned during the 1920s. During a labor surplus, black workers were not essential. Thus, employers frequently met their reduced labor needs by downgrading white workers to jobs that had previously been held by blacks, while black workers were dispensed with. In service as well as manufacturing occupations, increased white competition was displacing blacks from jobs where they had been dominant during times of prosperity. Unemployed whites began to compete with blacks for such jobs as janitors, waiters, cooks, and domestics. Major hotels that had traditionally employed black waiters frequently switched to white females during the early depression years. While blacks retained their relative share of jobs with some employers, displacement by downwardly mobile whites was sufficiently common to produce black unemployment rates that vastly exceeded white rates of joblessness in all northern cities. Because blacks were indeed the last hired and first fired, they suffered the effects of disproportionate massive unemployment until conditions of labor shortage appeared once again during World War II.

Coping with Mass Unemployment

Government relief was one possible alternative to wage income, but the ballooning numbers of urban unemployed strained the patchwork relief system to the breaking point. By 1932, roughly one-fourth of the unemployed in the United States were actually receiving relief, limited mainly to food.[3] In Chicago, the estimated 700,000 unemployed workers accounted for about 50 percent of the labor force, but in poorer black districts the rate of joblessness was sometimes as high as 90 percent. Local relief systems could not handle the burden.

Financed by a combination of private charity supplemented by state and local government contributions, relief provision in the early 1930s was locally administered and inconsistent in scope. As voluntary funds ran out, relief by 1932 became roughly 90 percent government funded. In New York City, about one-half of the unemployed family heads were on relief, which averaged $2.39 per family per week.[4] A more extreme situation arose in Philadelphia, where relief agencies—completely out of funds from all sources—discontinued every sort of payment to the needy for two months in the summer of 1932. Philadelphia's main relief agency, the Community Council, described the situation in July 1932 as one of "slow starvation and progressive disintegration of family life."[5] As local relief agencies ran out of funds, the sole response of Congress and the Hoover administration was to appropriate, in July 1932, $300 million for loans to state and local relief authorities. This meager amount had little effect. Systematic compilations of the deprivations endured by unemployed households were few, but numerous journalistic accounts of the era describe such conditions as widespread child malnutrition and deteriorating health conditions.[6] Relief was a poor substitute for wage income during the early depression years.

The condition of ghetto dwellers in the pre-Roosevelt depression years can be gleaned indirectly from data generated by landlord efforts to protect their real estate property. Specifically, millions of destitute tenants were unable to meet their rent payments, and the magnitude of their plight was recorded in the nation's courts that handled evictions. Destitution was commonly not accepted as a defense against eviction; property rights took precedence. In 1933, about 60 percent of Philadelphia's landlords were pursuing eviction preceedings against one or more of their tenants. Removals by compulsion were running at a 16 percent annual rate; "one family in every six was being forced out of its home under pressure from the landlord."[7]

A more systematic study of evictions and their side effects in Chicago was conducted by students and faculty members of the University of Chicago's School of Social Service Administration. Table 4.1 describes the activities of Chicago's Court of Forcible Entry and Detainer (renter's court) during the 1920s and early 1930s. Eviction by legal

Table 4.1. Chicago Renter's Court Activities

	Number of Forcible Entry and Detainer Suits Filed	Number of Writs of Restitution Issued
1920–1929 (annual average)	18,824	3,312
1930	28,462	5,442
1931	39,184	7,215
1932	56,246	63,152

Source: Edith Abbott, *The Tenements of Chicago: 1908–1935* (New York: Arno Press and the *New York Times*, 1970), pp. 433–34.

process for nonpayment of rent is a three-step legal process. The first step entails notifying the delinquent tenant that rent must be paid within a certain length of time; the landlord's "five-day notice." After the time limit set in the notice has passed, the landlord may consider the lease terminated and sue the tenant. This second step in the eviction process begins when the landlord sues for termination of the lease and possession of the premises; this entails filing a "forcible entry and detainer" suit in renter's court. The number of forcible detainer suits filed against Chicago tenants averaged 18,824 per year in the 1920s (table 4.1). Numbers of suits filed in the early 1930s rose very rapidly to a peak of 56,246 in 1932, a level that was almost exactly matched by the 56,158 forcible detainer suits filed against tenants in 1933. By 1933, widespread landlord bankruptcy had begun to reduce their propensity to sue nonpaying tenants.

Tenants answering to forcible entry and detainer suits typically pleaded inability to pay in the early 1930s and were ordered by the court to vacate their apartments within five days. In cases of severe hardship, tenants were allowed as much as fifteen or twenty days to move out. By 1932, however, an entirely new development altered the nature of landlord-tenant litigation: destitute tenants were defying the court orders en masse because they had no money and no alternative housing available. When tenants defy court orders to vacate, the landlords take the final legal step in the eviction process; they secure a writ of restitution to enforce the court's order. This writ is served by the bailiff upon the tenants and it informs them that they will be physically dispossessed within twenty-four hours. In other words, the police are coming to put the tenants and their possessions out into the street. Writs of restitution jumped nearly twenty-fold from their 1920s average of 3,312 to their 1932 peak of 63,152 (table 4.1). Whereas in the 1920s, court orders secured through forcible entry and detainer suits were sufficient to induce most delinquent tenants to vacate, by 1932 only the immediate reality of police force could remove most tenants from their dwellings.

Physical evictions on a massive scale produced related problems. Police forces were stretched thin by the magnitude of evictions being processed. This problem was exacerbated by the fact that residents in some ghetto areas were actively resisting police attempts to evict destitute tenants. The first of a series of rent riots occurred in Chicago in August 1931. A crowd of about two thousand resisted eviction of a black family in one of Chicago's poorest sections, leading to "disorderly proceedings in which three rioters were shot and killed, three policemen and a fourth rioter were seriously injured."[8] A group called the Unemployed Council organized systematic resistance to evictions in Chicago's ghettos. As soon as the police began evicting a tenant, word would spread to Unemployed Council members who would then gather together a group—often fifty to one hundred men—who would move the tenant's possessions back into the apartment as soon as the police had finished moving them out.

Many landlords faced a situation of nonpaying tenants, an eviction procedure whose effectiveness was declining, and a financial pinch exacerbated by the need to pay the legal costs of evicting tenants. To avoid eviction costs and delays, landlords often resorted to various schemes that would force out tenants by making the dwellings un-inhabitable, such as by shutting off the electricity, gas, and heat. In severe instances, landlords would resort to such illegal practices as turning off the water and removing the window frames. Normal building maintenance—for example, garbage removal and repair of pipes, windows, roofs,—was discontinued. Overt landlord malice was often unnecessary to achieve severe building deterioration. Faced with numerous nonpaying tenants, many landlords could not pay utility bills or mortgages on their property. Many lost their buildings through mortgage default. Predictably, utilities were shut off by the gas and electric companies and coal deliveries ceased because of nonpayment for previous deliveries. Lack of heat in the winter caused pipes to burst, and lack of water persisted because no money was available to pay for plumbing repairs. Rats were a serious problem in these buildings and disease and despair were rampant. Although the buildings were indeed unfit for human habitation, most continued to be occupied.

Nonetheless, those who remained in their apartments were often better off than those who were put out into the street. The following plea of a woman in Chicago's Renter Court typified the cases that the court dealt with every day in 1932. Her husband was very ill, her fourteen-year-old son was seriously ill (probably dying), her apartment had no electricity or gas, and she had no food. No one would help her; she burst into uncontrolled weeping, and finally threatened to kill the whole family.[9] Some of the dramatics could have been solely for the court's benefit, but many families did indeed face this reality. Instances of families dying in the streets, however, were extremely rare. Friends, neighbors, and relatives showed incredible generosity in helping those who were literally homeless. This often produced severe overcrowding and family breakups. A neighbor might take in one child while another would be allowed to sleep in a friend's car at night. Officials often looked the other way when the homeless took refuge in abandoned factories, warehouses, hotels, and so forth. Anywhere from one to two million people, predominantly younger males, simply hit the road, sleeping in boxcars and under bridges. Detroit dealt with the homeless by sponsoring a tent city to house evicted welfare families. The Michigan National Guard provided this endeavor with blankets, cots, and 300 large tents.

In June 1932, Chicago's Mayor Cermak vainly suggested that Washington send relief funds now rather than federal troops later. President Hoover did not act, but President Roosevelt in 1933 proved to be more willing to assist the destitute. In April 1933, the Federal Emergency Relief Administration (FERA) was funded with $500 million for grants to states.[10] FERA's energetic administrator, Harry Hopkins, had sent emergency aid to seven states before the conclusion of his second day in office. FERA was followed by Civil Works Administration (CWA) which managed to employ, under Hopkins' direction, four million workers by January 1934. CWA personnel built and repaired roads, schools, airports, parks, sewers, swimming pools, and similar projects. FERA, the CWA, and later federal programs coincided with an upturn in the private economy during 1933 and 1934. The worst of the Great Depression had passed. Nonetheless, severe unemployment and destitution were the norm in urban ghettos until World War II. "We have never given adequate relief," said Hopkins in 1936.

Recovery from the Great Depression was far slower in the urban ghettos than it was in the rest of the country. By the late 1930s, over 50 percent of the black households in many northern cities depended upon the federal government for some type of financial assistance.[11] In March 1940, black male unemployment rates ranged from 30 to 39 percent in New York, Chicago, Philadelphia, and Detroit, while white male unemployment rates in these cities varied between 12 and 18 percent.[12]

In the southern states, blacks often worked in traditional occupations that were racially stereotyped, virtually institutionalized as "black" jobs. In the North these lines of work such as cooking and cleaning were not widely recognized as black jobs even though blacks often filled them. This racial stereotyping of jobs, usually a hindrance, actually protected southern blacks during the depression because they were rarely pushed out of traditional jobs by whites. The firmly entrenched southern color caste system generated both greater security in traditional jobs and more difficulty in securing new and better employment opportunities in periods of labor shortage. Whereas northern black prosperity depended upon continuous economic growth and labor market tightness, increases in southern black economic well-being required breaking down of racial stereotypes in employment.

Impact of Government Programs

Black migration to northern cities slowed dramatically, but it did continue during the depression decade. Part of this migration was rooted not in the lure of economic opportunity but in agricultural displacement. While depression politics generated many relief and make-work programs that benefitted blacks, government programs in the 1930s often inadvertently reduced black economic well-being. The Agricultural Adjustment Administration dealt with farm problems by discouraging production of such key crops as cotton. Reduced cotton cultivation in turn caused planters to fire black field hands and it forced some sharecroppers to abandon farming.[13]

Similarly, federally funded construction projects in the early 1930s often served to force blacks out of the building trades. Blacks in the South often maintained their construction jobs by working for lower wages than whites. Since federal projects did not allow racial wage differentials, contractors who preferred to employ whites curtailed black employment because they now had absolutely no incentive to employ blacks. Later in the decade, Public Works Administration projects required that contractors employ some black workers, and other agencies adopted nondiscriminatory employment codes for their contractors. In 1940, for example, the U.S. Housing Authority required that 5.8 percent of the total payroll for skilled workers on public housing projects in 95 cities had to be paid to black artisans.[14]

In the housing realm, creation of the Federal Housing Administration (FHA) during the New Deal stimulated housing construction because this agency assumed the default risk of home mortgages issued by private financial institutions. Freed of loan default risk, lenders were willing to provide FHA insured home mortgages to middle-income home buyers who had previously been denied access to mortgage credit. The FHA's policies were blatantly discriminatory against blacks. The FHA encouraged construction of new homes in suburban areas or in vacant sites located in outlying areas of older cities. Blacks were not welcome in such neighborhoods. Since homes built with FHA mortgages typically carried racially restrictive covenants, blacks who could afford to purchase these homes were legally barred from doing so. Furthermore, FHA policies stressed that mortgages should not be insured in areas where "inharmonious racial groups" resided.[15] These policies amounted to a direct federal government endorsement of residential segregation and racial covenants. Developers, financial institutions, and real estate companies could now correctly state that the FHA was responsible for excluding blacks from most of the new housing that was constructed between 1934 and 1940. Government housing policies beneficial to blacks did exist. By May 1940, the U.S. Housing Authority had under contract about 140,000 housing units and over one-third of these units were designated for black occupancy. Like the FHA, this agency assumed that housing projects built under its jurisdiction would typically be racially homogeneous. Federal housing policies in the 1930s decade did in fact consistently promote and reinforce segregated housing.

Of all the various New Deal programs, labor reform legislation perhaps had the greatest long-term impact upon black workers. This is discussed in detail in chapter 7.

5

The World War II Interlude

Recovery Comes Slowly

By 1940, the employment gains of blacks in manufacturing had been eroded severely by the prolonged 1930s depression. As the nation's military buildup began to accelerate, black workers were distinctly on the sidelines of the industrial labor force. The black labor force stood as a vast reserve army that had been pulled into basic industry during World War I and the prosperous 1920s years, only to be massively expelled during the depression. This reserve army was destined to re-enter basic industry during the labor shortages of World War II on a scale that greatly exceeded any previous black employment in manufacturing. However, World War II production demanded less of the unskilled manual labor that blacks traditionally provided, and more of such skilled labor types as machinists, electricians, sheetmetal workers, and welders—areas in which few blacks had ever been employed or trained. Jobs and training in the expanding war industries were initially offered almost solely to white workers. In April 1940, for example, total black and white unemployment rates nationwide stood at 22.0 percent and 17.7 percent respectively. By October 1940, U.S. employment had grown by two million and the unemployment rate among whites had fallen to 13.0 percent; black unemployment meanwhile had declined by a mere one-tenth of one percent. Between January and March 1941, the U.S. Employment Service placed nearly 35,000 workers in foundry and forging, machine shop and machine tool, and metal processing industries; 245 of these were blacks. Proportionately fewer blacks were placed in aircraft and electrical equipment industries.[1] As in earlier periods of economic expansion, blacks were pulled into jobs vacated by upwardly mobile white workers. Thus black job gains in 1941 were concentrated in such areas as restaurant and hotel service work, janitorial services, and unskilled manual labor in low-paying industries. The twentieth-century urban employment cycle—last hired, first fired—once again typified black employment at the beginning of World War II.

Early wartime employment of blacks in manufacturing was more substantial in World War I than in World War II for several important reasons:

1. When the World War II economic boom began, large numbers of white workers were available to fill the jobs that war production was opening up.
2. The need for unskilled labor was relatively smaller than it had been during the previous war. Furthermore, blacks were grossly underrepresented in the vocational training programs that government had organized for war industry employees.[2]
3. Since most large manufacturing industries had accepted labor unions as bargaining agents for their blue-collar workers, their need for blacks as allies to keep out unions was greatly reduced.

The World War II Employment Boom

By the summer of 1942, black workers accounted for only 3 percent of the nation's war industry labor force. Nonetheless, wartime labor shortages were beginning to draw greater numbers of blacks into manufacturing jobs. On 25 June 1941, President Roosevelt issued Executive Order 8802, calling for full participation in the war effort by all persons regardless of race, creed, or color. The order stipulated that all defense contracts were to include clauses requiring nondiscriminatory employment practices. Furthermore, the executive order required that vocational training programs were to be conducted without discrimination. Although Executive Order 8802 was often ignored, it did encourage war material contractors to employ at least token numbers of blacks to create an appearance of compliance. Prosecution of discriminatory employers in war industries was never effective but the bad publicity that frequently focused upon those employers was a partial check upon blatantly racist practices. The executive order's greatest significance was to open up black opportunities in the federal bureaucracy. Traditional barriers to employing black females as clerical workers were abandoned by most government agencies. In the Washington area, 90 percent of the government's black employees in 1938 had been in subclerical jobs. By November 1942, federal government employment of blacks had increased substantially and nearly 50 percent were working in clerical and professional capacities.[3]

By late 1942, growing labor shortages and continuing government pressures were drawing blacks into industries that had traditionally been closed—communications equipment, aircraft, industrial machinery, plastics, etc. In traditional industries of employment such as autos and steel, blacks began to be upgraded into many skilled job categories. The occupational upgrading process was not always a smooth one. Detroit, for example, had an unusually large number of southern-born white workers, and the Klu Klux Klan was active in some of its war industries. Transfer of black workers to defense production, typically in skilled job categories, caused work stoppages among whites at Chrysler, Packard, and Hudson. When companies removed blacks in response to work stoppages, or practiced discriminatory transfer and promotion policies, black workers objected strenuously and sometimes resorted to work stoppages of their own. The United Auto Workers (UAW) demanded nondiscriminatory transfer and upgrading opportunities for black workers, suggesting that whites who were fired for opposition to these policies would receive no union support. When work stoppages by whites were firmly opposed by management and the UAW, black upgrading typically took place with minimal difficulty. The actual firing of whites who organized work disruption at Chrysler and Hudson demonstrated the commitment of management and the UAW to black worker upgrading. By late 1942, most of the Detroit area defense contractors had begun to utilize blacks in many semiskilled and skilled job categories that had previously been the domain of white workers only.

Another route to skilled job opportunities entailed completion of government-sponsored courses that taught such vitally needed skills as welding. Once again, in response to federal government pressure and growing labor shortages, these courses were opened up by 1942 to black workers residing in many northern and western cities. The southern response was less encouraging. In early 1943, there were twenty-five areas of acute labor shortage where government courses teaching skilled trades were vital for filling manpower needs. Seven of these areas were in the South, and five of the seven did not offer training for blacks. During 1943, over 112,000 blacks completed war production training and related courses, predominantly in shipbuilding, aircraft, and machine shop occupations.[4] Combined with the opportunity to utilize these skills in war industries outside of the South, this training represented a historically unparalleled upgrading of black workforce status. Some southern areas actually did allow blacks to move into skilled occupations during the war, but progress was slight, even in areas suffering from critical shortages of skilled workers. In Virginia's Hampton Roads area, four large government establishments and one large private shipbuilder employed 17,000 blacks: 2,000 were skilled, 7,000 semiskilled, and 8,000 unskilled. Mobile, Alabama, in contrast, was an area of severe labor shortage that clung to racist employment practices. In early 1943, the three largest defense contractors and one large government installation employed 12,000 black workers: approximately 83 percent worked as unskilled laborers and one percent held skilled jobs. Despite severe shortages of welders, no blacks held welding jobs.[5] It was not until late 1944 that some blacks were being trained and employed as welders in Mobile.

After a slow start, World War II finally opened to black workers the greatest occupational and industrial diversification and penetration that they had ever achieved in American industry. By September 1944, black workers made up 8 percent of the war industry labor force, and their major gains had occurred in semiskilled and skilled occupations. Black males were 5.9 percent of all operatives in 1940, and 10.1 percent of the total in 1944. Black females constituted 4.7 percent of all female operatives in 1940; by 1944 their share had increased to 8.3 percent.[6] Simultaneously, the proportion working as domestics fell from nearly 60 percent of all employed black women to less than 45 percent in 1944. Predictably, black participation in war industries was geographically concentrated in areas of greatest labor shortage. Nine large industrial centers accounted for 35 percent of all black defense industry employment in September 1944 (when 1.5 million blacks were working in the war industries): Chicago, Detroit, Cleveland, Los Angeles, San Francisco Bay, Philadelphia, Newark, Baltimore, and Hampton Roads. This heavy concentration in predominantly northern and very large cities closely resembled the pattern of black industrial employment that emerged during World War I. The First World War allowed blacks to establish themselves as unskilled workers in heavy industry, while World War II opened up semiskilled and some skilled employment in a much larger variety of industries.[7] The resultant economic advancement brought higher family incomes and it allowed black females in particular to achieve greater occupational diversity.

Black migration from farm to factory occurred on a large scale once labor shortages in centers of war production began to draw many thousands of unemployed blacks into industrial jobs. The migration patterns that emerged in 1942 through 1945 rather closely resembled World War I's migration flows. Black job seekers largely abandoned rural southern areas for destinations in large centers of industrial production. By 1944, Chicago and Detroit had received roughly 65,000 and 60,000 black migrants, respectively, which was somewhat greater than the black in-migration that these two cities had experienced during World War I. The most dramatic new migration flows brought large numbers of southern blacks to West Coast cities that were centers for shipbuilding and aircraft industries (table 5.1). Cities

Table 5.1. Black Population Increase in Selected Areas and Cities, 1940–1950

	Urban Black Population (in thousands)		Black Increase (in percentage)
	1940	1950	1940–1950
Areas			
Northeast	1,234	1,897	53.7
Northcentral	1,261	2,082	65.1
West	142	513	261.3
South	3,616	4,880	35.0
Total	6,253	9,372	49.8
All Non-South	2,637	4,492	70.3
	1940	1945, 1946*	1940–1945, 1946*
Cities			
Los Angeles	63,774	133,082	108.7
San Francisco	4,846	32,001	560.4
Oakland	8,462	37,327	341.1
San Diego	4,143	13,136	217.1

Sources: C. Horace Hamilton, "The Negro Leaves the South," *Demography* 1, no. 1 (1964):276; Robert Weaver, *The Negro Ghetto* (New York: Russell and Russell, 1948), p. 84.

*As of 28 January 1946 for Los Angeles; 1 August 1945 for San Francisco; 9 October 1945 for Oakland; and 21 February 1946 for San Diego.

that had very small black populations before World War II were often confronted with large numbers of migrants. For example, black inhabitants of the Portland Oregon area increased in number from 2,000 in 1940 to over 15,000 by 1944.[8] The total West Coast black population increased by 261.3 percent during the 1940s and this region was simultaneously absorbing a major expansion in white population (table 5.1).

For the first time, during the 1940s, black Americans became predominantly an urban people, and in non-southern states well over 90 percent of all blacks resided in cities. Between 1940 and 1950, the black urban population increased by 70.3 percent in northern and western states, while it grew by 35 percent in the South.[9]

During the 1940s trek to urban areas, black migrants lagged a year or two behind an earlier migration that had drawn several million whites into the cities. The San Francisco Bay region, for example, had experienced a total in-migration exceeding half a million people between 1940 and 1945. The industrial cities to which most blacks migrated were often crowded due to the earlier arrival of whites seeking jobs in war industries during 1940 and 1941. The newest wartime arrivals were predictably forced into already overcrowded black ghetto areas, and neighboring white districts were often similarly crowded by job-seeking migrants. Ghetto expansion was greatly complicated in cities where numerous white residents were competing for an inadequate supply of housing. This situation strengthened residential segregation, forcing chronic ghetto overcrowding to reach unprecedented proportions. Reminiscent of World War I, this situation produced race riots as well as terrorist attacks on those few blacks who sought to reside in white neighborhoods.

Thus, the World War II years produced a weakening of the color line in employment, but a hardening of segregation patterns in the housing market. It was economic necessity, of course, that was largely responsible for both developments. The suggestion that black migrant war workers, no less than whites, had to have housing was invariably met with a storm of protests. The vacancy rate for housing in black areas of Chicago fell to 0.1 percent in August 1943, and it remained at that level until after the Japanese surrender.[10] The Mayor's Commission on Human Relations in Chicago estimated that the excess population in the black belt was in the range of 100,000 persons.

The most publicized conflict over housing occurred in Detroit, leading directly to a small race riot while setting the stage for all-out strife in 1943. The Federal Works Agency (FWA) of Detroit announced, on 16 December 1941, plans to build a 200-unit housing project on the ghetto periphery, and the project was named Sojourner Truth after the famous black abolitionist. Two weeks later, the Detroit Housing Commission was authorized to open the project to black occupancy. White residents in the area, protesting this extension of ghetto boundaries, announced their intention to quit making mortgage payments. A congressional investigating committee visited Detroit and held a hearing on the intended racial occupancy of Sojourner Truth. The FHA advised the head of the investigating committee that black occupancy in the planned housing project would depreciate mortgages that the FHA had insured in the area. Under public pressure, the FWA announced that another site would be found for black housing; the Sojourner Truth project—name intact—was to be reserved for white occupancy!

Since no other site could be located, the mayor and the Detroit Housing Commission requested reassignment of Sojourner Truth to blacks. Subsequently, the FWA announced on 2 February 1942, the reassignment of Sojourner Truth to black war industry workers. When twelve black families attempted to move into the project later that month, they were blocked by several hundred whites. Blacks from the surrounding area arrived at the confrontation sight; police offered the would-be tenants no assistance or protection. Rioting started, leading to 100 arrests and the hospitalization of thirty-eight people. Under military protection, blacks who were producing the equipment and supplies necessary to defeat fascism abroad finally moved into Sojourner Truth.

The Sojourner Truth incident aggravated existing racial antagonisms and culminated in the largest outbreak of race riots of the World War II years, leaving thirty-five dead, over 500 injured, and producing millions of dollars in property destruction.[11] In a more disbursed manner, black residents spilling out of Chicago's overcrowded black belt were met with dozens of bombing and arson attacks that generally grew in frequency through 1947. Segregated ghetto living was clearly reinforced by World War II's housing shortages. Coexisting with wartime full employment and its attendant occupational and income gains was the reality of extraordinarily overcrowded ghettos fighting against housing segregation patterns that were becoming steadily more rigid.

6

The Collapse of Traditional Southern Agriculture

The Agrarian Roots of Urban Ghettos

Immediately before World War I, about 80 percent of the U.S. black population resided in rural southern areas. During World War I, agricultural workers from these regions made up the vast majority of black migrants to northern industrial regions. The rural to urban migration flow continued to grow in magnitude during the 1920s, slowed during the depression decade, and reached its greatest numbers during the 1940s and 1950s. By 1960, blacks residing in northern and western cities outnumbered the remaining rural southern black population. Of those staying in southern states, nearly 60 percent resided in cities.[1] The relocation from farm to city reshaped black existence in America more profoundly than the abolition of slavery. What caused the migration? How did rural southern society prepare black migrants for life in the city? What attitudes, skills, and educational backgrounds did the migrants possess when they arrived in urban America? Earlier chapters have emphasized the lure of economic opportunity, particularly during wartime labor shortages, as a major cause of black rural to urban migration. But abandonment of the rural South continued during the depression years and during recession years following World War II; in addition to the lure of jobs, the collapse of traditional southern agriculture was feeding the migration stream, forcing millions to abandon farming.

Mechanization was largely responsible for destroying the traditional role of black farm workers, just as it forced many white farmers off the land. But the unique problems facing the migrants who were driven out of southern agriculture were rooted in socioeconomic forces much more complex than mere mechanization. The black migrants typically left behind a system that was detrimental—to the fertility of the soil, to the people who worked the land, and to the social order that southern agriculture supported.[2] White migrants from farm regions, on the other hand, came from a far different cultural and economic background that made their adaptation to urban life far smoother. Other post–World War II migrant groups had some of the same difficulties as rural blacks in moving into the mainstream of American life, includng Puerto Ricans and many Appalachian whites displaced by the mechanization of coal mining. In all three cases, the roots of the difficulties were a complex set of social and economic institutions that had placed the migrants at the bottom of society prior to their migration.

The Cotton Belt

The cotton belt includes the most fertile soil in the South and contains a disproportionate number of the poorest people in the United States. As determined by soil, temperature, and rainfall, the traditional cotton region was between 25° and 37° north latitude, occupying a 300-mile-wide belt stretching from the Carolinas to western Texas. Traditionally, a larger acreage was devoted to cotton than the combined total of all other crops. Corn, the second largest crop, was merely the servant of cotton, feeding the mules that pulled the farm implements and the hogs whose meat was the dietary mainstay of the agricultural labor force. Before 1950, the cotton belt was the home of a few large planters, some independent farmers (predominantly white), and many tenants, both black and white. Where cotton was the most prevalent crop and the soil was richest, black tenants were most likely to dominate the workforce. Many thousands of these black tenants neither raised a garden, nor owned livestock or farm equipment—not even a hoe. They raised cotton under the supervision of white planters and their overseers. Rickets and pellagra, two diseases of poverty, were common among blacks who tilled the most productive soil in the South.

When cotton flourished one found a few large, well-maintained houses where the affluent planters resided and many small, unpainted shacks where the tenants lived. When the cotton crop was abundant and prices were good, there was no need to diversify into other crops. But when the cotton crop was poor or the price of cotton was low, there was little cash or credit available to invest in machinery for growing other crops. Besides, the labor force did not know how to raise crops other than cotton and corn. Cultivation of cotton year after year depleted the soil, perpetuated crude and obsolete agricultural practices, and left in its wake an impoverished people supported by crippled institutions. Throughout the 1920s and 1930s, the cotton crop was frequently poor *and* prices were low, bankrupting many of the large planters and driving the tenants (both black and white) into very deep poverty.

After the Civil War, cotton was raised increasingly by a system of sharecropping, whereby tenants worked the land "on halves." In 1880, 64 percent of all southern farms were owner operated but this figure was lower in the cotton belt. The percentage of farms operated by owners fell steadily, reaching 53 percent in 1900 and 44 percent in 1930.[3] The majority of tenants worked on small holdings rather than large plantations, and white tenants were more numerous than blacks. Whites, however, were most commonly working on the small holdings in hilly regions and in areas with less fertile soil. The plantations dominated the rich bottom lands where soil fertility was greatest. They relied more heavily on cotton, relative to the small farms, and the majority of plantation tenants were blacks.

Southern agricultural workers who did not own land were of four types: cash tenants, share tenants, share croppers, and wage laborers. The most affluent agricultural workers were tenants who paid a cash rental for use of the land. These tenants owned their own equipment and made their own decisions about growing and marketing crops. Cash tenants were the least common type of black agricultural workers. Share tenants, because they owned some of their own equipment, were able to rent land on the basis of paying the owner between one-fourth and one-third of the crop raised. Sharecroppers, in contrast, had nothing to offer but their own labor. The landowner provided the sharecropper with the mules and equipment necessary to raise a cotton crop and, in return, the sharecropper paid as rent about one-half of the cotton crop. In addition, share tenants and croppers had to pay (out of their share of the crop) for seed, fertilizer, and food supplies that were provided to them by the landowner. Share tenants and croppers were provided with a two-or three-room wooden shack, and they were often allowed to raise vegetable gardens for personal use. The poorest agricultural workers were wage laborers. They were not guaranteed any fixed amount of work; they were employed by the day when they were needed, and they may or may not be provided with a shack to live in. As the traditional cotton economy deteriorated in the 1920s and 1930s, blacks were increasingly downgraded from share tenant and cropper status to wage labor status. Early agricultural mechanization also encouraged downgrading to wage labor status.

Share tenants and croppers were designated as farmers in the census, but they closely resembled ordinary laborers in many ways. They were told what crops to plant, when to plant them, and the number of acres to be planted. Especially on the large plantations, their work would be regularly supervised by the landlord or his agents. Share tenants and croppers were entrepreneurs, however, in one important sense: they carried a considerable share of the risk involved in raising and marketing the crop. When the crop was bad or prices for cotton were particularly low, the cropper might find himself at harvest time with no remaining cash after the landlord had charged him for food, seed, and fertilizer. The tenant would then be entirely dependent upon home-raised produce plus cash advances or credit arranged by the landlord. Living in a perpetual state of indebtedness to the landowner was not uncommon. When the cotton crop was sold, the tenant had to take the landlord's word for the price that was obtained. Furthermore, the landlord kept all accounts on credit and supplies advanced to the tenant, and the landlord determined the rate of interest charged on all advances. Tenants were not allowed to question or even to check the accuracy of the landlord's accounting for crop proceeds, advances, and interest charges. Particularly when the landlords themselves were close to bankruptcy, the temptation to cheat the tenants at settlement time must have been strong. Blatant cheating of tenants, though, would make it difficult for the landowner to attract and hold good workers.

The advancing of food, clothing, and supplies to sharecroppers was quite normal because these workers typically had no resources of their own—otherwise they would not have been sharecroppers. The cropper would most commonly receive credit from the landlord, usually at a particular store or commissary, so that he could purchase food and other necessities up to a certain amount each month. Since this restricted the cropper to purchase only at the store where credit was available, it was an easy matter to mark up prices considerably on tenant purchases. A study of the Mississippi delta area in 1936 showed that the average subsistence advance per year was roughly $94 for sharecroppers and $138 for share tenants. An additional $68 and

$145, respectively, were advanced to sharecroppers and share tenants for seed and fertilizer.[4] A flat 10 percent interest rate was normally charged on these advances at settlement time after the crop was sold in the fall. Since the duration of the advance was much less than one year, the effective annual rate of interest paid by share tenants and croppers was several times the 10 percent rate. The burden of paying 20 to 30 percent interest for goods purchased on credit at high prices kept many of the tenants in a perpetual state of indebtedness. Under these circumstances, it was difficult to accumulate the wealth that would allow for upward mobility to share tenant or cash tenant status, much less actual land ownership. Some incentive was necessary to keep up the laboring efforts of the share tenants and croppers. Since the share tenants owned their own mules and equipment, they faced the threat of losing these to the landlord if their cotton crop was not sufficient to pay off debts at harvest time. For the cropper, there was the threat of being thrown out by the landlord if one did not appear to be working diligently on the cotton crop. Finally, there was always the possibility of producing a big crop when cotton prices were high, enabling the tenant to pay off the landlord's advances and to have enough cash to live on without further credit. Once clear of debt at usurious interest rates and high commissary prices, the tenant could then perhaps accumulate enough to become a cash tenant, to buy an automobile, or even to purchase land. Enough black share tenants and croppers achieved such improved economic status (especially if they worked for honest landlords) to serve as examples for the payoffs of hard work. At the other extreme, the perpetual failure to escape indebtedness and to get ahead created many disillusioned tenants whose chief concern was merely to get by.

It was difficult for the sharecropper to escape from his status. State legislation made it virtually impossible for share tenant and cropper families to leave the land except in the fall after harvest time. Although debt peonage had been declared illegal by the Supreme Court in 1911, similar types of bondage were common. Tenants who were in debt to their landlords could be prevented from moving away until they paid off the indebtedness. This practice was made effective by gentlemen's agreements among landlords that they would accept tenants from other planters only if the move was approved by the present landlord. Since dishonest landowners could readily keep their tenants in debt, the only possible escape was often to flee the community entirely. Tenant dissatisfaction with landlords did in fact generate much moving from place to place, with whites being generally more mobile than blacks, and the lowest class of tenants being more mobile than cash and share tenants. Indeed, black sharecroppers in Georgia cotton belt counties were estimated to have a median residence length of less than three years in 1934.[5] Frequent moving from place to place made it difficult to develop a good vegetable garden; it certainly did not encourage sound soil conservation practices.

Overall, the share tenants and croppers in the cotton belt lived very poor lives and their chances for upward mobility were slim. With the landowner having the power to determine crops, planting, and harvesting times, cultivation techniques, and final crop marketing, independent decision-making by tenants was certainly not encouraged. Many planters discouraged tenants from developing good gardens, fearing that vegetable gardening would interfere with cotton cultivation; some landlords would not permit tenant gardens. The tenant had no incentive to improve his living quarters, because all improvements were the landlord's property. Many landlords looked down upon efforts by black families to educate their children, preferring that the youngsters work in the cotton fields. Tenant families resided in wooden shacks that had glassless and screenless windows, as well as leaky roofs. Black tenant families were often provided with open privies, but about one-third of them had no privies at all. Diet was dominated by the three Ms—meat, meal, and molasses—foods rich in fats and low in vitamin content. Fat salt pork followed by cornmeal typically accounted for over 60 percent (up to 70+ percent) of the caloric intake of black tenant families.[6] Particularly among families that did not raise gardens for personal use, this diet frequently caused such vitamin deficiency diseases as pellagra. Poor diet also produced high susceptibility to contagious diseases, low vitality, and a high death rate. Black tenant families suffered from an extremely high incidence of tuberculosis when they moved to congested urban ghettos.

Incentives that did exist under this system were often perverse: it was often to the tenant's advantage to rob the soil of its fertility. The tenant's incentive was to make no repairs or investments that were likely to outlive his tenure at his present residence. Once he had decided to move, the tenant found it to his advantage to burn planks from the porch floor as firewood, and to take along any moveable materials that had not succumbed to the ravages of earlier tenants. The result was exhausted soil and buildings unfit for human habitation, but the soil often continued to be used for cotton cultivation and the buildings housed more groups of tenant families. The result was a growing group of tenants with the attitude "What's the use of trying?"

The white landowner, of course, rationalized his privileged position by claiming that the tenants were childlike and improvident, willing to work only when in need of food. He had to tell his tenants what to plant, how to plant it, and when to harvest it. Why, if he did not keep an eye on them, they might starve to death. The typical tenants, according to the typical landlord, would not even bother to grow a garden unless they were told to do so. Tenants were seen as naturally lazy and shiftless, incapable of making a living without supervision; tenants would not even fix their own leaky roofs. In financial matters, the landlord must maintain a watchful eye on tenant money; otherwise the tenant would throw it away on foolish expenditures. Sweet benevolence—at 30 percent interest rates. The southern planters' rationale for share cropping closely resembled their rationale for slavery.

Bad Times

Periodic bad times were a normal part of life in the cotton belt. The early 1890s, for example, produced several years of particularly poor weather, while the early twentieth century brought severe boll weevil invasions that devastated the crop in parts of the western cotton belt. During these bad times, the tenants fell deeper in debt to the landlords, and the landlords assumed a greater indebtedness with such creditors as banks and insurance companies. Some of the weaker planters failed during these periods, but the system in general continued, waiting for high prices and large cotton crops to restore profitability and reduce the debt burden. World War I produced high cotton prices, generating prosperity even in regions where crops had been reduced by boll weevil infestation. Many tenants actually shared in this wartime prosperity.

During the 1920s and early 1930s, however, the cotton belt was devastated by disasters of nature and the marketplace. Year after year of poor crops combined with low cotton prices drove planters and tenants deeper into debt. Prices of cotton lands plummeted in value, and hundreds of banks that had financed landowners were themselves driven into bankruptcy by the prolonged cotton belt depression. As credit dried up and millions of acres of land fell into the hands of creditors, the landlord's traditional willingness to provide for his tenants through advances of food and supplies became less and less common. Many creditors, such as life insurance companies, acquired land when plantation owners defaulted on their loans, and these new owners had no interest in supplying food, seed, and fertilizer to sharecropper families. They wanted to rent the land to cash tenants, but the sharecroppers could not afford to feed themselves, much less pay cash rents. When landowner advances were not forthcoming, many tenants had no way to plant a crop, or even to survive, so they left for villages and urban areas. Fortunate tenants with relatives in the cities were frequently provided with sufficient transportation money to leave the cotton belt, often moving to northern cities where their relatives were enjoying the benefits of a strong job market during the 1920s.

Greene County, Georgia, provides an extreme example of the combined impacts of boll weevil infestation and low cotton prices.[7]

Year	Number of Cotton Bales Ginned
1918	18,773
1919	20,030
1920	13,414
1921	1,487
1922	333
1923	1,490
1924	4,279

During the ten years following 1924, the annual cotton crop fluctuated between 4,400 and 8,700 bales. Green county was very prosperous at the end of World War I. The boll weevil invasion of the early 1920s devastated cotton yields, and consistently low prices for the meager crop drove most of the large planters into bankruptcy. Thousands of tenant families left the county entirely and large tracts of cotton land reverted to brush and pines by the late 1920s. By 1925, land prices had dropped to one-fifth of their 1919 level, and pine saw logs had displaced cotton as the leading agricultural cash crop in the county. Traditional cotton belt agriculture never again reached more than a faction of its former self in Greene County; most of the old plantation owners were gone for good, and the tenant families had scattered. By 1927, nearly 16,000 acres had been sold by the sheriff for back taxes; the unpaid taxes amounted to $5,870, less than 37 cents per acre on average. Throughout Georgia and South Carolina, many cotton farms and plantations were permanently abandoned during the 1920s.

The reduced output of cotton would have produced, via supply and demand forces in the marketplace, sharply higher prices in earlier times. In the 1920s, however, the United States was losing its share of the world cotton market (over 50 percent of the crop was sold abroad) to aggressively expanding cotton producers in Egypt, India, Brazil, and a host of other countries. Nations such as Russia and China were expanding cotton production rapidly to meet their domestic needs, while cotton cultivation was springing up in new producing areas such as Nigeria and Uganda. Domestically, a new kind of cotton cultivation was spreading in Texas and Oklahoma that was more mechanized and less dependent upon tenant labor than cotton production in the deep South.

Depression in the early 1930s produced even lower demand for cotton and hence even lower prices. A study of 2,000 cotton producing tenant families in Mississippi, Alabama, Texas, and South Carolina found that average cash income in 1933 was $105.43.[8] In that year the federal government instituted a series of agricultural programs, particularly the Agricultural Adjustment Program (AAA), that were destined to push additional tens of thousands of black families out of tenancy. The AAA paid direct subsidies to farmers who agreed to reduce their cotton crop acreages; its overall objective was to raise and stabilize farm income. Landlords of course divided the reduced cotton acreage among fewer tenants, and they expelled thousands of now superfluous tenants from their lands. Government payments to compensate farmers for their acreage reductions were supposed to be shared between the tenant and landowner, according to the usual share of the crop that each received. The landlord was given the responsibility for paying the tenant his portion of the government money. Since tenants were often deeply in debt to their landlords, their share of the funds was not given to them—it was merely applied to their outstanding debt. Other landlords simply cheated the tenants out of their rightful portion. One major problem regarding administration of the AAA programs, which were administered at the county level, was that blacks were politically powerless throughout the cotton belt. A 1937 study by the Brookings Institution concluded that the AAA had "found no way of writing a contract that would guarantee the cropper his share in the benefit payments."[9] Overall, the landlords had been given a strong economic incentive to reduce their tenant labor force when they drastically reduced their cotton acreage, and they had been given much of the responsibility for administering the AAA programs. The results were predictable.

Two additional strategies for taking the tenants' share of AAA benefit payments were reduction of tenants to wage labor status and mechanization; the two were closely interrelated. Tenants who were reduced to wage laborers were not entitled to a portion of the government subsidies. Increased mechanization was aided directly by the AAA's success in raising cotton prices and by the income supplement that benefit payments provided to landowners. In the mid- to late

1930s, sales of farm equipment increased dramatically in all parts of the United States. Over one-third of all the tractors in use in U.S. agriculture during early 1938 had been produced between 1935 and 1937. Farm equipment sales jumped from $90 million in 1932 to over $507 million in 1937.[10] During the 1930s, the number of tractors on southern farms increased by 86 percent, while the number of tractors in non-southern states increased by 67 percent.[11] Mechanization was particularly rapid in Oklahoma and Texas. As mechanization increased in the cotton belt, the demand for tenants fell and the numbers of employed wage laborers rose.

The mechanization of cotton farming was actually a three-stage process that started in the 1930s and reached completion in the mid-1950s. The older method of cotton production utilized mule power for soil preparation at planting time, and hand power for weeding and picking the crop. This labor intensive technology dominated until the early 1940s, but declined rapidly during the late 1930s. The first stage of mechanization entailed using tractors to prepare the soil for planting; weeding and picking were still done by hand, increasingly by wage laborers. Texas in the 1930s began to rely on Mexican migrant labor for cotton picking. This first stage of mechanization was dominant throughout the 1940s, although it began to lose ground to stage II mechanization late in that decade. The second stage of mechanization utilized tractor power for soil preparation and crop cultivation; herbicides largely replaced handweeding, but picking was still done by hand. Stage II was dominant in the early 1950s only; perfection of mechanized cotton picking equipment caused elimination in the 1950s of the only remaining labor intensive step—handpicking of cotton. The need for vast numbers of black workers in the cotton belt was thus eliminated by the mid–1950s. From 1940 to 1960, output per man hour in cotton production increased more than threefold.[12] In Mississippi alone, nearly one million people left agriculture, a decline of 62 percent in two decades.

Mechanization was aided in the 1930s by government-sponsored agencies that increased the availability and reduced the cost of credit to farmers. Overall, acreage reduction programs increased crop prices, government payments compensated landowners for acres not planted in cash crops, and farm incomes were increased. The combination of higher farm incomes and easier access to credit made it possible for many landowners to finance mechanization of their operations. Mechanization reduced the need for agricultural workers, and those who were employed in the remaining labor intensive phases of crop production were able to find work a much smaller number of days each year, relative to the pre-mechanization phase of farming. The 1940 census revealed that the number of southern tenants declined by 342,000 during the 1930s decade, and 192,000 of these displaced tenants (including croppers) were blacks.

As blacks were increasingly pushed out of tenant status, some remained in their plantation shacks and worked as wage laborers part of the year. Others moved to local villages and tried to make a living from a combination of part-time agricultural work, non-farm employment, and relief. Some displaced tenants left the cotton belt entirely, moving to southern and northern cities where employment was sparse but government relief was more available than it had been in the rural South. Those who tried to survive as agricultural workers found that the landowners were largely unconcerned about any lack of life's necessities that they might experience in the farming slack seasons. The wage laborer was on his own; his ability to survive in the South was no longer of much concern to the planters. Cheap labor could be hired in abundance by southern planters throughout the depression decade. The later 1930s, however, were relatively good times for one group of black agricultural workers. Those remaining share tenants and croppers benefited directly from the higher cotton prices resulting from the AAA's acreage reduction programs. These tenants also shared in the prosperity of high World War II cotton prices, but they were displaced en masse in the years following the war.

Preparation for Urban Life

Blacks residing in the rural South were the poorest, least healthy, and least educated group of citizens in the United States. They were denied the elementary rights to which citizens are entitled in a democratic society; they could not vote, and their participation in government administration was minimal. The cotton belt's education system typified the position of blacks in southern society.

The average annual salaries paid to black public school teachers from 1911 to 1913 ranged from $310 in Kentucky to $111 in South Carolina.[13] It is little wonder that 70 percent of these teachers had less than a sixth grade education. In Macon County, one of Georgia's most prosperous cotton belt counties, 88.9 percent of all public school funds were used to operate white schools in 1928, but 70.1 percent of the students attended all black schools. Between 1928 and 1934, per capita expenditures on white students fell by 12 percent, while black student expenditures decreased by 40 percent. Expenditures per Macon County schoolchild were $47.10 for whites and $1.82 for blacks during 1934, a 25.9 to 1 ratio.[14] By contrast, in 1978 the average per capita education expenditures in South Africa were 654 rand and 57 rand, respectively, for whites and Africans, an 11.5 to 1 ratio.[15] The Georgia General Assembly in 1928 appropriated $17,883 for Macon County black schools, but $7,628 of this amount was diverted to white schools by local officials. Average Macon County salaries for public school teachers were $994 for whites and $142 for blacks in 1934. The educational picture was the same throughout the cotton belt. The larger cities devoted the most resources to black education and the rural areas devoted the least. Black schools in rural areas typically convened in dilapidated buildings provided by the government, or in churches and lodge halls when school buildings were unavailable. Teachers were poorly trained and underpaid, classrooms were overcrowded, and students often lacked such basics as desks. In the entire state of Georgia, over 50 percent of all black schoolchildren were enrolled in the first two grades during 1934. The average level of school attainment for the state's black population was third grade; for whites it was eighth grade in 1934.[16]

White tenants often lived in poverty that was comparable to that of black cotton belt tenants, but at least the rural white population was offered the possibility of upward mobility via the educational system. White poverty was based more upon meritocracy while black poverty was institutionalized. The political impotence of southern blacks gave them no real channel for protesting the condition of black schools. Indeed, the same can be said regarding all of the injustices that they suffered at the hands of cotton belt local governments. The only real alternative was migration.

Traditionally, it has been the better-educated blacks that have migrated out of the rural south. Those who remain in rural areas of the home county are most frequently the illiterate and least-educated adults. Aside from rare times of mass exodus, black migrants before World War II most commonly moved to smaller towns in their own states. This small town population in turn supplied most of the migrants to large cities. The small town was therefore a critical link, having roots both in the rural areas and the large cities. When opportunity beckoned, as it did during the labor shortages of World War I and II, the small town residents spread the word of big city job availability. The small towns also offered better school systems and a greater diversity of occupations to its black residents. These town residents made the smoothest transitions in the large cities, while those migrating directly from the rural South—as large numbers did during

the two world wars and during the final stages of agricultural mechanization—had the greatest difficulty adjusting to big city life.

The Final Collapse

Blacks were pushed out of southern agriculture in two stages. Initial
cotton mechanization during the 1930s and 1940s did not eliminate
the need for a vast labor supply at harvest time. Rather, the initial
stages of mechanization served mainly to reduce the income levels
and the economic security of those tenants who were downgraded to
wage worker status. As partial mechanization increasingly characterized the cotton belt, agricultural wage workers were employed, on
average, fewer and fewer days each year. This decline in economic
status persuaded many to migrate out of the cotton belt, but migration
trends were complicated by two factors. During the 1930s, city jobs
were very hard to obtain and unemployment was extraordinarily high
in black ghetto areas. These circumstances discouraged but did not
halt migration. During the 1940s, urban jobs were indeed available,
especially in centers of defense production, and black migration from
the cotton belt was high. Prosperity, however, returned to the rural
South in the 1940s, and the demand for workers was increasing at
precisely the time when migration to the cities was reducing the cotton
belt's population. Black workers remaining in the cotton belt therefore
found more days of work each year at wage levels that were generally
rising. Despite continued mechanization, rapid expansion of crop
acreage sustained a strong demand for farm workers. Their improved
economic circumstances in the 1940s encouraged the large majority
of the cotton belt's black population to retain their attachment to
southern agriculture, albeit as wage laborers rather than tenants.

　　Table 6.1 reveals the technological underpinnings of the two-stage
push out of agriculture. During the 1940s, labor productivity was
increasing steadily due to mechanization, and black farm workers were
becoming wage hands rather than tenants, small village dwellers rather than farm residents. Cotton in 1949, however, was still a very labor
intensive crop requiring a huge labor force at harvest time, and mechanized picking was just beginning to catch on. By the mid-1950s,
complete mechanization had reduced the need for agricultural workers to a mere fraction of the 1949 level; this was true for corn as well
as cotton (table 6.1). The post-1949 second stage of the push out of
agriculture, via complete mechanization, broke the connection between cotton raising and the large cotton belt black population. A big
labor force was no longer needed; hundreds of thousands of black

Table 6.1. Estimated Labor Input per Unit
of Output in Mississippi Delta Region

Year	Cotton, Hours of Labor per Cwt	Corn, Hours of Labor per Bushel
1940	33.82	1.40
1949	20.70	1.23
1954	6.39	1.03
1957	4.90	.50

Source: Richard Day, "The Economics of Technological Change and the Demise of the Sharecropper,"
American Economic Review 57, no. 3 (1967):438.

farm families were now economically obsolete, displaced by the mechanized cotton picker. The cotton belt economy no longer required the
labor services of most black farm workers, tenants and wage workers
alike.

Cotton belt population figures also reveal a two-stage push out of
agriculture. During the stage of partial mechanization in the 1940s,
the Mississippi delta rural farm population declined by 19 percent,
reflecting migration to both northern and southern cities and towns.
During the stage of complete mechanization in the 1950s, the delta's
rural farm population fell by an astounding 54 percent, while the
entire farm population fell by 50 percent in Mississippi—a drop in
ten years from 1,097,000 to 543,000 inhabitants.[17]

Table 6.2 reveals the dramatic shift in black population that accompanied the overall agricultural displacement process. The greatest
shift occurred from rural southern to urban residence in northern
and western states. During the 1940s when economic opportunities
were luring workers to industrial cities, the number of blacks residing
in northern and western cities increased by over 1.85 million. The
"pull" migration of the prosperous 1940s, however, was smaller in
magnitude that the "push" migration that agricultural displacement
produced in the 1950s. During the latter decade the number of black
inhabitants residing in northern and western cities grew by 2.7 million.
By 1960, less than one-quarter of the nation's black population resided
in the rural South. Most of the migrants in the 1950s were utterly
unprepared for big city life, while the cities, in turn, were unprepared
for the massive black in-migration. If government relief agencies to
alleviate human suffering had existed, they would have found much

Table 6.2. Urban and Rural Residence of U.S. Black Population

	Rural		Urban		Entire U.S.
	South	*North, West*	*South*	*North, West*	
Population *(in thousands)*					
1940	6,289	324	3,616	2,638	12,867
1960	4,704	355	6,608	7,193	18,860
Distribution *(in percentage)*					
1940	48.9	2.5	28.1	20.5	100.0
1960	24.9	1.9	35.0	38.1	100.0

Source: C. Horace Hamilton, "The Negro Leaves the South," *Demography* 1, no. 1 (1964):276.

to do in the cotton belt during this period. Their response to rampant rural unemployment was, instead, to tighten welfare eligibility criteria; relief rolls in the rural South actually declined in the 1950s.[18] Displaced black farm workers often faced two alternatives: to migrate or to starve.

7

Organized Labor and Black Workers

TRACES OF THE RELATIONSHIPS THAT HAD BOUND BLACK SLAVE TO white master (and vice versa) endured the throes of the transformation of the southern slave economy into the twentieth-century industrial city. As explained in chapter 2, the nineteenth-century heritage of southern race relations produced antiunion attitudes among black workers and a tendency for blacks to view prosperous whites as their allies. White labor unions typically reinforced this heritage by pursuing discriminatory policies towards black workers. The result was often a vicious circle that exacerbated racial antagonism: blacks would work as strikebreakers for many reasons, but their resentment towards the discriminatory white unions was a major part of the rationale for being scabs; white workers, in turn, would justify discriminatory union policies partially on the grounds that blacks were undercutting their unions. By playing off black against white workers, the unity of labor could often be undermined by management.

The web of paternalistic relations that bound blacks and affluent whites in the old South was often recreated in varying degrees by companies that sought to weaken organized labor. An extreme example of this occurred in the 1930s when Henry Ford attempted to defeat unionization drives at the Ford Motor Company. The "paternalistic" Ford employed more blacks than any other auto company. He employed some blacks in skilled, technical, even subexecutive capacities; he had two black personnel officers. He invited George Washington Carver to his home and arranged to have Marian Anderson sing on the "Ford Sunday Hour." He helped finance the all-black village of Inkster and provided jobs at one dollar per day to its unemployed residents. He donated the Parish House of St. Matthews Episcopal Church to blacks and gave large sums of money to the Second Baptist Church (a black church) of Detroit.[1] What union had ever showed so much concern for black well-being?

In some instances, the only entry for blacks into new fields was through the back door as a scab. From the black perspective, the new white employer had done more for black workers than any white labor union. Blacks were sometimes referred to as "good strike insurance."[2] Certain nineteenth- and early twentieth-century unions such as the Industrial Workers of the World adopted truly nondiscriminatory policies, but these unions did not endure. The American Federation of Labor (AFL) grappled with the race issue in a variety of ways, largely unsuccessfully, and it was not until the 1930s that a major drive was made that did indeed bring black workers into labor's mainstream. That drive was conducted by the Congress of Industrial Organizations (CIO) and it offered the first substantive alternative to the kind of race relationships that the antibellum South had fostered.

American Federation of Labor Racial Policies

The American Federation of Labor emerged in the early twentieth century as the nation's dominant labor organization. From a membership of over two million in 1904, the AFL grew to five million members in 1920, but it entered a period of stagnation during the intensely antiunion 1920s. The AFL was a national association of craft (as opposed to industrial) unions; rather than organizing workers on an industry-wide basis, craft unions typically organized workers who possessed a particular skill, such as carpentry or steel puddling. Groups of craft unions such as the Stock Yards Labor Council sometimes launched industry-wide strikes, but the individual craft unions typically retained great autonomy even when they were acting in concert with related unions. Craft unions that belonged to the AFL, in fact, retained considerable autonomy, making it difficult for the AFL to prevent racial discrimination among its member unions. Since the AFL did not work overly hard to eradicate the discriminatory practices of its members, a wide variety of racist policies flourished.

Unions whose constitutions limited membership to whites included the Railway Mail Association, the Brotherhood of Railway Carmen, the Order of Sleeping Car Conductors, the Commercial Telegraphers, and a host of others. When union constitutions did not mention race, firm tradition often served the same purpose as in the case of electrical workers, granite workers, structural iron workers and a number of other unionized crafts. Outright black exclusion could be a foolish, self-defeating union policy, as was the case in the late nineteenth-century steel industry. Therefore, many craft unions devised strategies for integrating blacks into their organizations on a separate, usually unequal, basis. Particularly in trades where black employment was traditional, craft unions sought to organize blacks in the late nineteenth and early twentieth century as a matter of self-defense.

Voluntary separation was the least common type of union strategy for segregating black workers from the union mainstream. In the few places where blacks and whites voluntarily separated themselves into racially distinct union locals, separation was strictly an unofficial union policy. Blacks in such locals often claimed to prefer separation because it allowed them to elect their own local union officials and to gain experience in union government. Since this type of separation often generated race consciousness rather than working-class consciousness, it was always a potentially disrupting force within unions.

Involuntary separation at the local union level was common, particularly in the South, in those international unions which claimed to eschew discrimination against black workers. Separate white and black union locals were set up as a matter of racial expediency, and they were often permitted to function on parity. Black organizers were sometimes used to set up black local unions, but they were not allowed to organize white workers. This strategy was used successfully in the early twentieth century by the nominally nondiscriminatory carpenter's union, which organized twenty-five southern locals comprised exclusively of black carpenters. A common source of friction between black and white union locals, however, concerned job allocations which frequently favored white at the expense of black union members.

A third type of segregationist union strategy was adopted by many national unions that, as official policy, sought to introduce blacks into their unions as distinctly subordinate members. Common types of discriminatory policies included: barring blacks from union office, designating certain types of skilled work as "white only" jobs, organizing blacks into auxiliary union locals that were commonly subordinate to the nearest white local, representation of black union members at conventions by whites only, and making blacks ineligible for transfer to white union locals. Unions which established these dual discriminatory arrangements also tended to give preference to white members regarding a whole range of normal union functions, from attention given membership grievances to allocation of jobs among union members. These blatantly discriminatory unions had difficulty recruiting black members. Unions with official nationwide racist membership policies gave credence to the widely held black attitude that the union movement sought only to promote the interests of white workers.

Another common union discriminatory device used for barring blacks from skilled trades entailed union participation in the governmental process of licensing skilled workers. The plumbers' union, for example, had an informal policy of excluding blacks. License laws require that workers wishing to practice a skilled trade, such as plumbing, within a certain geographic area must pass a competency exam administered under municipal authority. Members from local unions were commonly included on the board of examiners who evaluated those seeking licenses to pursue skilled trades. Plumbers' union members of municipal boards of examiners would simply rule that every black applicant for a plumbing license was unqualified to pursue the trade. In a number of cities, such as Philadelphia, the licensing board would never grant a license to a black plumber.[3] When black plumbers nonetheless attempted to pursue their occupations in these cities, the plumbing supply stores would refuse to sell to them. If certain firms did sell supplies and fixtures to black plumbers, then white plumbers would boycott those firms. Thus, blacks were pushed out of some skilled trades by a combination of government authority, union policies, and diligent policing by skilled white workers to whom black competition was anathema.

Rise of the CIO

President Roosevelt's New Deal legislation in the labor reform field set the stage for the CIO's emergence. The late 1930s CIO organizing drives in such mass production fields as steel and autos marked the first time that national attention was focused on black civil rights. They contained the seeds of what was later to become the civil rights movement.

Three pieces of legislation in particular—the 1932 Norris-LaGuardia Act, section 7a of the National Industrial Recovery Act, and the 1935 Wagner Act—generated a great burst of enthusiasm for unionization in the mass production manufacturing industries. The main product of this enthusiasm was the CIO, the Committe for Industrial Organization (changed in 1938 to the Congress of Industrial Organizations), which effectively challenged many racist practices of the AFL unions, and encouraged integration of blacks into the mainstream of American labor. The three major pieces of labor legislation restricted the use of injunctions against unions, gave workers the right to organize and bargain collectively through representatives of their own choosing, and outlawed a number of practices that employers had adopted to discourage unionization. Although section 7a was declared unconstitutional in 1935 along with the rest of the National Industrial Recovery Act, its unionization safeguards were relegislated by passage of the Wagner Act in that same year.

The resultant great opportunity to organize new unions was largely bungled by AFL indecisiveness and by jurisdictional disputes among its constituent craft unions. This paralysis in the midst of widespread worker enthusiasm for unionization generated great conflict at the AFL's 1935 convention. The CIO arose out of this conflict and although it initially retained its affiliation with the AFL, the CIO broke ranks with its parent federation in 1937. The industrial unionism practiced by the CIO was incompatible with the craft union philosophy of the AFL. Unionization efforts in the steel industry typified CIO criticisms of AFL inflexibility and ineffectiveness. The twenty-four craft unions involved in organizing steelworkers could not agree among themselves on how workers involved in the various aspects of steel-making were to be divided amongst the unions.[4] The 1935 AFL convention delegates complained that mass production industry workers felt discouraged and confused when they could not organize due to the jurisdictional disputes of the craft unions. These AFL dissidents formed the CIO to organize industrial unions; by the time of their separation from the AFL, the CIO had grown to thirty-two unions spanning America's largest manufacturing industries.

CIO industrial union operating procedures were not conducive to barring blacks from union membership. The CIO unions attempted to organize all workers employed in the various manufacturing industries, regardless of race, and the unions sought no control over industry hiring practices. The AFL unions, in contrast, frequently tried to control the hiring practices of employers. AFL craft unions sought to restrict the supply of labor, first by limiting union membership, and second, by demanding that employers hire AFL union members only. The process of restricting union membership to control the labor supply frequently entailed keeping blacks out of AFL unions, or limiting their participation in various discriminatory ways. In addition to practicing egalitarian union racial policies, the CIO also endorsed many government programs and policies—minimum wage, unemployment insurance, and the like—that were very popular within the black community. The AFL unions not only did little to support social legislation beneficial to blacks and poor people generally, they often actively opposed such legislation.

The CIO needed black support for the success of industrial unions in basic manufacturing industries and for passage of the progressive social legislation that the CIO so vigorously endorsed. The CIO actively sought that black support by courting black community leaders as well as workers. Strategies included CIO contributions to the NAACP, donations to black churches and newspapers, and participation of CIO officials in black organizations such as the Urban League. These seemingly sincere efforts eradicated much of black community's traditional hostility toward organized labor. The NAACP and the National Urban League encouraged black worker support of CIO unions. In the 1941 strike to organize Ford Motor Company, NAACP executive secretary Walter White effectively persuaded thousands of blacks not to become strikebreakers. This great historic turnaround with respect to organized labor on the part of black community leaders helped the CIO establish strong unions in most major previously nonunion basic industries. Furthermore, the CIO's impressive organizing successes encouraged its competitors, the AFL craft unions, to drop some of their racially restrictive practices.[5] Although the CIO preached racial equality and enjoyed wide black community support, it could not eradicate completely the racism that was embedded both in the union movement and the labor force. Particularly in the South, a few CIO union locals either barred blacks from membership or segregated them into separate locals. Residual segregation always plagued CIO unions to some degree. Nonetheless, the CIO brought black workers into the mainstream of organized labor. By the end of World War II, hundreds of thousands of black workers belonged to unions in such major industries as auto, shipbuilding, steel, electrical machinery, and meatpacking. The long and bloody era of widespread black strikebreaking had come to a close.

Labor Unions and Blacks: The Honeymoon Ends After World War II

World War II was a watershed period for black American workers. The war years represent the dividing line between blacks clinging to bottom rung jobs and blacks moving into more skilled positions in the labor market. Phenomenal occupational gains were made as a result of both union pressure and the favorable full employment demands of World War II; this thrust was given a further boost by the moral power of an antidiscriminatory federal employment policy. Thus, the war experience gave the black worker the opportunity, for the first time, to move vertically as well as horizontally within the labor market. But it did more. The World War II experience strengthened the black labor–CIO alliance that had been forged during the 1930s and brought blacks into the mainstream of organized labor. It was the black labor–CIO alliance that marked the beginning of effective agitation on the part of blacks for equal employment opportunities. This added a new dimension to industry's thinking, because such agitation challenged the common view that it was too much trouble and hence bad economics to hire blacks for skilled jobs.

Union or no union, the reality of labor shortages would have dictated widespread wartime use of black workers in industry. The vital contribution of the CIO unions was not black employment per se, but rather the insistence that blacks be granted access to skilled jobs. In the absence of this pressure, blacks would have been much less likely to move up from the lowest-paying, dirtiest, most dangerous jobs that they had traditionally entered en masse during periods of labor shortage. As discussed earlier, unions such as the Auto Workers actively fought against both employer reluctance and the resistance of their own white members when the issue of black occupational upgrading surfaced. Furthermore, the CIO used its influence at the federal level to support equal employment opportunity policies for both government workers and the employees of federal government contract recipients.

That the black worker–CIO honeymoon was over by the end of World War II seems obvious in retrospect. It was an easy matter to support black worker upgrading when skilled worker shortages were widespread; periods of black-white competition for scarce skilled jobs greatly lessened union dedication to equal job opportunity issues. Those black occupational gains were based on the special circumstances of a wartime, full-employment economy which followed on the heels of the CIO's union drives during the 1930s. As those conditions changed, so did the security and status of the black worker. Circumstances shifted and posed employment problems for black workers even before the peace was made.

As victory for the Allies approached, war industries began cutting back in production, which affected blacks even before World War II finally ended in September 1945. The areas where blacks had made the most significant gains were the very industries—shipbuilding, aircraft, munitions, and explosives—with the least potential for reconversion to peacetime production. Therefore, a large proportion of blacks were threatened with unemployment when war production ceased. Almost one-half of the blacks in war industries had been concentrated in aircraft, shipbuilding, iron and steel, and government jobs related to war services.[6]

In addition, there was the problem faced by unorganized black workers who would be displaced when whites encroached on the tightened job market situation. This was a problem particularly in the South where there were proportionately more unorganized workers when the war ended than in the North. The southern textile industry, for example, was only about 20 percent organized in 1946 as compared to 70 percent in the North.[7]

The third problem blacks faced at the end of World War II was that of seniority—preference in employment based on length of service. By V-E Day (Victory in Europe), most unions were advocating seniority contracts to guide layoffs and subsequent rehiring. Since wartime prosperity came to blacks last, they were particularly vulnerable to seniority issues and were more likely to lose their jobs than whites.

In the latter half of 1945, the reduced employment of blacks in general reflected all the above factors, despite the generally prosperous employment atmosphere of the postwar years. According to the final report of the Fair Employment Practice Commission (FEPC): "Of the seven war production centers studied by FEPC during reconversion, all but Chicago showed a heavier loss of jobs by Negroes than by white workers, plus a necessity on the part of Negro workers to accept the lowest paying jobs."[8] And, whereas during the war some blacks had risen into the skilled and semiskilled categories, by 1946 such openings for them had dwindled. The employment of blacks as skilled craftsmen and foremen, for example, declined after the war in contrast to a significant increase in the proportion of craftsmen and foremen among whites.[9] However, although occupational gains were precluded for many of the blacks who migrated to cities after 1945, neither was unemployment for blacks as severe as it might have been during the immediate postwar period. That blacks did not suffer greater downgrading was largely a result of the relatively full employment situation during the postwar years.

Black workers and community leaders looked to the CIO for protection of their wartime occupational gains. It was, after all, the CIO that first focused attention on the civil and economic rights of black citizens in the 1930s. Thus, most black labor and their leaders agreed with the *NAACP Bulletin* that the CIO stood for "our people within the unions and outside the unions."[10] But, blacks were to be disappointed with the CIO during the postwar period.

The national political situation was a significant factor in the disruption of the CIO-black relationship during the postwar years. Unions, after all, reflect their environment, and during the postwar era the nation was generally antiunion as well as anti-Communist. Both political trends put the CIO in a particularly vulnerable position. The antiunion drift had its foundations in the widespread and large-scale strikes from 1945 to 1946 and the wage drives from 1946 to 1947. Since the CIO led the wave of strikes and wage wars, much of the public wrath against unions was aimed specifically at the CIO. Furthermore, the issue of Communist involvement in the union movement was a particularly difficult and divisive issue for the CIO.

Anti-communism as a national issue developed with the deterioration of Russian-American relations, particularly after the March 1947 declaration by President Truman that asked all Americans to join in a global commitment against communism. The CIO unions were thus put on alert since from their earliest days they had relied on the organizing efforts of Communists.

Communists occupied many key positions in the new industrial unions. By 1940, it was generally known that they controlled locals in electrical, radio, woodworking, fur, and leather industries, and the unions of municipal, transport, and maritime workers.[11] Thus, unlike the AFL, which had a long history of opposition to communism, the CIO in 1946 either had to purge or be purged. It chose the former alternative and by the early 1950s the CIO had so completely ousted Communists from its ranks that it made a claim for political purity equal to that of the AFL. During this period of the Cold War and McCarthyism, Communist and left-wing influence declined in all unions and all aspects of American life. The left-wing was precisely that segment of the union movement that had traditionally fought hardest and most consistently for the rights of black workers.

CIO efforts to purge itself of Communists created internal dissension which fragmented and dissipated any sincere efforts it may have entertained to help black workers. The CIO was increasingly pre-occupied with questions of its own survival. By the late 1940s, most blacks—labor and leaders alike—suspected that the alliance with the CIO had been merely a marriage of convenience and claimed the CIO no longer had time for black issues. Union leadership felt that there were more pressing matters for the CIO to worry about than the problems of black workers. In race relations, as in other matters, unions reflect their environment. Black problems were a low national priority in the postwar period.

Increasing membership in the CIO during those decidedly anti-union days was a higher priority item, and both the AFL and the CIO organizations found time to devote to this problem. They went after the large reservoir of unorganized southern labor in textiles, lumber, furniture, chemical, and food processing industries in 1946. In addition to membership, both organizations were concerned with the flood of antiunion legislation in the South and hoped to weaken that thrust through their respective unionizing efforts. Both the AFL and the CIO were hampered by the race issue, the violent antiunion attitude of employers, and the ruthless determination of local officials to keep northern unions out of the South. Neither union federation was successful. The AFL curtailed its campaign at the end of 1947 for financial reasons and the CIO failed to get many new members after 1948, even though its southern drive continued until 1953.

The CIO drive, called Operation Dixie, played upon past success in using its favorable racial image to organize mass production southern industries. Indeed, CIO President Philip Murray described the southern organizing drive as "a civil rights program . . . which not only encompassed the organization of workers into unions . . . but the freedom of southern workers from economic and political bondage . . ."[12] In turn the CIO position and reputation among blacks was a factor in causing the AFL to try for the first time to project to blacks a more favorable image. The AFL policy board thought that special efforts should be taken to give special attention to blacks and to counteract the CIO appeal to black labor. Obviously, this change in strategy was rooted more in survival and growth than in any ethical change on the part of the AFL.

Initially, the CIO image cost the AFL some members. In particular, the CIO woodworkers won the Masconite Corporation of Laurel, Mississippi, the largest employer in that state, away from the AFL. The black vote was decisive in that election and sparked even more interest by the AFL in the black union vote. The AFL redoubled its efforts by launching a three-pronged attack against the CIO. First, it claimed that the CIO offered the black worker "pie in the sky" with little chance of delivery while the AFL "does not offer you words, but results." Second, the AFL took on claims that it was discriminatory, and countered that it had segregated locals where required by law or when preferred by black workers themselves. Third, the AFL emphasized the CIO link with communism.[13] Furthermore, AFL organizers claimed it was mostly the Communist-dominated CIO unions that had high-ranking black officers.[14] Juxtaposing union progress for black CIO members and Communist infiltration linked civil rights and union integration with communism and confused the issues in the minds of both black and white workers. Nevertheless, the AFL campaign did not bring in many new union members; but then neither did the CIO gain from its more favorable reputation among blacks in the long run.

The truth is that both the AFL and the CIO plunged into the southern snare—that long tradition of racial antagonism between southern blacks and whites—and got swamped in its complexities. Racial difficulties emerged when organizers tried to organize blacks first—a common procedure, because it was usually easier to persuade black workers to sign up than whites. Both the CIO and the AFL followed this pattern and both succeeded in alienating white workers. Then, in most cases, the propaganda hijinks of the AFL against the CIO boomeranged against both organizations because, in many cases, people would not believe that only the CIO was evil; thus, they fought all unionization efforts. It is problematic how much black resistance to or lack of enthusiasm for the CIO was related to the CIO-communism link. But it was generally known by blacks that Communists actively downgraded the issue of black rights during World War II.[15]

Finally, although the CIO did indeed have a good track record for routing out racism, it too discriminated, especially in the South. For example, certain CIO unions such as United Rubber Workers and the United Paperworkers had segregated locals which had long been accepted. Such accommodations to prevailing pattern and local customs were not lost on blacks. They noted that, as a result of the public reaction and the Red Scare that put unions on the defensive, the CIO was fighting to save its white neck and was in no position to initiate bold policy positions, especially for black workers. Thus, the erstwhile favorable reputation of the CIO in the black community began to fade long before the AFL-CIO merger in 1955. The specific target that the black community chose to vent its frustrations on was the CIO Civil Rights Committee (CRC).

The CRC was established in 1942 to abolish racial discrimination, but all along was opposed by some unions who either gave it only token support or who ignored it entirely. It was clear from the beginning that the CRC was to be basically and fundamentally a public relations arm of the CIO with only advisory powers on racial issues. The CRC had no power to handle racial cases. Although the CRC received bad press from blacks from the start, it was not until 1949 that the committee was considered totally worthless. The *Pittsburgh Courier*, an influential black newspaper, even suggested that the CRC be abolished.[16]

Black workers within the CIO were not about to quit the organization, but neither were they going to give in to the lack of an effective strategy for dealing with black economic problems. They continued to air their complaints during the late 1940s and their grumblings spurred the CIO leadership to call a special meeting to discuss the CIO's declining reputation among blacks.

Ray Marshall claims that the CIO, for all its defensive posturing between 1945 and 1955, exerted a significant influence over the AFL on racial matters and caused it to "abandon its discriminatory practices and try to project a more favorable image."[17] However, the CIO's influence extended largely to public utterances by the AFL, not policy changes within that organization. Indeed, Herbert Hill, legal advisor to the NAACP, claimed that during the early 1950s the status quo ante remained in most unions. For example, in 1953, when the International Brotherhood of Electrical Workers won the contract at Bauer Electric Company in Hartford, Connecticut, "it characteristically demanded that all Negro electricians be dismissed from their jobs, as Negroes would not be admitted into union membership."[18] Nevertheless, there was a heady dose of optimism when the AFL and the CIO merged in December 1955. Resolutions were adopted at the merger convention to eliminate racial discrimination and segregation within labor unions and to bring the benefits of trade unionism to millions of exploited blacks. So what was new? There was some justification for the optimism: the color bar was lifted from all but two AFL-CIO union constitutions; the CIO was to have a salubrious effect on the AFL, it was generally conceded; the new AFL-CIO constitution established a Committee on Civil Rights to be backed and aided by a new Department of Civil Rights; resolutions were passed to create the internal machinery for the settlement of civil rights complaints, the enactment on union initiative of antidiscrimination clauses in all collective bargaining agreements, and for legislation that would set up a federal fair employment practices system. What was more, James B. Carey, president of the CIO's International Union of Electrical Workers (IUEW) and who had an excellent reputation among blacks, was the chairman of the Committee on Civil Rights.

In actuality, a number of features of the AFL-CIO merger widened the gulf between the labor movement and the black community. First, two-thirds of the official positions of the merged organization went to the AFL, which was still more suspect to blacks than the CIO. Second, the AFL-CIO Executive Council admitted two unions with race bars in their constitutions, which in itself was not particularly alarming. However, neither Carey nor Walter Reuther nor other CIO leaders cast a dissenting vote against these organizations.[19] Then, in December 1957, Carey resigned from his chairmanship of the Committee on Civil Rights. According to the *New York Times*, he felt, "that he had not been given enough power or freedom to do an effective job of stamping out racial bias in unions . . . he felt he was being ham strung. . . ."[20] These circumstances, occurring at a time of increasing unemployment among blacks, contributed to the growing feeling that union discrimination was adding to the economic plight of black workers.

Meanwhile, black social and legal activism within the larger society was increasing, as reflected in freedom marches and civil rights sit-ins. Simultaneously, the level of frustration felt by the majority of blacks was also increasing, triggered by social and economic segregation, lower incomes, the dilapidated, segregated housing they were forced to live in, and the realization that white liberal and labor organizations could not be counted on. The great migration of blacks northward during the 1940s and 1950s had been accompanied by hopes that the North was the Promised Land for people of color. But race riots, low incomes, and the erosion of World War II economic and occupational gains contributed to disillusionment with the North, as well as with the unions.

Thus, as the unions turned their backs on the black community, the onus fell on blacks within the unions to act decisively, and even sometimes forcefully, to secure some measure of racial equality in the workplace. One response was the Trade Union Leadership Conference (TULC), formed by a group of Detroit unionists in 1957. This group, considered fairly militant for the times, evolved out of the growing dissatisfaction with civil rights progress within the AFL-CIO. Basically, TULC sought to direct the power of the labor movement in broad civil-rights activities as well as " . . . to interpret the Negro community to the labor movement and the labor movement to the Negro community."[21] Among other issues pushed by TULC was the inclusion of blacks on most international executive unions boards. TULC succeeded in 1962 on this last issue when the UAW Executive Board elected a black for the first time. While black community leaders found it to their advantage to make an alliance with unions in the 1930s, by the end of the 1950s, blacks had less need for the union organizational umbrella since the unions did so little for blacks. Thus, the unions that had spawned the egalitarian ideals and, at least initially, had given blacks a taste of the power that black-white unity harbored, now forced black leaders to rely more on their own organizations and themselves.

Civil Rights Movement Roots in the CIO

Thurgood Marshall, while chief legal advisor to the NAACP, called the CIO's program no less than a "Bill of Rights for Negro Labor in

America."[22] In a broad sense this was still true in the late 1950s, but attainment of this bill of rights was now largely in the hands of black organizations. The CIO dissipated the paternalistic cloud that had hung over black-white relationships for so long and provided blacks with an interim infrastructure that could reshape and refocus priorities. The importance of the CIO infrastructure was not that it broke down racial barriers completely, but that it forced blacks and whites to interact as equals and, more important, put blacks in positions of responsibility so that they were leading as well as being led, making decisions for whites as well as for blacks. Through this process, new images were formed and a new pattern of social relationships was shaped. The suggestion that "unionization of Ford led to a basic change in the social structure of the Detroit Negro community"[23] is thus plausible.

The ground broken by the CIO–black worker alliance did not lie fallow. Once dependence upon the CIO became fruitless, blacks realized that they had to go beyond the unions to the legal and political institutions within the society that curtailed their rights. Left-wing whites who had been thrown out of the CIO also realized that other avenues had to be found to carry on the spirit of the original CIO organizing drives. Such institutions as the Highlander School in Tennessee helped both blacks and radical whites in this endeavor. Highlander was a piece of the CIO infrastructure that typified the kinds of alternatives that blacks and whites pursued when the CIO no longer emphasized progressive programs.

Highlander was a school for organizers to lead disenfranchised blacks and whites to exercise their democratic rights as American citizens.[24] Most of its participants in the late 1930s were textile or mine union members who showed promise of becoming organizers or local union leaders. A handbook called "How to Build Your Union", widely used by CIO organizers, was written by Highlander students and staff. The CIO severed its relationship with Highlander in the 1950s because of the school's alleged Communist connections. After this break, Highlander students tended increasingly to be civil rights activists.

Rosa Parks recalled that, "At Highlander, I found out for the first time in my adult life that this could be a unified society, that there was such a thing as people of differing races and backgrounds meeting together in workshops and living together in peace and harmony. . . . I gained there strength to persevere in my work for freedom, not just for Blacks but for all oppressed people."[25] Perhaps it is no coincidence that Parks balked at the bus driver's orders to move to the back of the bus several months after her Highlander studies. The ensuing

Montgomery, Alabama bus boycott in 1956 was a great impetus to the civil rights movement's growing momentum.

Highlander's activities were vast and varied during those years. Zilphia Horton, a Highlander staff member, and Pete Seeger (a frequent participant) revised an old union song to create "We Shall Overcome." Dr. Martin Luther King was a frequent participant at Highlander. Highlander School participants of the 1930s began sending their children to study there in the 1950s. The Student Nonviolent Coordinating Committee (SNCC) exemplified this link. Many SNCC founders were second-generation Highlander participants; during a January 1960 SNCC meeting at Highlander before a Greensboro North Carolina sit-in, the school was attacked and a Howard University student—Stokley Carmichael—was narrowly missed by a bullet. Education for social change helped to transmit the spirit that prompted one generation to "sit-down" (in the late 1930s) to the next generation who made the "sit-in" demonstration an effective tool in the civil rights struggles.

Blacks who had been part of the CIO experience were not prone to commit themselves to a web of paternalistic relationships that tended toward obliging, compromising behavior designed to undermine one's sense of self-worth. When the CIO backpedaled on black worker rights, paternalism no longer held those blacks captive. Thus, they were free to fashion their own synthesis based on relationships of class and race and to continue the struggle for civil rights. Together with radical whites, they capitalized on both the experience gained and the momentum set in motion by the CIO to transcend the labor movement, becoming a fullblown civil rights movement. Even if the CIO had never existed, a civil rights movement might have been in the offing because of black urbanization and changes in occupational structure. The ground broken by the CIO campaigns shaped the timing, the content, and the ultimate success of this nation's civil rights movement. This movement, in turn, succeeded in altering the legal environment in which businesses and unions function. Discriminatory employment policies are now limited by Title VII of the Civil Rights Act of 1964 which outlaws discrimination based on race, sex, or national origin by private employers. Executive Order 11246, issued in 1965, requires that federal contractors refrain from discrimination in employment. Acting as a unified voting bloc on civil right issues, blacks have been a continual factor in shaping the conditions of their employment. The black worker–labor union dynamic will continue to be an important determinant of that employment environment for the foreseeable future.

8

The Changing Economic Base
of Metropolitan Areas

This chapter investigates the nature and the consequences of urban structural changes as determinants of black economic well-being.[1] Ghetto economic and social problems are too often examined in an overly narrow, ghetto-oriented fashion that tends to confuse the symptoms of poverty and disorder with their underlying causes. Practitioners of this narrow approach to studying the inner city often claim that ghetto problems are caused largely by the deficiencies of ghetto residents themselves.[2] Rather, ghetto poverty is a symptom of more fundamental forces, particularly those forces that shape job availability, but there are, indeed, feedback mechanisms that cause the conditions of ghetto life to reinforce poverty.[3] Comprehension of the larger forces that shape cities is a prerequisite for understanding ghetto problems.

Declining industrial cities characterized by massive loss of blue-collar manufacturing jobs and increasing local government fiscal difficulties do not provide an economic environment conducive to long-run improvements in black economic well-being. Many black residents who have in the past found relative prosperity and economic opportunity in older cities such as Detroit and Cleveland now face bleak future prospects in these environments. Thoughout the twentieth century, periods of widespread prosperity have consistently produced substantial employment gains for urban blacks, and the 1960s decade was no exception.[4] The prosperous 1960s, however, did not reverse ominous trends in black job availability that have been apparent since the end of the Korean war. Declining manufacturing industries and general economic stagnation in the 1980s pose a growing threat to black economic well-being, particularly in the nation's older industrial regions.

The Transformation of Urban America

This section analyzes the post–World War II transformation of two types of metropolitan areas: older industrial snowbelt areas in the northeast quadrant of the United States and "sunbelt" cities in the South and Southwest. Terms such as snowbelt and sunbelt have substance insofar as they relate to city "age," that stage of economic development during which the city became a major center of economic activity. Population densities, dominant transportation modes, vintage of physical capital stock, and, in general, the overall nature of the infrastructure, are key traits that are systematically related to city age. Certain technological changes and economic phenomena have interacted with government policies to produce simultaneously growth of sunbelt cities, decentralization of economic activity in snowbelt metropolitan areas, and rapidly changing composition of business activities in older, densely populated industrial cities.

This suggests, in conjunction with information cited later, the following broad portraits of snowbelt and sunbelt urban SMSAs (standard metropolitan statistical area) since World War II.

Sunbelt SMSAs

These areas are characterized by a more diversified service and trade-oriented economic base relative to the snowbelt SMSAs, and have grown rapidly. Manufacturing employment has grown moderately, with production and nonproduction jobs increasing steadily. Nonproduction manufacturing employment (white-collar) has grown more rapidly than production jobs. Rapid employment growth has been experienced in trade, services, and government employment. As early as 1963, employment in the retail and wholesale trades exceeded total manufacturing employment. Growth in services has been most substantial, with business services accounting for the largest job gains within this category.

Snowbelt SMSAs

These areas were characterized originally by an economic base that was strongly oriented toward manufacturing. These areas have grown moderately but in a very unbalanced fashion with population shifting from the central cities to the suburbs. Manufacturing production employment has largely moved out of the central city. Wholesale and retail employment has declined substantially while central city jobs in services, government, and nonproduction manufacturing have increased. Growth in business service employment has been rapid and sustained, along with substantial growth in finance, insurance, and real estate. In contrast to the central city, the suburban periphery has experienced strong growth in retail, wholesale, and manufacturing industries. Unlike the sunbelt, employment in manufacturing industries is greater than in trade and services, but it is becoming relatively less important over time because it is not a growing sector. Manufacturing employment increasingly consists of nonproduction jobs.

Many years before rising sunbelt cities caught the attention of economists, decentralization of economic activity in older industrial cities became a major concern.[5] Decentralizing manufacturing employment, the leader of the shift from the central city to suburbia, was motivated by both technological and economic changes, such as changes in production methods, developments in transportation, and changes in the relative attractiveness of suburban and central-city tax and service programs.[6]

Decades of decentralization have coincided with important changes in the nature of business enterprise, especially in the large corporation, that brought increasing use of white-collar as opposed to blue-collar workers. It is customary to emphasize technological advancement to explain changes in manufacturing location and employment. But this is only a very partial explanation. A fundamental shift in the nature of the corporation, which is only partly rooted in considerations of production efficiency, is largely responsible for both shifting manufacturing employment patterns and the changing nature of the central city. The modern corporation is increasingly oriented toward marketing rather than production, toward development of new products rather than mass production of products at minimum unit costs. Production efficiency is still important, but the modern corporation executive has found that the high profits accrue to the firm that gets there first with something new and attractive. Furthermore, the modern corporation is increasingly shaped by government tax and expenditure policies. The Reagan tax cuts of 1981 epitomize government efforts to shape the business sector.[7] In many instances it is more enlightening to envision this process as one whereby business interests persuade government to act in ways that will, in turn, reshape the modern corporation. Major results of this business–government interaction are greater capital intensity and larger employment of white-collar as opposed to blue-collar workers—relative to the capital intensity and employment patterns that would have prevailed in the absence of government efforts to shape business.

The Changing Nature of the Corporation

Chapter 3 partially described the late nineteenth and early twentieth-century period during which large corporations were initially formed. Because of such key developments as the presence of an extensive nationwide railroad system, giant national corporations increasingly produced and marketed their products over many regions throughout the country. Industrial cities that developed in this era relied primarily on rail transit and secondarily on water transit. Thus, shipping considerations restricted potential factory locations to centrally located sites near ports and/or rail terminals.[8] Similarly, a central-city location was usually a prerequisite for attracting a large factory labor force. Since most workers either walked or utilized mass transit to get to their jobs, factories that did not locate in central cities were not within commuting reach of their potential labor force. Large factories that were located away from the central city therefore found it necessary to provide housing—indeed whole communities—for their employees, an added expense that most employers preferred to avoid. In fact, manufacturing production was heavily concentrated in zones of central cities where transit access was excellent, and factory workers resided in nearby, densely populated areas where two- and three-story multifamily housing was the norm. Living close to one's job site minimized the time and money costs of commuting, which tended to be very substantial if the distance to work was more than a few miles.

Prevailing production technology as well as the high cost of city land encouraged the construction of multiple-story factories in the late nineteenth century. The flow of production was vertical: raw materials entered the production process on the top floor of the factory, and these materials were processed in stages as they descended to lower floors. The finished product arrived at the bottom floor, which was typically devoted to shipping and perhaps storage. A steam engine located on the ground floor drove the plant machinery via a series of belts; multiple-story factory design was often the most efficient way to utilize steam power since it minimized machine distance from the steam engine, and hence the length of the belts needed to drive the machinery.

Corporations were largely production-oriented in that era, meaning that the corporate focus was upon mass producing standardized products at low unit costs. As huge factories rose to exploit the economies of large-scale production as well as the expanded markets that rail transit opened up, great industrial cities flourished. The large corporations required sophisticated management procedures to plan and coordinate their far-flung activities. The smaller firms that typified the nineteenth-century U.S. economy were run by a few individuals, often members of one family, who were in close touch with all aspects of the company's operations. In the twentieth century, the family firm management style increasingly was replaced by the administrative pyramid of the corporation.

Corporate managers were apt to be highly specialized—attached to a specific function such as a finance department or an engineering group. Managers often devoted all of their efforts to one narrow function such as purchasing, personnel, or sales. The activities of individual, specialized managers had to be coordinated by higher levels of management, just as the various specialized departments within the management hierarchy had to be directed from above. Furthermore, techniques created by the railway companies were widely copied to administer the geographically dispersed operations of national corporations.[9] This entailed creation of field offices to oversee local operations, while a head office was created to direct the field offices. Not only did top corporate officers devote themselves largely to managing lower levels of management, but the entire head office of the corporation became an administrative unit whose primary reason for being was to manage lower level administrative units. Armies of clerical workers kept the corporate records in order and provided support functions for the various management levels.

In terms of urban development, creation of the corporate management hierarchy produced growing numbers of corporate headquarters buildings in the central business district (CBD) of large cities.[10] In the pre–World War I years of the twentieth century, great stone buildings, ten to fifteen stories tall, were built to house the corporate administrators. During the 1920s, numerous "skyscrapers" were built in the big cities to house the proliferating corporate pyramids. Corporate managers, professionals, and clerical workers by the thousands descended upon the CBDs each day to coordinate and plan the activities of the growing national corporations.

After World War I, a few forward-looking corporations (General Motors and Du Pont initially) began to combine the practices of managerial specialization and hierarchy with the notion of decentralizing their operations into several divisions. This multidivisional corporate form was often adopted by firms that emphasized new product development and marketing as their dominant concerns.[11] The multidivisional corporation could enter a new market by adding a new division while leaving its old divisions largely undisturbed. Similarly, a new division could be created to introduce competing product lines in the same market, thereby expanding the range of products available to consumers. General Motors, for example, created separate divisions to produce economy cars, luxury cars, and cars that fell between these two extremes. A separate division produced locomotives and another produced trucks. To meet the challenge of a changing market, a new division could be added while an old division was dropped entirely. The multidivisional corporation was admirably adopted to capitalism's product proliferation phase. Because each division had its own corporate administrative pyramid as well as considerable independence from its corporate parent, acceptance of the multidivisional corporate structure further extended the management bureaucracy. With Chevrolet, Oldsmobile, Buick, Pontiac, and Cadillac defined as separate divisions—each competing for the customer's dollars—General Motors had five separate marketing departments in the automotive field rather than one. Furthermore, the top layer of management at General Motors need not concern itself with the problems of individual divisions unless problems arose. Rather, top management would concentrate on allocating investment capital to its most promising divisions, creating new divisions and searching the globe for opportunities.

Marketing-oriented mutidivisional corporations became the rule in the decade following World War II, and this development had important ramifications for cities and inner-city ghettos. Horizontal and vertical expansion of corporate hierarchy in the big cities generated large and sustained demands for white-collar workers. Blacks in the past enjoyed upward economic mobility only in those periods when manufacturing industries were rapidly expanding their blue-collar worker ranks and blacks moved first into the low-level unskilled jobs and later into the more skilled categories. Big cities have emerged as centers of administration rather than production, and black economic well-being depends critically upon the ability of black workers to adjust to this new reality.

Management activities are spread geographically across America in very distinct, city-shaping patterns. Multidivisional corporations have at least four major management levels of supervision and control: local, regional, divisional, and corporate head office.[12] The lowest level of management—local—takes place at the actual site of production such as the factory, where the day-to-day production activities of firms are supervised. Thus, local management is spread geographically throughout the country (and the world), wherever corporations conduct their business. The three higher levels of management—regional, divisional, and corporate head office—are concentrated in the larger metropolitan areas, particularly in big city CBDs. A few very large cities such as New York, Chicago, Houston, and Los Angeles possess numerous corporate head offices as well as divisional, regional, and local management facilities. As these largest cities have increasingly specialized in management activities, their demand for white-collar workers has expanded rapidly relative to both blue-collar employment and white-collar worker demand in the entire nation. Furthermore, professional and management functions that are complementary to the task of managing giant corporations have proliferated in the largest metropolitan areas. Specifically, corporate law firms, large banks, CPA firms, advertising agencies and a number of similar professional business services have proliferated in those places where their large corporate clients are concentrated. The dynamic, expanding sector of such very large cities as Chicago has therefore increasingly become administration-and-management-oriented, and the resultant demands for workers have been in the white-collar fields: clerical, professional, and managerial.

Below the very largest cities are those that possess a few head offices of giant corporations as well as the head offices of smaller regional corporations; divisional, regional, and local management functions are often heavily concentrated in these cities. Examples of this city type include Atlanta, Denver, Seattle, and Cleveland, and these cities have typically generated very rapid increases in white-collar employment.

In the smaller cities, specialization in management functions declines, and the proportion of the local labor force employed in the professional, managerial, and clerical fields drops accordingly. Smaller cities that possess significant corporate operations—such as Gary, Flint, Dayton, and Peoria—typically claim only local corporate managers, and these cities are not likely to house concentrations of such corporate services as advertising agencies and large accounting firms. The fate of these cities is controlled by higher level corporate managers located in the distant large cities. Loss of a major corporate facility such as a large manufacturing plant can be devastating to these smaller cities because they have often failed to develop rapidly expanding white-collar lines of economic activity. Thus, an old manufacturing area such as Chicago can experience an absolute decline in manufacturing production, but the overall area can continue to prosper because of continued growth in white-collar employment. In contrast, termination of steel production in Gary or auto production in Flint would utterly devastate those cities.

Not all large cities possess substantial amounts of managerial and administrative activities, and some small cities do indeed possess large and growing amounts of these white-collar job generating functions. Detroit, for example, possesses relatively few of the higher-level management and professional functions. Proximity to Chicago undoubtedly discourages many large corporations from locating major regional management facilities there. By contrast, rapid white-collar employment gains have generated growth in smaller cities such as Columbus, Ohio, but this type of growth has often been derived from the presence of a major university or a state capital complex. Particularly in the industrial Northeast and Midwest, the post–World War II health of cities and SMSAs has been linked to their ability to attract employers offering jobs in managerial, administrative, and professional areas. Generally declining blue-collar industrial employment has often weakened the economic vitality of those areas which have failed to generate rapid increases in white-collar employment.

As a group that has relied historically upon blue-collar manufacturing work for upward mobility, blacks of course have been affected directly by the long-term urban shift from industrial production to administration and finance. As early as the 1920s, blacks living in centers of booming white-collar employment such as Chicago were pulled into blue-collar industrial jobs partially because whites—the traditional factory proletarians—were increasingly seeking cleaner, better paying white-collar work. In turn, the severe plight of urban blacks during the Great Depression was partially due to the competition that downwardly mobile whites caused as they once again sought the production jobs that many blacks had moved up to during the 1920s. The prosperous 1960s were similar to the 1920s in that blacks often filled better paying blue-collar jobs that were being vacated by upwardly mobile whites. Furthermore, the demand for clerical workers in the big cities was so strong in the 1960s that younger black females were able to move in substantial numbers into the lower echelons of this occupation. In both the 1920s and the 1960s, black economic progress was derived from the interrelated phenomena of rapidly expanding white-collar employment and the upward occupational mobility of white workers. The 1960s, in contrast to the 1920s, did allow blacks, particularly young women, to benefit directly from white-collar job availability. But the shift to white-collar employment coincided with the last stages of the transformation of southern agriculture in the decade after World War II. Blacks moved in large numbers into the central cities where corporate headquarters were expanding.

But the educational system in the rural South had not prepared them for the new white-collar jobs. In addition, white-collar employment for men was largely a white occupation. Finally, the informal labor market networks that black men were involved in were oriented largely to blue-collar employment. These factors—poor education, segregated employment patterns for many white-collar jobs, and the informal organization of the labor market—combined largely to exclude black men from the opportunities created by the post–World War II development of the large corporation. The transformation of large cities from centers of production to centers of administration bypassed much of the black community.

In the 1970s, black income gains relative to that of whites stagnated as the nation's economic growth slowed and, in the early 1980s, blacks and whites throughout large parts of the Midwest are once more engaged in job competition reminiscent of the 1930s. In the past, such competition reversed black employment and income gains. Chapter 9 summarizes evidence suggesting that similar trends are reappearing.

Government Tax and Expenditure Policies

Government tax and expenditure policies that shape capital formation in the private sector are other factors that undermine the economic position of blacks. Investment tax credits and tax code provisions for accelerated depreciation are two key policies that have destroyed numerous jobs that black workers would have otherwise held. Government policies that lessen the cost of capital relative to labor predictably induce employers to replace workers with machines. Conventional economic wisdom holds that labor and capital are substitutes, but this notion is in fact an oversimplification. Blue-collar workers and capital equipment are indeed substitutes for each other, but capital and white-collar employees are complements. Thus, government tax policies have caused blue-collar workers to be replaced with a combination of capital and white-collar employees, further biasing job competition against the less-skilled manual worker. A study of the impact of the investment tax credit upon total U.S. labor input from 1962 to 1971 concluded that employment of blue-collar workers would have been about 1.1 percent higher, while employment of white-collar workers would have been about 0.3 percent lower over the period in the absence of the investment tax credit.[13] Accelerated depreciation and the method of financing social security are two government policies that have an even greater magnitude than the investment credit upon relative labor, capital costs.

The policies discussed thus far represent only a few of the many government policies that tend to destroy blue-collar jobs while white-collar employment and more capital intensive production methods are encouraged. The impact of government on the tradeoff between capital and labor is most apparent in two areas: education and the integration of capital accumulation and technical change. Government foots much of the bill for training managers, scientists, and engineers, and finances most of the research in advanced technologies, either directly or through tax expenditures. Government investment in education and technology (social investment) and business investment in plant and equipment (private investment) have increasingly become one process: the integration of education, science, and production technology in a single process means that private investment largely embodies social investment. The investment process that has been eliminating blue-collar jobs is heavily dependent on public policy.

Social investment in human capital is financed by government because scientific-technical knowledge and skills cannot be monopolized by any one business interest. Capital in the form of knowledge and skills is the property of the workers themselves. In the absence of prohibitions on labor mobility, individual firms often find it unprofitable to train their own labor. They will, instead, seek to hire workers who already possess requisite skills. To a lesser extent, this same line of reasoning applies to business spending for research and development. Patents on particular products do not enable firms to capture all of the benefits that flow from innovation, particularly when research efforts are pushing on the frontiers of existing technical knowledge. Furthermore, high costs and the uncertainty of realizing economically utilizable results discourage corporate investment in research and development. R and D is therefore largely financed by the state while the benefits of advanced research accrue to the technologically sophisticated firms.

Today no single large corporation could afford to train its own scientific and technical personnel and maintain its own research and development apparatus. Government has assumed a large part of the cost of providing industry with a labor force whose skills are tailored to fit the technical requirements of modern production and distribution, and government both funds and coordinates most research and development. The result has been a rapid and accelerating rate of scientific discovery and technical advancement that continually shapes and reshapes the economy. It also continually alters the urban landscape, the composition of the labor force, and the products that we consume—indeed, the content of life.

The mode of operation of large firms, and for small firms operating on the technological frontier, stresses the combination of skilled labor with technically advanced plants and equipment. This style is fostered by government tax and spending policies that subsidize advanced capital equipment, and government training of the skilled workers that this type of production process requires. Because this sector of the economy expands output primarily by combining additional skilled laborers with additional units of technologically advanced capital, output expansion can coexist with an actual reduction of job opportunities for less-skilled workers. This growth in manufacturing capacity often displaces blue-collar workers, who then flood other sectors of the labor market where they depress wage levels and build up pressures for growth of the welfare system. An expanding high technology sector is perfectly capable of simultaneously producing rising average incomes and a growing surplus population in which blacks are disproportionately represented. Growth of the economy and changing technology can readily be a long-run cause of, rather than the cure for, the underemployment and poverty of urban blacks.[14]

There is another, less rational, aspect of government policies that merits discussion at this point because of its generally detrimental impact upon the well-being of urban blacks. The process of metropolitan growth has been accompanied by local government fragmentation, suburban exploitation of the central city,[15] and a growing tendency for the tax base, increasingly suburban, to be divorced from social needs, which are increasingly conconcentrated in the central city. Urbanization generates myriad interdependencies in industrial, commercial, residential, transportation, and recreational development patterns. Absence of overall social planning produces political boundaries that may relate in no systematic way to the interrelated developmental patterns of industry, commerce, housing, transportation, and so forth. Metropolitan areas, therefore, typically contain a central city and an uncoordinated mass of suburbs dotting the urban periphery. The resultant muddle leads to a proliferation of uncoordinated, overlapping government services. Expenditures by local governments are invariably large and often highly wasteful. Continued urbanization and suburban proliferation produce urban "crisis" and the national government is called upon to provide a new bundle of goods which, superimposed upon the existing disarray, will hopefully correct some of the more glaring irrationalities of the anarchical patterns of metropolitan development.[16] Nonetheless, irrational patterns exist as manifested in the fiscal crises facing many of the nation's older industrial cities. The burdens of central-city fiscal crisis fall disproportionately, of course, on the poor, the aged, and the minority populations who are least able to flee the central city.

The Changing Make-up of the City

In the past decade, it was often fashionable to envision America's older, larger cities as an endangered species.[17] Particularly in the manufacturing sector—the traditional economic base of so many large cities—production jobs were moving out of the old central city, and employment opportunities were increasingly located in suburbia. Paralleling the employment dispersals, population shifts to the suburbs have been the second factor in changing metropolitan spatial structure. Intrametropolitan migration has been highly selective. It has disproportionately been young, employed, and white populations of central cities that have resettled in suburban peripheries, leaving the old, unemployed, and black inhabitants behind.

At the same time that decentralization was eroding the white population of central cities, blacks streamed in from the South. Primarily due to the mechanization of southern agriculture, black migration to cities limited net inner-city population declines. Five major cities— Chicago, Baltimore, Cleveland, Detroit, and Philadelphia—illustrate shifting central-city racial composition. While these cities experienced a net loss of 1,018,479 people from 1950 to 1970, out-migration of whites to the suburbs reached a grand total of 2,575,646. In-migration of blacks plus net births over deaths among existing residents added 1,557,167 to the combined population of the five cities, so that while blacks composed only 16.7 percent of the population of these cities in 1950, by 1970 this percentage more than doubled to 37.3 percent.

Demographic transition and net population decline notwithstanding, most of the large cities clearly are not dying. Rather, they are adapting to corporate and government policies, to the existing state of technical know-how, and to a resultant pattern of economic development that is increasingly transforming large cities into centers of administration and dispersers of business services.

The transition of central-city economic base from industrial production to administrative and service functions may entail a permanent reduction in inner-city population. This transition may also be most traumatic for those industrial cities such as Detroit that are less successful in attracting corporate management facilities and the diverse providers of business services that employ white-collar labor. Those few cities that do indeed die out will be those old industrial cities that are least successful in generating white-collar jobs to offset generally declining blue-collar employment. Our earlier discussion of the geographic distribution of corporate management functions suggests that the smaller rather than the larger industrial cities should be the leading candidates for nonviability.

Transit considerations that shaped factory locations early in the twentieth century have been dramatically altered in recent decades, particularly since World War II. Widespread automobile ownership has enabled employees to commute many miles to work. Freed from the need to locate near mass transit lines and working-class residential districts, manufacturers have located their production facilities farther and farther from the central city. This has been especially true for those that rely primarily upon truck transit, including wholesale distributors, as well as manufacturers. Particularly in the age of automoblile proliferation, the older, densely-populated central cities have become extremely congested. Transportation costs are often minimized by leaving the central city's traffic behind, locating instead at an outlying site near a freeway.[18] The suburban freeway interchange has therefore become the preferred location for manufacturers and other shippers who do not rely heavily upon rail or water transit. The lower population densities and reduced congestion of suburbia, as well as the greater availability of single-family housing, has proved appealing to workers; millions of them have left the central city for suburban housing in the years since World War II.

Multiple-story factories that characterized nineteenth-century cities and the production techniques of that period largely became relics after World War II. Electricity had replaced steam power to drive machinery. New assembly-line techniques made it economical for most manufacturers to adopt a horizontal production flow. Raw materials were introduced at one end of a long, singe-story factory, processed as they were moved horizontally, and the finished product emerged at the other end of the factory. The modern production technology increasingly required spacious, single-story plants which were expensive to construct in built-up central-city areas.

Outlying suburban areas were the logical sites for the sprawling single-story manufacturing facilities that utilized modern assembly-line techniques. Vacant land was more readily available and cheaper in suburbia as opposed to the central city. In addition, lower property taxes and insurance costs encouraged suburban plant location. Suburban sites also offered a more pleasant commuting and working environment for the employees: relative to the city, there was less crime and pollution. Reduced congestion made commuting by car more pleasant, and employers at suburban sites invariably offered abundant free parking immediately adjacent to the factory. Growing reliance on truck transportation also favored suburban plant location because central-city congestion was a particularly severe handicap for truckers. If rail transit had to be utilized as well, it was possible to find suburban locations adjacent to railroad lines.

Whereas the old factory was typically a multiple-story structure in a crowded central-city district, new facilities were overwhelmingly single-story buildings located by freeways in suburbia. Unlike his or her predecessor who walked to work or rode the trolley, the modern day factory worker usually drives. Past advantages of a central-city location are now detriments and the multiple-storied factories that thrived a century ago now stand largely as abandoned relics of another age. The multifamily residential areas that surrounded the old factories are now largely ghetto housing for a growing central-city black population.

While a part of the central-city economy has been dying, another part has flourished. Disadvantages of a central-city location such as the ones previously discussed are counterbalanced in the eyes of some employers by advantages such as proximity to complementary businesses, proximity to amenities, and favorable labor market conditions for certain types of employees. These advantages have generated rapid growth of central business districts in cities such as Chicago, where administrative activities are concentrated. In the CBD, corporate headquarters benefit from the proximity of big banks, advertising agencies, corporate law firms, relevant government offices, and so forth. Amenities complementary to certain corporate management functions—restaurants, hotels, entertainment—also exist in abundance in CBDs.

Data summarized in table 8.1 describe some of the broad economic base transformations that snowbelt cities have undergone in the post–World War II period. Data were gathered describing employment in manufacturing, trade, and services for all major metropolitan areas in six states that typify the snowbelt region: Pennsylvania, Ohio, Michigan, Illinois, Maryland, and Missouri.

Total manufacturing employment for these twenty-six snowbelt SMSAs grew slightly from 4.234 million in 1947 to 4.472 million in 1972; after 1972, the number of manufacturing jobs declined. Interestingly, the 1977 figures on manufacturing employment are buoyed by very strong automobile industry production in that year.

Table 8.1 reveals the depth of snowbelt central-city job loss in manufacturing production, retail, and wholesale. The near constancy of overall snowbelt SMSA manufacturing employment masks the fact that central cities have experienced a massive exodus of manufacturing production jobs. Between 1947 and 1977, the twenty-six central cities described in table 8.1 collectively lost 51.1 percent of their total production jobs in manufacturing (a total of 1,131,494 production jobs). In terms of numbers of jobs, the second largest industrial grouping was retailing, and these same twenty-six central cities lost 29.8

percent of their retail trade employment in the 1948 through 1977 time period. Although service employment expanded by 27.5 percent between 1948 and 1977, the absolute growth of this industrial grouping was small compared to losses in manufacturing and trade. Finally, growth in selected service employment has been absent in these central cities since 1972.

Government employment is heavily concentrated in central cities, especially in their CBDs, and employment by state, local, and federal government units has expanded substantially in the post–World War II period. Large cities have typically experienced rapid growth in industry groupings such as business services, finance, insurance, real

Table 8.1. Post–World War II Snowbelt Employment in Three Major Industry Groupings

A. Mean Employment for 26 Central Cities in 6 Snowbelt States				
	1948	*1963*	*1972*	*1977*
Manufacturing—Production	85,221	57,817	48,722	41,692
Manufacturing—Nonproduction	19,362	25,986	24,126	22,048
Trade: Wholesale, Retail	60,346	50,250	46,744	42,915
Selected Services	14,401	16,735	18,902	18,364
Total	179,320	150,788	138,494	125,019

B. Mean Employment for 26 Suburban Peripheries in 6 Snowbelt States				
	1948	*1963*	*1972*	*1977*
Manufacturing—Production	48,788	56,941	67,717	69,362
Manufacturing—Nonproduction	9,485	23,098	31,432	33,759
Trade: Wholesale, Retail	20,064	36,494	62,932	77,321
Selected Services	3,363	7,414	14,915	19,935
Total	81,700	123,947	176,996	200,377

C. Suburban Jobs as Percentages of Total SMSA Jobs				
	1948	*1963*	*1972*	*1977*
Manufacturing—Production	36.4	49.6	58.2	62.5
Manufacturing—Nonproduction	32.9	47.0	56.6	60.5
Trade: Wholesale, Retail	30.7	50.9	63.0	68.5
Selected Services	18.9	30.7	44.1	52.1
Total Suburban Share	31.3	45.1	56.1	61.6

Sources: U.S. Census of Manufacturing, U.S. Census of Business: Retail Trade, Wholesale Trade and Selected Services.

Notes: Suburban periphery employment is defined as total SMSA employment minus central-city employment. Manufacturing data listed under "1948" actually refer to 1947 data.

estate, and government, in services such as hotels and entertainment, and in administrative jobs of manufacturing concerns. Declining industrial activity and expanding administrative and service functions are transforming the economic base of older industrial cities, while economic advantages such as greater access to customers and suppliers have spurred decentralization of wholesale and retail firms. The exception to this pattern is found among the smaller snowbelt cities that have not attracted expanding administrative and service sector activities. Their condition is typically one of substantial absolute employment declines in all fields.

Table 8.2 describes the sunbelt counterpart to the northern metropolitan areas listed in table 8.1. Data were gathered for manufacturing, trade, and service employment trends for all major cities in nine states: Virginia, North Carolina, Georgia, Alabama, Louisiana, Oklahoma, Texas, Arizona, and Colorado.

The newer sunbelt cities are quite different. They are typified by either abundant open space within city boundaries or the legal authority to annex their suburbs. These cities have therefore experienced rapid increases in both administrative employment, manufacturing, and trade. Their manufacturing sectors are overwhelmingly post–World War II in vintage and their transit infrastructures are modern.

The sunbelt cities were centers of development for the rapidly growing industries that spearheaded the long wave of economic growth of the 1950s and 1960s. These industries, such as electronics,

Table 8.2. Post–World War II Sunbelt Employment in Three Major Industry Groupings

Mean Employment for 23 SMSAs in 9 Sunbelt States				
	1948	1963	1972	1977
Manufacturing—Production	—	29,900	43,326	46,565
Manufacturing—Nonproduction	—	13,150	18,961	19,696
Trade: Wholesale, Retail	31,445	44,583	69,349	84,634
Selected Services	7,136	13,112	23,430	29,241
Total	—	100,745	155,066	180,136

Sources: U.S. Census of Manufacturing, U.S. Census of Business: Retail Trade, Wholesale Trade and Selected Services.

Note: Manufacturing data listed under "1948" actually refer to 1947 data. The 1947 data were missing for several of the sunbelt SMSAs because of the very small size of their manufacturing sectors in that year.

computers, and aerospace, were among the leaders in developing the high technology that combined capital-intensive production methods with skilled labor. Rapid rates of technological change and development of new products also required emphasis on marketing, with consequent emphasis on white-collar jobs in those sectors of business. Many of the sunbelt cities, particularly in the West and Southwest, spearheaded the transformation of production and administration to the new post–World War II pattern.

We should note that the cities of southern New England, in the snowbelt, made a similar transition. Decline of the older manufacturing industries there, which had been going on since the 1920s, made available a redundant but relatively well-educated labor force. An urban infrastructure and developed transportation system was available. Strong educational institutions devoted to scientific research provided both needed skills and the basis for technological innovation. And the early development of the electronics and aerospace industries in New England during World War II, also an important factor in the West and Southwest, gave those industries an important initial start.

The growth of the sunbelt cities, and those of New England, has also been uneven, however. Continuing technological change has greatly simplified production processes in such industries as electronics, computers, communication equipment, and other industries that use advanced technology. The result has been a growing imbalance in the workforce. A relatively small number of highly-trained technical, scientific, and professional personnel are engaged in administration, marketing, product development, and supervision of production. These are the high-salaried component of the workforce in those industries. Meanwhile, production jobs have been broken down into increasingly simplified component parts that require little skill. Production workers, then, are generally in the low-wage category, and there is a growing gap between the incomes of production workers and those employees that carry the high technology skills. Thus, in the electronics industry, wage rates are considerably below those of production workers in such older industries as steel and automobiles. Just as the decline of manufacturing industry in the older snowbelt cities tends to create a growing low-wage sector in the labor market along with a growing high-income sector, so the economic development of the sunbelt cities is creating a similar pattern of economic inequality.

Overall, snowbelt and sunbelt SMSAs, are quite different regarding industrial composition of employment and rates of employment growth. The more rapidly growing sunbelt SMSAs, in contrast to their snowbelt counterparts, are relatively less reliant upon manufacturing employment and more reliant upon the service industries. Available evidence indicates that the sunbelt SMSAs rely more heavily upon government employment (especially federal jobs) relative to the snowbelt SMSAs.

Government employment has produced long-term job growth in both snowbelt and sunbelt central cities. Consistent time series data on local government employment in central cities are available for most central cities over the 1957 to 1977 time period. For the cities being considered herein, these data were available for 11 of the 26 snowbelt cities and 19 of the 23 sunbelt cities.[19] The number of city government employees rose from 291,059 to 431,717 between 1957 and 1977 in the snowbelt central cities, while the sunbelt central cities registered more than a doubling—from 139,728 to 308,952—in the number of city government employees. Data on federal government employees are complete from all cities and suburban areas, but they are only available for 1975. Overall federal government employment levels indicate that federal employees collectively represent an industry grouping that is rather small in comparison with the industry groupings appearing in tables 8.1 and 8.2. Significantly, government employment is heavily concentrated in white-collar occupations. Charlotte Freeman estimates that professional and technical categories account for about 32 percent of total government employment, while clerical accounts for another 33 percent.[20]

Available data on government employment are consistent with the portrait of snowbelt central cities as atrophying centers of industrial production and emerging centers of service and administrative functions. Although overall decline in employment and population characterize these cities, administrative and service activities have increased fairly consistently since 1948. In terms of relative employment growth, snowbelt central cities are increasingly dominated by government, service, finance, insurance, real estate, and nonproduction employment (largely administrative) in manufacturing. These trends are most dominant in the largest northern central cities. In Chicago, Baltimore, Cleveland, and Philadelphia, for example, growth in service employment has been much more rapid than it has been in the other twenty-two snowbelt central cities under consideration. Furthermore, these larger cities have, relative to the other twenty-two snowbelt cities, experienced greater losses of manufacturing production jobs, greater gains in manufacturing nonproduction jobs, greater losses in retailing employment, and greater gains in finance, insurance, and real estate. The largest central cities, therefore, are transforming themselves most rapidly away from industrial production and towards service and administrative activities.

Overview

Large urban areas in the United States have been rapidly reshaping their employment and residential patterns in recent decades. Extensive decentralization of residential, trade, and industrial production activities has occurred, while administration and business services have tended to cluster in big city CBD areas. On balance, jobs and residential locations have been spreading out, and the typical large urban area of today has a much lower population density than its nineteenth-century counterpart. Either thinly populated or previously empty areas adjacent to cities have captured most of the post–World War II growth in employment and population. These growing regions have typically been suburbs in snowbelt urban areas, but in sunbelt cities such growth has often taken place within city boundaries. The older, densely populated cities that flourished during the late nineteenth century have typically lost both employment and population to their suburban peripheries. Plagued with congestion, aging infrastructure, and many obsolete manufacturing facilities, these snowbelt cities have lost ground because their traits which were once advantageous—high density, rail and water transit access—are now often outright liabilities in a decentralizing society where auto and truck transit are dominant. Government policies as diverse as the Highway Defense Act of 1956 and the FHA's role in financing suburban housing development have aided this shift in urban form from high density cities to sprawling urban areas where low density patterns of employment and population are the norm. Another group of government policies labeled loosely as "urban renewal" has aided high-density CBD development, but this has not offset the declines in population and employment that older big cities have experienced.

In addition to the spreading out of jobs and people in the non-CBD portions of urban areas, major shifts in the composition of employment have been occurring in large metropolitan areas. The CBDs are often the only dynamic, expanding sector in older central cities and labor demands in the CBDs are predominantly for white-collar workers. Even in the decentralizing industrial production sector, labor force composition is increasingly skewed toward the skilled white-collar worker, while unskilled jobs for blue-collar employees are generally declining except in the most rapidly growing regions. These shifts in labor force composition were associated with the changing nature of the corporation. They've been accelerated by government policies ranging from tax policies permitting rapid depreciation write-offs to state financing of research in advanced technologies. By subsidizing production processes that utilize sophisticated capital-intensive techniques and highly-skilled workers, government has encouraged blue-collar employee displacement.

In 1980, 58 percent of the U.S. black population resided in central cities, compared to 25 percent for the rest of the population. These cities and their surrounding suburban peripheries showed widely varying degrees of economic health, reflecting their differing abilities to adopt to changing economic circumstances.

In a ranking of the nation's 121 largest cities, Anthony Downs found that blacks disproportionately reside in the least healthy areas.[21] Among cities ranked as "severely declining" that were located in SMSAs that were declining as well, blacks accounted for 27.4 percent of central-city population. Among the growing cities located in growing SMSAs, blacks made up 14.5 percent of the central-city inhabitants. Residence in the older, more densely populated sections of declining central cities is a growing handicap in the struggle for jobs and income.

These ghetto areas are often adjacent to obsolete manufacturing facilities that are typically underutilized and sometimes completely abandoned. Furthermore, the typical less-efficient and aged manufacturing facility is precisely the sort that is most apt to be closed during a business downturn. Ghettos are often located close to expanding CBDs and this can be highly advantageous for those ghetto residents who can compete successfully for the predominantly white-collar jobs that CBDs offer. But these opportunities are more readily available to whites than to blacks, who often lack the educational background and access to informal labor market networks that are available to whites. Finally, ghettos are typically far removed from the suburban areas where manufacturing and trade employment is most likely to be available. In sunbelt central cities where employment is growing rapidly, ghetto dwellers are nonetheless most likely to be housed in the oldest densely-populated sections that are farthest removed from the expanding trade and manufacturing jobs. The equivalent of snowbelt suburban areas is often incorporated within the boundaries of sunbelt central cities; indeed these cities often annex their suburbs. Even in the sunbelt cities, jobs in the decentralizing fields of manufacturing and trade are to be found largely in the low density outlying areas of sunbelt central cities that are least accessible to ghetto residents.

Overall, growth patterns in big urban areas favor the white-collar worker over his blue-collar counterpart. Aside from the CBD, development is of a low density sort often known as "suburban sprawl." The typical worker drives via automobile to his employment site. Mass transit commuting is common only among those employed in the CBD. Black workers rely disproportionately upon blue-collar employment; most reside in high-density residential areas; incidence of automobile ownership is relatively low. Evidence on how they have fared in the urban labor market is examined extensively in the next chapter.

9

Black Economic Well-Being Since the 1950s

HAS BLACK ECONOMIC WELL-BEING IMPROVED SINCE WORLD WAR II? There are no simple answers. This chapter will document areas of improvement as well as deterioration, and we will explore the causes of these diverse trends. Overall, the evidence points to polarization within the black community: the younger and better-educated are registering strong and sustained gains in income and occupational status; those who are not highly educated—yet not below average in skills and years of schooling—continue to ride the cyclical roller coaster, prospering in periods of labor shortage and suffering during prolonged recessions; those on the bottom appear to be positively worse off, perhaps representing a semipermanent lumpenproletariat facing very uncertain prospects for future job market upgrading. Regional trends, interacting with major shifts in industry employment patterns—the decline of automobile industry employment for example—complicate all generalizations about trends in black well-being.

Future income and employment prospects for black workers are assessed rather pessimistically in this chapter. Particularly among black male workers the future may bring about an affluent elite of white-collar workers, a greatly diminished number of middle-income blue-

collar workers, and a large and growing number of low-income unemployed and underemployed workers whose labor force attachment
is quite marginal.

The Evidence For Major Economic Progress

Black progress in education and occupational status has been quite
pronounced in recent decades. Income trends are less clearcut, but
evidence that incomes of blacks have been rising relative to incomes
of whites, summarized in table 9.1, has been widely cited to demon-
strate long-term, sustained improvements in the well-being of blacks.
Although black family incomes have fallen relative to white incomes
in the 1970s (table 9.1), long-term improvement is still apparent. Furthermore, there are a number of valid reasons for using incomes of
individuals, as opposed to families, as the "more accurate" measure
of trends in relative black income position.[1] For example, much of
the decline in black family incomes since 1970 is directly related to
the rise of single-parent families rather than changes in labor market
status. Table 9.1 clearly shows that black male incomes improved
dramatically during the prosperous 1960s (the relevant black-white
income ratio rose from .47 in 1959 to .59 in 1969); furthermore, some
additional improvement occurred during the recessionary 1970s—
black male incomes rose from 59 percent of white incomes in 1969
to 65 percent in 1979. An even more clearcut improvement in relative
incomes is apparent in data describing relative black female incomes
in table 9.1. In each of the last three decades, black female incomes
(expressed as a percentage of white female incomes) have increased
dramatically. Whereas black females received only 46.3 percent as
much as their white female counterparts in 1949, their 1979 relative
incomes were 93.1 percent of white incomes. By 1979, black females
actually exceeded white cohort incomes in every area of the United
States except the South. Now that's progress. Or is it? We will argue
that nationwide black relative income comparisons (or black-white
income ratios) are severely flawed measures of black economic well-
being. Essentially, data such as those summarized in table 9.1 obscure
more than they reveal, actually setting back our understanding of
complex issues by relying upon overly simplistic measures of black
income position.

The issue of black educational gains since World War II is much
more straightforward than a comparison of relative incomes. Progress
in the education realm has been widespread, as shown in table 9.2.
Among black adults, median years of school completed in 1980 was
12.0 years, only slightly behind the 12.5 years reported by the white

Table 9.1. Incomes of Black Individuals and
Families, States as Percentages of White
Individual and Family Incomes

Year	Black Families*	Black Males†	Black Females†
1947	51	—	—
1948	53	54	43
1949	51	48	46
1950	54	54	45
1951	53	55	42
1952	57	55	39
1953	56	55	59
1954	56	50	54
1955	55	53	52
1956	51	52	57
1957	53	53	58
1958	51	50	59
1959	52	47	62
1960	55	53	62
1961	53	52	67
1962	53	49	67
1963	53	52	67
1964	56	57	70
1965	55	61	73
1966	60	59	79
1967	59	57	80
1968	60	61	81
1969	61	59	85
1970	61	60	92
1971	60	60	90
1972	59	62	96
1973	58	63	93
1974	60	64	92
1975	61	63	92
1976	60	63	95
1977	57	61	88
1978	59	64	92
1979	57	65	93
1980	58	63	96
1981	56	63	92

Sources: U.S. Bureau of the Census, *Current Population Reports*, ser. P-60, no. 137, table 15 (Washington, D.C.: Government Printing Office, Mar. 1983), pp. 39–42. Ibid., table 16, pp. 43–46.

*Figures prior to 1967 include blacks and other races; figures since 1967 include blacks only.
†Figures for blacks refer to blacks and other races.

Table 9.2. Trends in Black Educational Attainment

A. Median Years of School Completed by Persons 25 and Older

	Nonwhite	Black	White	Difference
1940	5.8	—	8.7	2.9
1960	8.2	—	10.9	2.7
1980	—	12.0	12.5	0.5

B. Number of Blacks Enrolled in Colleges and Universities

1965	274,000
1970	522,000
1975	948,000
1980	1,007,000

Sources: Census of population data, cited in John Reid, "Black America in the 1980s," *Population Bulletin* 37, no. 5 (1982):25; U.S. Bureau of the Census, *Current Population Reports,* ser. P-20, no. 373, table 3 (Washington, D.C.: Government Printing Office, Feb. 1983), p. 5.

adult population. The incidence of teenagers (16 through 19 years of age) out of school with no high school diploma in 1981 was 13.6 percent for blacks, 11.7 percent for whites.[2] The incidence of black college enrollment for those eighteen to twenty-four years old rose from 10.3 percent in 1965 to 19.4 percent in 1981; the corresponding enrollment rate for whites was roughly 26 percent throughout this period. Although college enrollment of black students peaked at 1,103,000 in 1977, 1,080,000 were enrolled in 1981 which suggests approximate stability rather than enrollment declines. Available evidence indicates black educational gains throughout the 1960s and 1970s, with no trend towards backsliding emerging to date in the 1980s.

Educational achievements have translated into occupational gains for many black workers, especially among young college graduates. Black male college graduates twenty-five to thirty-four years old earned in 1959 only 59 percent as much as their white college graduate cohorts; by 1979 this figure had jumped to 84 percent. In the case of students holding MBA degrees, black-white parity has apparently been achieved. The Association of MBA Executives reports MBA degree holders hired in 1980 started out with average salaries of $24,259, with blacks and whites receiving approximately equal pay.[3]

Penetration into white-collar occupations has been prevalent among younger black women. In 1980, 49.4 percent of the black females who worked during the year were employed in white-collar jobs. The incidence of white-collar employment for black males was 23.9 percent; over 17 percent were employed as skilled craftsmen, however, while another 25.2 percent worked as operatives—which is commonly well-paid factory work. These occupational figures must be interpreted with one important qualification in mind: those not working are excluded.[4] Similarly, income figures such as those summarized in table 9.1 include *only* those persons having income. Of course, the incidence of blacks working in any given time period is lower than the incidence of employed whites; the same pattern applies to income recipients. Nonetheless, real occupational gains have been realized by black workers since the 1950s, and this is especially true for females.

One final piece of evidence indicating black progress in recent decades is the increase of blacks in highly visible, prestigious positions. The traditional areas of high visibility—entertainment and professional sports—are now overshadowed by blacks serving in top elected offices. Since the 1960s, blacks have also served at very high levels in government bureaucracies: the presidential cabinet, the Supreme Court, major state government positions. In fact, increased representation of blacks is apparent at all levels of government (table 9.3).

In the private sector, blacks account for rapidly growing numbers of younger executives at major corporations. In the media, black stereotypes of thirty years ago have been largely relegated to the dustbin of history; blacks now appear in authoritative roles such as newscasters.

Table 9.3. Growth in the Number of Black Elected Officials

	1970	1982
Federal	10	18
State, Regional	169	397
County	92	465
City	623	2,451
Judicial, Law Enforcement	213	563
Education	362	1,266
Total number of elected black officials	1,469	5,160

Source: E.R. Shipp, "'63 Marcher sees gains but a 'Long Way to Travel,'" *New York Times* 28 Aug. 1983, p. 30.

In light of all the above—relative income gains, narrowing the educational gap, upward occupational mobility, including penetration of society's most prestigious positions—it is not surprising that most respondents to a 1980 Gallup poll felt that the quality of life for blacks had improved during the 1970s.[5]

The Evidence Suggesting that Black Economic Well-Being Is Declining

Most of the respondents to the Gallup poll mentioned above were whites. Among black respondents, the majority felt that their quality of life had stayed the same or gotten worse during the 1970s. The broad generality of the question—How have blacks fared over time?—is apt to produce oversimplified answers supported by simplistic evidence. Some are better off; others are worse off. While widespread economic and social progress was clearly the norm during the 1960s, much evidence indicates regression in black economic status in the 1970s. According to Vernon Jordan, former president of the Urban League, "For Black Americans the decade of the 1970s was a time in which many of their hopes, raised by the civil rights victories of the 1960s, withered away."[6]

The economic well-being of black Americans has traditionally improved during periods of labor scarcity: World War I, the 1920s, World War II, and the Vietnam War. Relative income gain has also accompanied the twentieth-century residential shift from the rural South to northern and southern urban areas. But aside from boom periods that have drawn black workers into better-paying jobs, how widespread and enduring are the black income and occupational gains of recent decades? Has the change from a predominantly southern rural to a predominantly urban America drastically lessened racial discrimination, or have new forms of racial inequality arisen in the cities? Long-term occupational gains appear to endure, particularly for black females, but other labor force trends are ominous. Abstracting from the cyclical ups and downs, blacks since World War II have experienced rising unemployment rates and falling labor force participation rates; the labor force status of urban black males shows signs of long-run deterioration. By 1980, 15 percent of all black males twenty-five to sixty-four years of age were telling the Census Bureau that they had earned absolutely nothing during 1979. In 1969, median black family incomes in the north central states were $19,182 (in 1981 dollars); by 1981 the comparable median figure had plummeted to $15,474.[7]

Relative incomes of urban blacks have not risen dramatically in the post–World War II era. Incomes of blacks in the cities still ride the cyclical roller coaster: up in the 1940s, down in the 1950s, up in the 1960s, down in the 1970s. Numerous studies that argue otherwise invariably fail to sort out the one-time-only income gains accompanying urbanization, labor market cyclical swings, and the income gains of the highly educated.[8] Gains of migration, of boom periods, and of a fortunate few are incorrectly interpreted as evidence of overall black economic uplifting.

The simplest way to clarify trends in black economic status is to segment blacks geographically into those residing in southern states, and northern and western states.[9] Blacks residing in the nonsouthern states are overwhelmingly urban, and table 9.4 shows that their relative incomes—for both males and females—fell between 1959 and 1979. The drop was particularly pronounced for black males, whose in-

Table 9.4. Income of Blacks* by Region and Sex Stated as Percentages of White Incomes (*calculations based on medians*)

A. North, West	Black Males	Black Females
1953	74	85
1959	73	106
1964	75	110
1969	78	120
1974	75	113
1979	70	105
1981	66	103
B. South	Black Males	Black Females
1953	46	45
1959	33	42
1964	46	53
1969	54	62
1974	54	74
1979	60	81
1981	58	74

Sources: U.S. Bureau of the Census, *Current Population Reports,* ser. P-23, no. 80, table 30 (Washington, D.C.: Government Printing Office, 1979) p. 46. Ibid., ser. P-60, no. 129, table 47 (Nov. 1981), pp. 183–193. Ibid., ser. P-60, no. 137, table 43 (Mar. 1983), pp. 133–40.
*Data for 1964 and earlier refer to black and other races; post-1964 data refer to blacks only.

comes, stated as a percentage of median white male incomes, fell from
78 percent in 1969 to 66 percent in 1981. Recall that this *excludes* all
zero income earners, thereby understating the extent of relative black
income decline for the entire population.[10] The picture in the South
was entirely different. Agricultural transformation, as described in
chapter 6, increased the impoverishment of many southern blacks
during the 1950s. This is reflected in table 9.4: the ratio of black to
white incomes fell from .46 to a rock bottom .33 for males between
1953 and 1959, and the female ratio fell from .45 to .42. Starting
from a position of widespread southern poverty and deprivation in
1959, steady and sustained improvement took place in the next two
decades. During this period of transition, blacks residing in the South
shifted from being predominantly rural to largely urban in residence.[11] Their shift from agriculture to the urban job market was
facilitated by strong southern urban economic expansion (see chap.
8, especially table 8.2) which continued in the 1970s despite recessionary national conditions. In other words, the large relative income
gains of southern blacks (table 9.4) reflect the one-time-only gains
accompanying urbanization and integration into nonagricultural lines
of work.

Rural to urban migration was, of course, part of a nationwide redistribution of black population. Table 9.5 shows that, in addition to
rural to urban migration within the South, the net migration out of
the South was nearly 4.5 million for blacks from 1940 to 1970. This,
too, reflected a movement that was predominantly rural to urban.
Nationwide gains in relative black incomes (table 9.1) that accompanied this population shift, however, did *not* produce proportionate
increases in black economic well-being. Rural areas of the South have

Table 9.5. Net Migration of Blacks by Region (in thousands)

	South	Northeast	North Central	West
1940–1950	−1,599	+463	+618	+339
1950–1960	−1,473	+496	+541	+293
1960–1970	−1,380	+612	+382	+301
1970–1980	+ 209	−239	−103	+132
Total	−4,243	+1,332	+1,438	+1,065

Sources: U.S. Bureau of the Census, *Current Population Reports*, ser. P-23, no. 80
Tables 8 and 9 (Washington, D.C.: Government Printing Office, 1979), pp. 15–16.
Ibid., ser. P-20, no. 368, table 42 (Dec, 1981), p. 130.

the lowest cost of living of any region of the United States, much lower than comparable living costs in urban areas.[12] In fact, black migrants of this era disproportionately moved to large cities where living costs are among the highest in the nation. The 1980 census reported that 34 percent of all blacks resided in just seven urban centers: New York, Chicago, Los Angeles, Philadelphia, Detroit, Baltimore, and Washington, D.C. A rural South Carolina family subsisting on $2,500 a year may or may not be better off subsisting on $7,500 a year in Harlem. Rural South Carolina housing rental rates are certainly dwarfed by the cost of comparable housing in big city ghettos. Higher living costs obviously consume a share of the gains realized by rural to urban migrants, significantly offsetting relative black–white median income gains.

The validity of black–white income ratio comparisons over time is suspect for many reasons. Forms of noncash compensation, for example, have augmented white real incomes faster than that of blacks in recent decades. Especially in the professional and managerial occupations (disproportionately white), compensation in such forms as educational stipends, pensions, insurance premiums, and expense account living has increased more rapidly than actual wages and salaries. One study showed that black employees were much less likely than whites to participate in private pension plans, and those who did participate were eligible for or receiving pensions that were far smaller than those of white recipients.[13]

Another severe conceptual problem for black–white income comparisons concerns exclusion of some forms of income—such as capital gains and undistributed profits—from the census income definition. Nor are the wealthy the only ones receiving such uncounted income; families at the other end of the spectrum are often recipients of food stamps, medicaid, and other forms of uncounted income. The list of biases goes on and on. The rich, for example, disproportionately receive property income, and income from property is systematically underreported to the government on a much larger scale than wage income.

Do the corporate elite, with their company cars, country club memberships, dining and entertainment expense allowances, generous pensions, etc. bias the reported income statistics more or less than poor blacks who receive free school lunches and subsidized housing? We really have no idea. Black–white income comparisons lose their validity increasingly as such forms of uncounted income expand over time. Reported income is a crude measure of actual income, and long-term comparisons of black–white income ratios should be viewed as even cruder measures of relative black well-being.

In summary, the evidence cited in table 9.1 does not show that blacks as a group are relatively better off than they were in the early 1950s.

1. A large share of reported income gains is negated by the shift from low cost of living areas in the rural South to high cost of living urban areas.
2. Income figures include only those earning income; the proportion of black males with zero income rose absolutely from 1953 to 1981 and it rose relative to whites. In contrast, the proportion of black women with zero income fell in absolute terms, but rose relative to whites.
3. Black–White income ratios obscure trends in income distribution within the black community. Black incomes could, for example, be a constant percentage of white incomes during a time period when rapid gains by the well-educated are forcing up this percentage, and income losses by the less-educated are pulling down relative black incomes. When one abstracts from the rural to urban shift (which produced major gains for low-income blacks), it turns out that the post–World War II period is indeed characterized by rising income inequality within the black community.
4. Differences in reported versus actual income are present due to income concealment, income measurement peculiarities, as well as conceptual problems as to what is and is not income. These problems tend to make the precision of black–white income comparisons highly uncertain.

Among less-educated and less-skilled black Americans, absolute improvement in economic well-being may indeed be absent. Our inability to adjust accurately for cost of living differences between rural southern and urban areas alone makes it impossible to compare the well-being of less-skilled blacks in the 1950s with that of the 1980s. Measures of unemployment and labor force participation, however, suggest deterioration among less-skilled male workers.[14] The proportion of black males employed full-time for the entire year of 1955 was 56.6 percent. During the prosperous year of 1969 this percentage had fallen to 51.7 percent, and by 1980 only 45.0 percent of those who worked were employed full-time year-round.

Black teenagers face employment problems that dwarf those of older black workers.[15] Black teenagers have closed most of the education gap with their white cohorts, suggesting that their labor force status should begin to resemble more closely that of white teenagers. The opposite has in fact occurred (table 9.6). Indeed, education ad-

vances may be having a perverse effect on the labor force status of
young blacks. Stronger educational credentials often create an unwillingness to accept jobs to which particularly low status is attached.[16]

The most disturbing statistics on black well-being are not directly
related to the labor market. Signs of breakdown in the social fabric
of low-income urban black communities, although poorly understood,
are undoubtedly exacerbated by labor market problems. In 1979, for
example, 15 percent of all deaths among black men were attributable
to accidents, homicide, and suicide. Black males twenty-five to thirty-
four years of age experienced death rates two and one-half times
higher than whites in the same age group. The age-adjusted black
death rate from homicide was over six times higher than the corresponding white rate.[17] Throughout the 1970s, the incidence of im-
prisonment of young black males rose dramatically. On an entirely
different matter, black families of the form "single-parent female with
her own children" increased in number 91.6 percent from 1970 to
1980. During the same time period, married couple families with their
own children decreased in number by 5.9 percent.[18]

Table 9.6. Civilian Labor Force Participation Rate *(in percentage)*

	Male		Female	
	Black*	White	Black*	White
A. *Participation Rate for Persons Age 16 or older*				
1969	75.0	78.7	48.0	40.5
1971	75.5	79.7	47.4	42.7
1973	71.3	78.7	47.6	42.8
1975	72.1	78.7	48.2	45.7
1977	70.9	77.8	49.3	47.0
1979	71.7	78.5	52.3	49.9
1981	70.4	77.8	52.7	51.4
1983	69.5	76.2	53.6	52.2
B. *Participation Rate for Persons 18–19 Years Old*				
1969	62.3	59.6	41.8	48.1
1971	54.0	65.5	33.5	52.6
1973	59.7	69.3	41.0	53.9
1975	54.2	71.8	38.4	58.5
1977	55.5	71.4	40.6	58.7
1979	58.6	73.8	42.3	63.7
1981	59.0	72.8	43.0	61.6
1983	49.1	65.6	41.0	60.8

*Includes all nonwhites
Sources: U.S. Bureau of Labor Statistics, "Employment and Earnings" (Washington,
D.C.: Government Printing Office), various issues.

The proportion of black families living in poverty has increased since 1970, from 29.5 percent to 30.8 percent in 1981. This development is related to the increasing incidence of households headed by females; 52.9 percent of all such black families were below the poverty level in 1981. High rates of out-of-wedlock births exacerbate the trend of more black children being raised in households whose income is sub-poverty level. Rates of out-of-wedlock childbearing are particularly high among black teenagers.[19] Childbearing typically terminates the education of young mothers, resulting in limited job access. Young single women with small children, little education, and few skills often end up on welfare. A recent study found that approximately 40 percent of all black families with children under 18 are getting AFDC (Aid to Families with Dependent Children) benefits, compared to 6.8 percent for white families.

Causes of all the above, from violent death to the rising incidence of female-headed households living in poverty, are only dimly understood, but they do not suggest a pattern of widespread, across the board increases in black well-being. Rather, they suggest the sort of deterioration in community cohesion that would accompany declining labor market opportunities. High and rising unemployment rates among the young, falling labor force participation rates, a rising incidence of violent death and of incarceration in prisons—these are traits of an emerging class of disaffected young urban blacks. They are the emerging lumpenproletariat.

The Unanswered Questions

The progress portrayed in the first section, "The Evidence For Major Economic Progress," is the picture that dominates existing social science literature. It is so filled with overgeneralizations and so reliant upon one analytical tool—the black–white income ratio—that its message is largely wrong. And yet, very real educational gains do exist and it is important to understand why they have not resulted in more enduring and widespread income gains. Racial discrimination in the labor market along with more sophisticated forms of statistical discrimination (chap. 12) account for part of the problem. Many of the mysteries about trends in black economic welfare, though, can be clarified by putting them in the context of events described in previous chapters. Changing patterns in the demand for labor (chap. 8) have simultaneously improved female labor force status and undermined male prospects. The role of organized labor has shaped black occupational access, as has civil rights activism (chap. 7). Trends in major industries that employ blacks disproportionately—manufacturing, government, services—determine the value of educational credentials and thus shape black occupational access and earnings. These factors have varied greatly from decade to decade, producing diverse trends in black earnings. Furthermore, these are the factors that will shape black economic status in the years ahead.

The 1950s

In several important ways, the 1950s reflected the beginnings of trends that were to become dominant determinants of urban black well-being in the 1980s—gains in white-collar occupations for the more educated and an increasingly tenuous employment situation for the less-educated. During the decade, rural to urban migration continued at a brisk pace and the largest black population gains were registered by major industrial cities. Most of the employed black males worked in the major blue-collar occupations—operative, general laborer, craftsmen, and foremen—and the majority of these were employed in manufacturing. Black females were concentrated primarily in low-wage service occupations and secondly, in the operative category. The frequency of white city residents in the white-collar occupations—professional, manager, clerical, and sales—was three to four times greater proportionally than the incidence of blacks in white-collar jobs.

Factory jobs were the highest paying type of employment that was widely available to urban blacks. They provided the route to upward mobility for the less-skilled, and the early 1950s, spurred by the Korean War, brought sustained gains in manufacturing employment. Nationwide unemployment rates for nonwhites stood at 4.1 percent in 1953, and the teenage unemployment incidence was 7.3 percent. In this era of 20 percent plus unemployment rates (early 1983 figures) for prime working age black males, it is useful to recall that 30 years ago, blacks with fewer skills and much less education experienced full employment in urban America.

The 1950s decade was not, however, a period of uninterrupted black economic gain. While blacks were being ejected en masse from southern agriculture, their economic fortunes in the cities ebbed and flowed along with the uneven demands for their labor services.

There were two very distinct sides to the coin of black economic prospects in northern and western cities: opportunities were more diverse and the pay was generally higher, but black unemployment in the North was much higher than it had been traditionally in the rural South. After the Korean War, an ominous new trend developed: 1953 was the last year of relatively low black unemployment—4.4 percent for males and 3.7 percent for females. The corresponding rates for prosperous years in the 1960s were typically more than double the 1953 black unemployment rates. These were years of retrogression rather than progress. Whereas nonwhite unemployment rates as a percentage of white rates averaged around 170 percent during the late 1940s and early 1950s, in 1955 the nonwhite unemployment rate was more than double the corresponding white rate.[20] After 1955, black unemployment rates were consistently more than twice as high as white unemployment rates. During the 1950s, the relative income of black males declined significantly in every major region of the country. For the entire United States, though, the black–white income ratio for males declined only moderately, attributable solely to black migration from low-income rural southern areas to higher-income northern states.[21]

Black migration in the 1950s was heavily responsible for the decline in relative black economic well-being experienced in northern and western states. As machinery displaced men on a large scale in the most backward areas of the rural South, a northward stream of black migrants engulfed inner cities in the North and West. The migrants of the 1950s found a different situation in the cities than did their counterparts of earlier periods. There were few jobs available for them in the northern cities. The reasons were chiefly to be found in labor market structural difficulties as well as national economic trends. Briefly, the migrants were moving to the big city at the wrong point in history.

First, the southern refugees of the 1950s were among the least-skilled and the worst-educated of all Americans. The skills that they had were largely agricultural; the little education that they had was obtained in rural southern schools of poor quality. Their few skills and talents were not widely demanded by urban employers.

Second, the mass production industries in northern cities were hiring few blue-collar workers. Many large employers of earlier black migrants—automobile, steel, and electrical equipment—were actually reducing their unskilled and semiskilled labor forces. Job availability in manufacturing was greatest for white-collar workers such as engineers and technicians, but blacks generally lacked the skills required for entry into these jobs. Manufacturing growth no longer required vast numbers of unskilled workers.[22]

Third, black migrants from the South faced competition in the labor market from whites displaced from farms, particularly in the Midwest. Technological transformation of agriculture was a national phenomenon. When the decline in farm employment began in 1920, some 11.5 million persons were employed in agriculture. By 1940, the figure had fallen to 9.5 million, but by 1964 it had dropped to

4.7 million.[23] The white workers displaced from agriculture also moved into urban areas. Since they were better educated and more highly skilled than the southern black migrants (and were not black), they tended to get the more desirable jobs.

Fourth, national economic growth had slowed down. The nation's gross national product increased at a rate of only 2.4 percent annually between 1953 and 1960, as compared to 4 percent per year from 1946 to 1953. Unemployment rose throughout the economy, and a substantial amount of economic slack developed. Under these conditions, the uneducated black migrant was not only the last hired, but in many instances he or she was not hired at all.

Fifth, what economic expansion there was took place on the fringes of metropolitan areas. Jobs created in suburban locations were often not easily accessible to the poorest of the black migrants who settled mainly in the central cities.[24]

The economic experience of black migrants after the Korean War was often one of unemployment and underemployment. By 1958, nonwhite unemployment had reached 12.6 percent nationwide, and it stayed between 10 and 13 percent until the escalation of the Vietnam War in 1964. The unemployment rates do not include those involuntarily restricted to part-time work or those employed at very low wages—the subemployed. The ranks of the subemployed typically exceeded the ghetto unemployed, often by wide margins.[25] Ghetto joblessness had always been widespread during recessions and depressions. Since the 1950s, however, high rates of black unemployment have been a permanent feature of ghetto life—in boom times as well as during recessionary periods. This is entirely a post–Korean War phenomenon.

The decade of the 1950s was not entirely bleak for urban blacks. The brunt of increased unemployment and underemployment was absorbed by recent migrants and young people. The more educated, long-term ghetto dwellers made occupational gains in the white-collar fields, particularly in clerical work (table 9.7). Increased penetration into clerical occupations was particularly beneficial to black females in the 1950s, and it helped to boost black female incomes relative to their white female counterparts. Many of the older industrial cities that had experienced heavy black in-migration were, during the 1950s, experiencing CBD expansion; a number of large-scale employers of clerical labor—corporate headquarters, banks, insurance companies, and government agencies—were expanding their central-city operations.

Aside from gains in certain white-collar areas, though, the dominant features of black labor market involvement in the 1950s were

Table 9.7. Occupation of Employed Blacks by Sex, for Central-City Residents of Chicago, Baltimore, Cleveland, Detroit, and Philadelphia *(in percentage)*

	1950	1960	1970
A. *Male*			
Professional, Technical	2.3	4.0	5.8
Manager, Proprietor	2.7	2.4	3.0
Sales	1.9	2.4	2.6
Clerical	6.4	9.7	10.0
Craftsmen, Foremen, and Kindred	11.4	13.0	16.0
Operative	30.9	33.9	34.4
Laborer	26.8	18.5	12.5
Service	16.5	15.6	15.2
Private Household	1.0	0.5	0.4
(% White Collar)	(13.3)	(18.5)	(21.4)
B. *Female*			
Professional, Technical	4.8	8.4	11.1
Manager, Proprietor	1.4	1.3	1.6
Sales	2.3	2.9	3.4
Clerical	7.5	16.9	30.8
Craftsmen, Foreman, and Kindred	1.2	1.2	1.7
Operative	27.6	22.9	18.3
Laborer	2.5	1.3	1.8
Service	21.1	23.6	22.9
Private Household	32.6	21.5	8.4
(% White Collar)	(16.0)	(29.5)	(46.9)

Source: U.S. Census of Population.

rising unemployment and underemployment, restricted opportunities in manufacturing after 1953 (the traditional route of upward mobility for unskilled blacks), and deteriorating incomes of black males relative to their white counterparts.

Problems in manufacturing employment were exacerbated by discriminatory policies concerning layoff and job upgrading. As explained in chapter 7, union concern for black worker rights fell rather dramatically during the 1950s, and unions were often supportive of unfair treatment of black employees. The seniority system was a particular irritant. There are a number of seniority system designs, each with its own set of problems for black workers. During full employment periods, blacks benefit from the widest possible seniority base (one that is commonly plant-wide in scope). Seniority may then be a basis for maximum upgrading and promotion opportunities *if* the system is applied in an impartial manner. But, during periods of employment contraction, blacks benefit most from a narrow-based seniority system (departmental or occupational) since their high concentration in several occupations and departments provides protection from being bumped by whites who have greater seniority. In fact, plants often used departmental seniority for job upgrading and plant-wide seniority for layoffs. This arrangement clearly favored white workers over blacks, and it directly reflected the balance of racial power in the unions.[26] While the job upgrading opportunities went mainly to white workers, black workers were most likely to be laid off during recessions. These discriminatory practices were widespread in such supposedly progressive unions as the United Auto Workers. Although blacks accounted for 8 to 9 percent of all auto workers in the 1950s, they never accounted for as much as one-half of 1 percent of skilled craftsmen. General Motors had over 11,000 skilled workers in the Detroit area; fewer than 100 were black.[27]

The 1960s

During periods of labor shortage, the swollen ranks of unemployed and underemployed urban blacks are drawn off to staff more stable and renumerative jobs. Black workers often find it possible to move from low-wage competitive sector jobs into higher-wage work with large corporations or the government. Second, job upgrading invariably becomes an issue during boom periods, and barriers to black occupational advancement are challenged. It is no coincidence that concern about racially discriminatory employment practices always appears to be most prevalent during periods of rapid economic expansion and job creation. This was the situation in the 1960s: jobs were available in areas where black penetration had traditionally been minimal, and discriminatory hiring practices were reduced, allowing black employment gains in skilled and white-collar lines of work.

In important ways the World War II era provided the model for 1960s black employment gains. As discussed in chapter 5, the federal government lead the way to expanded job access in the early 1940s. Executive Order 8802, signed by President Roosevelt in 1941, required that all defense contractors adopt nondiscriminatory employment practices. The federal government reformed its own hiring practices during World War II and employed hundreds of thousands of black workers in white-collar jobs. Hiring black females as clerical workers on a large scale thus began in the 1940s. One important difference between World War II and the 1960s, however, was the role of organized labor as a champion of black rights. While the CIO unions played this role in the early 1940s, blacks themselves—via the civil rights movement—won many victories in the struggles of the 1960s for improved job access.

Two major themes dominate the improvement in black economic well-being during the 1960s. First, this long period of sustained economic growth created strong labor demands that translated into widespread income and occupational gains for black workers (table 9.4 and 9.7). Second, civil rights activism produced an outpouring of legislation designed to curb racial discrimination as well as an avalanche of court rulings that advanced the cause of equal rights. All of this produced a reshaping of public attitudes about the roles of minority groups in U.S. society: black willingness to assume subservient economic, social, and political roles fell, and whites increasingly accepted the notion that equality of opportunity should apply to blacks as well as to themselves.

Trends in the Demand for Labor

In the urban labor markets (particularly the big city job markets) where most black workers compete for jobs, long-run trends toward expanding white-collar employment accelerated, while trends toward stagnant or declining manufacturing employment were reversed during the 1960s. Even in the older northeastern and midwestern cities, the long-term loss of manufacturing jobs was actually halted. Cleveland, for example, is an old industrial city that has lost well over 50 percent of its manufacturing production jobs since 1947. Between 1963 and 1967, Cleveland manufacturing employment actually grew slightly—from 168,900 to 171,300 jobs.[28] Baltimore typified the employment trends of many snowbelt cities. This city experienced a net increase of nearly 9,000 manufacturing jobs between 1962 and 1967. Bennett Harrison and Edward Hill estimated that, in those lines of Baltimore manufacturing offering high-wage blue-collar work, employment had declined by 19 percent between 1953 and 1959, stabilized from 1959 to 1962, and then increased by 5 percent between 1962 and 1970.[29] In the suburban areas of snowbelt cities, manufacturing production jobs were typically growing in availability, inducing the more mobile elements of the ghetto labor force to commute to suburban jobs. Black males in Detroit made particularly large gains in numbers of jobs held in high-wage manufacturing employment. By 1970, over 33 percent of the employed central-city black male Detroit residents were commuting to suburban jobs.

Declining manufacturing employment after the Korean War severely reduced black employment prospects during the mid- to late

1950s. Rapidly increasing unemployment was the result. The long 1960s boom partially reversed this situation, predictably bringing falling black male unemployment rates and rising real incomes. For the snowbelt cities, however, the prosperous 1960s were merely an interlude; manufacturing production work had already resumed its long-term decline by 1970, and the trend has been straight downhill ever since. Furthermore, the suburban periphery is no longer a source of growing manufacturing employment for blue-collar workers. This long-term decline is one of the key factors behind the sharp drop since 1969 (table 9.4) in the relative incomes of black males who reside in northern and western states.

Chapter 8 argued that long-term growth patterns in major urban areas favor the white-collar worker over his blue-collar counterpart. During the prosperous 1960s, both blue- and white-collar job holders progressed, but opportunities were greatest in the white-collar occupations. Ghettos are usually located near central-city CBDs, where white-collar employment is most heavily concentrated. For those black urban residents having the educational background necessary to compete for these jobs, expanding CBDs in the 1960s offered numerous possibilities. Younger, better-educated black females benefited most from this situation, moving heavily into clerical occupations while also registering some gains in the professions. In 1950, "cleaning lady" had been the most common job title among urban black females. By 1970, private household employment was a distant fourth, and clerical work was in first place. In cities such as Chicago during the 1960s, it was commonplace to observe tripling and even quadrupling of black female clerical employment in industries like banking.

Rapidly expanding government employment probably provided the greatest opportunities for black female gains.[30] Over half of all government jobs are clerical or professional and these are the two occupations that black females have penetrated most rapidly since 1950. Indeed, most of the employed black women who work as professionals are employed by the government; among them, teaching is the most common profession. In many northern cities such as Baltimore and Chicago, over 25 percent of all employed black females in 1970 worked for the government.

The shift in black female occupational structure has been profound since 1950. While black males were still overwhelmingly employed in blue-collar and service occupations, black women were in the 1960s rapidly narrowing differences in occupational structure with white females by moving into white-collar jobs. Like whites, black females have been steadily shifting away from the operative occupational category but black male operative employment grew in both absolute and relative terms after 1950, following a trend that dates back to World War I. Black men remain heavily employed in manufacturing, which is a highly cyclical sector of the economy that is shrinking in significance, while black women rely increasingly on administrative and professional work that is both less cyclical and growing. Although blue-collar manufacturing jobs for men and white-collar clerical work for women provided important gains for blacks in the 1960s, low-wage work continued to be a major employer of ghetto labor. Services and retail trade are major low-wage employers. Even in manufacturing, certain sectors such as apparel offer poor paying, dead-end, unstable work of the least desirable sort. Employment growth in these low-wage sectors during the 1960s was particularly prevalent in the sunbelt cities.[31]

Civil Rights Activism

Comprehensive treatment of the civil rights movement would require more than a chapter; it requires a separate volume. Here we simply highlight those aspects that are most directly relevant to the employment status of blacks. The Civil Rights Act of 1964 is one obvious landmark. Title VII of that act outlawed discrimination based on race, sex, or national origin by private employers, unions, and employment agencies; the Equal Employment Opportunity Commission (EEOC) was set up to investigate charges of discrimination. In 1972, the Commission's powers were expanded, allowing it to file suits on behalf of those injured by employment discrimination. Another major piece of the fair employment infrastructure grew out of Executive Order 11246, issued in 1965, which prohibits employment discrimination by recipients of federal contracts. The Office of Federal Contract Compliance (OFCC) was created to monitor compliance with the order. Given the subjective nature of much employment discrimination, actual government policy in this realm has varied from year to year, and numerous court cases have been necessary to define boundaries between discrimination, nondiscrimination, and affirmative action.

The EEOC and OFCC lack the personnel necessary to enforce adequately their legislative mandates, but the effectiveness of anti-discrimination efforts in the employment realm is not totally dependent upon these two agencies. Quite aside from the EEOC and the OFCC, the law permits injured parties to seek redress through the courts. Nonetheless, the EEOC's record has been disappointing. In 1973, for example, nearly fifty thousand individuals filed complaints with the EEOC alleging discrimination, many more than the approximately one thousand EEOC professional staff could handle. By 1977, the backlog of cases had grown to 130,000.[32] The OFCC has the power to cancel or suspend government contracts and it sometimes exerts strong pressure on government contractors. In 1969, for example, the OFCC issued the Philadelphia Plan for affirmative action by federal construction contractors in that city: contractors were ordered to increase their employment of minority craftsmen from the current 2 percent to goals of 4 to 9 percent within one year, and 19 to 26 percent within four years.[33] Thus affirmative action plans became part of civil rights law.

Aggressive use of EEOC and OFCC powers is rare. The OFCC debarred no contractors between 1965 and 1970 and debarred an average of two per year between 1971 and 1977. All EEOC litigation through 1977 resulted in estimated back pay settlements of only $65 million. Nonetheless, a few well-publicized settlements have induced many employers to hire at least a few blacks for better-paying jobs. In 1973, American Telephone and Telegraph signed a consent decree that included a multi-million dollar package providing back pay and future promotions for women and minorities. Large firms in general have established minority hiring plans and, at a minimum, pay lip service to minority hiring and promotion.

Estimating the exact impact of anti-discrimination laws on black employment and earnings is quite impossible, but several conclusions are warranted. First, blatant discrimination as formerly practiced by such unions as the AFL building trades has been sharply curtailed. Second, it is now the norm for large companies to employ at least a few blacks in both skilled blue-collar ranks and managerial white-collar jobs. Third, fair employment laws depend upon active enforcement for much of their effectiveness. Proponents of these laws face a constant battle to insure that the enforcement agencies possess the resources and the willingness to combat employment discrimination. The record to date suggests that comprehensive enforcement has never been attempted. Fourth, employers are most likely to adhere to the spirit of anti-discriminatory laws during periods of economic expansion. Tough questions such as racial implications of various seniority systems need not arise when black employees are being hired and upgraded. During economic downturns, however, the last hired are most apt to be the first fired; these are black workers disproportionately.

One difficulty in assessing the impact of measures as controversial and subjective as anti-discrimination laws is the fact that they are inseparable from overall attitudes on the status of minorities. One major impact of civil rights activism is that black workers themselves are less likely to tolerate discrimination on the job in a milieu where equal rights concerns are paramount. In the 1920s, blacks were grateful for access to any kind of position in better-paying industries. In contrast, the charged environment in the 1960s encouraged black workers to speak out against discrimination in the work place, in unions, and in society in general. Most employers, especially those large enough to attract the attention of the EEOC or OFCC, wanted to avoid the publicity that was apt to accompany allegations of discrimination in hiring and promotion. Firms hiring numerous blacks for several occupations (such as clerical or operative) often improved promotion opportunities and upgraded at least a few blacks. Creating the perception of better job opportunities helped to legitimize employment practices, thus perhaps lessening black disenchantment in all ranks. Less discriminatory hiring practices were widely adopted as pragmatic business practices: an expanding economy generated the need to hire additional workers, and greater access to job openings for blacks not only helped to avoid government scrutiny, it was also a wise public relations gesture.

The 1970s

The three major industry groups employing black workers are manufacturing, services, and government. Job growth in manufacturing was moderate during the 1960s, while employment creation in government and services was quite rapid and widespread. Black employees benefited from these strong labor demands. But the 1960s also created job gains in traditionally discriminatory industries such as construction that lessened racial barriers because of government scrutiny and declining public acceptance of racist hiring and training policies. Similar pressure, plus growing clerical worker needs, caused industries traditionally employing few blacks—finance, communications, utilities—to recruit black workers actively during the 1960s. Rapid educational gains also helped to deepen the industry-occupational mix open to black job seekers. In the more rapidly growing sunbelt regions of the United States, this 1960s pattern of improved job access continued well into the 1970s. Declining labor demands in the slower growing, more recession-prone snowbelt economy set the stage for losses in black economic well-being during the 1970s. Job losses in manufacturing were heavily concentrated in several high-paying, unionized industries where black male employment gains of the 1960s had been particularly strong. Job losses in government were much less widespread, but they were concentrated heavily in areas such as New York City and Cleveland, where black employment in government had risen substantially in the 1960s.[34]

The impact of manufacturing sector decline upon black workers is shown clearly by the situation in motor vehicles. Blacks prospered disproportionately from auto industry prosperity in the 1960s. The proportion of all motor vehicle industry employees who were black rose from 9.1 percent in 1960 to 13.4 percent in 1970; 138,609 blacks worked in this one industry at the end of the 1960s.[35] The rule of thumb that the auto companies employ at least one million workers during a good year—valid as late as 1978 when employment reached 977,000—is no longer applicable. The industry in the 1980s is investing heavily in labor-saving equipment and use of foreign-made parts is increasing. Researchers for the United Auto Workers Union estimate that 1985 auto industry employment may be as low as 527,000, only 54 percent of the 1978 total.[36] Future industry employment, of course, depends upon the market share of imported autos: the 527,000 job estimate assumes a 30.9 percent import share of the U.S. car market. The U.S. Chamber of Commerce estimates that communities lose, on average, two service jobs for every three manufacturing jobs that disappear.[37]

A study of workers displaced from manufacturing industries in the early 1970s found that average annual percentage earnings losses, during the first two years after job loss, were: autos, 43.4%; steel, 46.6%; aerospace, 23.6%; electronic components, 8.3%; shoes, 11.3%; and women's clothes, 13.3%.[38]

Re-employment was the norm for workers displaced in the early 1970s, and the severity of earnings loss is associated with two obvious factors: wages before displacement, and alternative opportunities for employment. Since autos and steel are both high-wage industries heavily concentrated in slow growth snowbelt states, their displaced workers predictably experienced high earnings losses. Displacement from lower-wage manufacturing industries produced the smallest earnings losses, especially in instances such as electronic components where employment is concentrated in the healthier sunbelt states. These patterns of earnings losses may actually be accentuated in the 1980s, due to the severity of regional employment declines in the Midwest, where steelmaking and auto manufacturing and assembly are so heavily concentrated.

Industrial cities like Cleveland, Chicago, and Pittsburgh no longer provide the route to upward mobility via manufacturing employment for less-skilled workers. The massive losses of blue-collar manufacturing jobs in the 1970s and 1980s, interacting with local government fiscal difficulties, are effectively reversing many of the employment gains captured by blacks in the 1960s. Yet these are the same cities in which highly educated blacks continued in the 1970s to gain jobs in the expanding management and administrative sectors. It is precisely in these older industrial cities where the contrast between the haves and the have nots is sharpening most rapidly: a portion of the smaller white-collar group prospers while the larger blue-collar urban black workforce is undermined. In the aggregate regional statistics (table 9.8), the misfortune of the many swamps the progress of the few, and the income gains of the 1960s are decisively erased. The severity of the losses recorded in table 9.8 undoubtedly reflects, too, weakening local government employment, which reduced the ranks of the more affluent white-collar group. The fact that Michigan is the only state registering a gain since 1959 in relative black family incomes partially reflects the superior unemployment compensation benefits received by autoworkers.

The situation in the South was altogether different in the 1970s. A stronger regional economy has created blue-collar as well as white-collar jobs, and local government fiscal difficulties were less severe

Table 9.8. Ratio of Nonwhite to White Family Median Incomes in Selected States, 1959–1979

	1959	1969	1979	Change: 1959–1979
A. Snowbelt Industrial States				
Illinois	.68	.70	.60	−.08
Ohio	.70	.74	.67	−.03
Michigan	.68	.75	.69	+.01
Pennsylvania	.71	.74	.62	−.09
B. Sunbelt Southeastern States				
Alabama	.42	.49	.55	+.13
Georgia	.44	.52	.56	+.12
North Carolina	.43	.57	.63	+.20
Virginia	.50	.59	.62	+.12

Sources: U.S. Bureau of the Census, *Advance Estimates of Social, Economic, and Housing Characteristics—Supplementary Report: Counties and Selected Places* (by State) Alabama ser. PHC80-S2-2 (Washington, D.C.: Government Printing Office, 1983), p. 39; ibid., Georgia S2-12, p. 79; ibid., Illinois S2-15, p. 75; ibid., Michigan S2-24, p. 67; ibid., North Carolina S2-35, p. 55; ibid., Ohio S2-37, p. 67; ibid., Pennsylvania S2-40, p. 63; ibid., Virginia S2-48, p. 75. U.S. Bureau of the Census, *Census of Population: 1970, General Social and Economic Characteristics, Final Report PC (1)-C2, Alabama* (Washington, D.C.: Government Printing Office, 1972), pp. 2–164; ibid., *Georgia*, pp. 12–238; ibid., *Illinois*, pp. 15–336; ibid., *Michigan*, pp. 24–246; ibid., *North Carolina*, pp. 35–201; ibid., *Ohio*, pp. 37–327; ibid., *Pennsylvania*, pp. 40–308; ibid., *Virginia*, pp. 48–209.

than in the snowbelt cities. Relative black incomes continued their 1960s trajectory. Regional differences are particularly apparent in the unemployment data. In March 1980, black male unemployment rates in Illinois and Ohio exceeded 16 percent; the corresponding rates in Georgia and North Carolina were 8.7 and 8.3 percent. The differential in female unemployment rates for blacks was less pronounced: 13.6 and 13.2 percent in Illinois and Ohio, versus 11.2 and 11.1 percent in Georgia and North Carolina.[39] The female differential pattern reflects the fact that sunbelt black women workers have penetrated white-collar jobs to a much lesser degree than their snowbelt counterparts. Continued black economic gains in the South were brought to a halt, however, by the severe recesssion of the early 1980s, as shown in table 9.4.

The 1980s

Has the twentieth-century transition of blacks from a predominantly southern rural to a predominantly urban America drastically lessened racial discrimination, or have new forms of racial inequality arisen in the cities? Black economic progress in the sunbelt cities sheds the most light on this question. Table 9.8 shows a trend toward convergence in snowbelt and sunbelt black–white income ratios. Relative black incomes were still slightly higher in most of the northern states in 1979, but the continued 1980s decline of blue-collar jobs in high-wage manufacturing industries pulled the regional wage ratios into closer alignment. Briefly, the labor market in northern cities is increasingly resembling the southern job scene: blacks in both regions face most rapid job growth at the higher and lower ends of the market, and least opportunity in the middle occupational echelons.

Harrison's study of sunbelt cities shows that blacks there have traditionally had a much higher proportion of low-wage and part-time jobs than their snowbelt counterparts.[40] Chapter 8 revealed that southern and southwestern cities were more service and trade oriented, while snowbelt cities and SMSAs were more manufacturing oriented. Declining snowbelt manufacturing along with growth in services is lessening these differences in industrial composition as well as wage structure; service work is very low in pay relative to manufacturing. Furthermore, the sunbelt manufacturing production jobs, relatively low paying, are frequently in those fields that are most likely to be growing nationwide in coming years. Electronics, for example, is expected to expand in snowbelt as well as sunbelt regions, but it rarely offers blue-collar workers the wages paid by such traditional employers as the metal shaping and manufacturing industries. As described in chapter 8, the expanding lines of manufacturing tend to produce jobs for highly trained technical, scientific, and professional personnel, and production jobs staffed by low-wage workers. Rapidly rising productivity per worker also characterizes this sector, minimizing high tech industry's ability to create new jobs (fig. 9.1). Data Resources Incorporate (DRI) estimates that output per high tech worker will rise by 46 percent between 1983 and 1993, double the projected increase for services (23 percent) and manufacturing (24 percent).[41] The manufacturing sector lost roughly three million jobs between 1980 and 1982. Neither a cyclical upswing in manufacturing industries nor continued growth in high tech areas is predicted to replace, by 1990, the production jobs lost during the early 1980s.[42]

Those industries where job growth is most rapid, services and trade (fig. 9.1), are primarily low-wage industries; high-wage sectors—construction, transportation, public utilities, government, and manufacturing—have been stagnant since the 1960s, with available job openings concentrated in white-collar, skilled fields. Aside from the 1960s, these trends in job growth have actually been apparent since the end of the Korean war. In Baltimore, for example, 31 percent of all private sector jobs in 1953 were found in the low-wage nonmanufacturing industries; by 1974, 43 percent of the jobs were found in this sector.

FIGURE 9.1. Employment by Industry: 1983 and 1993 *(in millions of workers).*

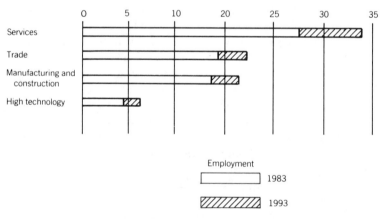

Employment

[ ] 1983

[///////] 1993

Assumptions:
    1983-88: 3.4 percent average annual increase in GNP; 2.1 percent
        average annual increase in nonfarm employment.
    1988-93: 2.7 percent average annual increase in GNP; 1.2 percent average
        annual increase in nonfarm employment.
Source: Data Resources, Inc.

During this same time period, high-wage manufacturing work fell from 32 percent to 25 percent of Baltimore's private sector employment. While high-wage sectors tend to offer full-time year-round work predominantly, low-wage industries such as services and retail trade more frequently offer only part-time work to their employees.[43]

Sources of future income gains for black workers in urban America are not readily apparent. Even in the best paying occupations, the outlook for gains is not all together bright. In the professional and technical occupations, for example, most blacks are employed as teachers, nurses, health care technicians, social workers, and counselors.[44] These represent the lowest paying types of jobs available in this heterogeneous occupational grouping, and they are largely lines of work where career opportunities for upgrading in pay and responsibilities are minimal. Furthermore, black professionals rely heavily on government, particularly city government, for employment, and they are concentrated in older, larger cities where fiscal problems are most severe. Not only are future employment gains unlikely, but outright employee reductions are the norm in cities such as Chicago and Detroit.

The situation in the clerical occupations is brighter, since long-term employment growth in this line of work is expected to continue into the foreseeable future. While government workforce reductions have a negative impact on clerical job opportunities, this has been offset by growing private sector demand for workers in this field. Jobs in computer-related fields, such as data entry, should continue to grow rapidly. Clerical work, however, offers few opportunities for occupational advancement, and pay is below average relative to wage and salary levels in the overall economy. While the large-scale shift of black workers into clerical occupations does represent a long-term upgrading in labor force status, it certainly does not represent a move towards long-term equality in labor force status. In fact, the social status and remuneration associated with clerical work have been steadily declining, relative to the other occupations, throughout the twentieth century.[45]

Nonetheless, prospects in clerical and professional occupations are brighter than those facing blue-collar workers. Advances in education and training can lead to further gains in growth areas such as the managerial and non-government professional occupations, and younger black workers are increasing their penetration in these lines of employment. Yet it is among the young that polarization appears to be most pronounced: rapid income gains for the best educated coexist with very high unemployment rates and falling labor force participation rates for the majority of young blacks. Long-term economic trends suggest that the latter group is most likely to find work in low-paying but growing industries, particularly services. Night-watchman, dishwasher, janitor—these are the types of low-wage, unstable work that will increasingly typify job opportunities for ghetto residents.

High unemployment and low labor force participation rates among black teenagers are often cited as evidence of declining job prospects. The unemployment problems of this group are indeed staggering— the unemployment rate for blacks sixteen to nineteen years of age actually topped 50 percent in August 1981—but we feel that teenagers are not an appropriate group for illustrating labor market trends. Part of the black teenage employment problem reflects improved education and training opportunities. These opportunities have in-duced many young blacks to substitute schooling or military service for work. Because those with better than average employment pros-pects are most likely to pursue advanced education and training, the attractiveness to employers of the remaining out-of-school civilian black youth population is reduced.[46] This process partially explains both the rising incidence of black youth unemployment and the oc-cupational and income gains realized by educated young blacks.

To illustrate the polarization process we focus not upon black teen-agers but upon those twenty to twenty-four years of age. Trends in their labor market status are documented utilizing data from the Census of Population Public Use Samples for Illinois and Ohio. Similar data for North Carolina and Georgia are used below to explain dif-ferences in snowbelt/sunbelt employment situations facing young black males. The labor force participation rate of black males twenty to twenty-four years old in Ohio and Illinois resembles that of all adult black males in those states—70.3 percent for the former versus 70.7 percent for the latter—but the similarities end there. These younger blacks are better educated than the overall black workforce and they have entered the labor force during the time when all of the forces promoting polarization discussed above were fully operative. Census data yield the following information: (1) the labor force participation rate of black males twenty to twenty-four years of age fell from 76.5 percent in 1970 to 70.3 percent in 1980; (2) their unemployment rate rose from 12.5 percent in 1970 to 29.3 percent in 1980; (3) they were heavily concentrated in manufacturing employment in both 1970 and 1980, and the majority of those in manufacturing worked in three high-wage sectors: metal (predominantly steel mills), machinery, and transportation equipment; (4) 43.8 percent of this group worked in manufacturing in 1970, versus 31.1 percent in 1980; (5) their incidence of white-collar employment rose from 23.6 percent in 1970 to 28.1 percent in 1980; (6) their incidence of employment in service occupations rose from 10.4 percent in 1970 to 20.1 percent in 1980.

Overall, the proportion of black males twenty to twenty-four years of age in Ohio and Illinois who held jobs fell precipitously between 1970 and 1980. Whereas 63 percent were working in 1970 on the date when they filled out their census forms, only 41 percent were employed in 1980. Job loss in the traditional manufacturing sector was partially offset by growth of white-collar employment, but it was in the low-wage service sector where job expansion was most pronounced. Table 9.9 compares earnings and employment stability in the manufacturing and service areas. Relative to manufacturing, service work is low paying. In 1979, mean wage and salary incomes for black male service workers in Ohio and Illinois reached only $8,137; mean wage incomes of their cohorts employed in manufacturing stood 75.3 percent higher, at $14,263. The service workers receive low hourly wages, but they are also handicapped by their higher incidence of part-time work. According to table 9.9, average weeks worked in 1979 was 37.2 for service workers and 44.4 for manufacturing employees.

Table 9.9. Selected Data on Black Male Employees in Ohio, and Illinois in 1979 *(means only)*

	Manufacturing	Services	All employees
Total wage and salary income	$14,263	$8,137	$12,346
Total income from all sources	$14,742	$8,609	$12,882
Weeks worked in 1979	44.4	37.2	42.0
Average number of hours worked per week	40.0	35.8	38.4
Weeks unemployed in 1979	3.6	5.6	4.2
Total number of observations	4,723	2,282	13,285

Source: Sample A of the 1980 Census of Population and Housing: Public Use Microdata Sample.

Notes: This table represents a 2.5 percent random sample of the population of Ohio and Illinois. According to the data source, 2.5 percent of the universe of black male employees 16 years of age or older in 1980 in these two states constituted 15,079 observations. In performing the above mean calculations, 1,794 of the observations were excluded because they had not worked as employees during 1979. Unpaid workers in family businesses were excluded from the above sample of 13,285 observations.

Similarly, the average number of hours worked per week was a lower 35.8 hours in services, versus 40.0 hours in manufacturing. Finally, the typical service worker portrayed in table 9.9 spent 5.6 weeks unemployed in 1979 (versus 3.6 in manufacturing) and he spent 9.2 weeks as a nonparticipant in the labor force (versus 4.0 weeks in manufacturing). The educational credentials of black workers employed in manufacturing and services were quite similar overall: 23.0 percent of those in services had attended school beyond the high school level, as had 22.8 percent of those in manufacturing. Both groups, however, lagged behind the average educational credentials of black males employed outside of the service and manufacturing areas.

Rising unemployment rates and declining labor participation of blacks twenty to twenty-four years of age are partially caused by the nature of the service jobs that increasingly typify their employment alternatives. Many service industries do not offer full-time, year-around work. Employment in services frequently entails enduring bouts of unemployment and labor force nonparticipation. Seven specific types of industries employed nearly 81 percent of the black male service workers summarized in table 9.9. In order of importance they were: restaurant (employing 20.3 percent of the service workers), public administration, hospital, education, service to building firms, real estate, and hotel. Restaurants and hotels that cater to tourists are normally seasonal employers, and educational institutions often have reduced needs for service workers in the summertime. Other major service employers such as hospitals often provide stable work, but wage rates for their service employees are typically very low. Employment in hospitals has grown quite rapidly for all blacks in Ohio and Illinois in the last two decades. It was the largest single industry in which black females in these two states worked in 1980; over 16 percent of all black working women listed hospitals as their industry of employment in 1980, and while most were service workers, 27.2 percent worked as professionals, primarily nurses.

While younger snowbelt black males shifted rapidly out of high-wage manufacturing work in the 1970s and toward unemployment as well as low-wage service jobs (and white-collar employment), their sunbelt cohorts experienced no such tumultuous changes in labor force status. Southern blacks are protected from the trauma of losing high-wage manufacturing jobs because they had few of them in the first place. Among the black males working in manufacturing in North Carolina and Georgia, three lines—textiles, wood products, and food processing—provide over one-half of the jobs. These three low-wage industries employed 54.2 percent of the Georgia and North Carolina black males working in manufacturing in 1970, versus 55.2 percent of those in manufacturing in 1980. Among those twenty to twenty-four years of age, black males in these two states relied on manufacturing for 38.6 percent of their jobs in 1970, and 36.7 percent of them in 1980. White-collar and service work did increase in incidence over the 1970s decade, but the changes were minor ones. Black males twenty to twenty-four years old saw the incidence of service employment rise from 13.4 percent to 15.7 percent while the percentage of those in white-collar jobs rose from 15.7 percent in 1970 to 17.1 percent in 1980. Their incidence of unemployment did rise slightly over the decade, but the 2.4 percent rise from 12.6 to 15.0 percent in the unemployment rate was dwarfed in magnitude by the 16.8 percentage points (from 12.5 to 29.3 percent) that were tacked on to the unemployment rate of their northern cohorts.

The changes in labor force status among twenty to twenty-four year-old black males of course reflect changes that in varying degrees shape the economic well-being of all black male workers. Thus, the declining incidence of employment in manufacturing is undercutting the job status of all snowbelt black workers. Among all employed Ohio and Illinois black male employees, 40.1 percent worked in manufacturing in 1970 versus 34.4 percent in 1980. Rising unemployment and falling rates of labor force participation typify black male workers from twenty-five to fifty-four years of age. For those in Illinois and Ohio, the incidence of unemployment rose from 4.4 to 13.5 percent between 1970 and 1980, while their labor force participation rate fell from 87.4 to 82.7 percent. In contrast, their cohorts in Georgia and North Carolina experienced stable labor force participation rates and an increase in the incidence of unemployment from 3.1 to 6.8 percent. During the recessionary early 1980s, snowbelt black workers fell further behind their sunbelt counterparts because of their greater dependence upon the most cyclical segments of manufacturing—steel, autos, and related durables. Indeed, in 1982, the North Central region actually surpassed the South for the first time in history as the region having the highest rate of black poverty (39.8 percent).[47] It would be incorrect, however, to conclude that southern black economic well-being is surpassing that of northern blacks precisely because of the highly cyclical nature of much northern durable goods manufacturing. Although the long-term outlook for employment in snowbelt heavy industry is dim, upturn phases in the business cycle are still capable of alleviating (partially) the large cyclical component of black unemployment.

Increasing Government Representation May Not Improve Black Economic Well-Being

History suggests that strong and sustained economic growth periods improve black labor force status in both absolute and relative terms. Overall health of the economy will continue to be a vital determinant of black economic well-being in the future. A strong political voice, typified by 1960s civil rights activism, may also produce economic dividends for the black community. Gains in local government, though, may offer little potential unless the fiscal crises of the older, larger cities are alleviated.

Black political goals in central cities have been city hall power, improved city services for black neighborhoods, and a larger proportion of city government jobs.[48] Winning city hall, though, is increasingly a hollow political prize. Facing constant job loss, disinvestment, and tax base deterioration, black leaders in cities like Detroit, Gary, and Newark are increasingly dependent upon state and federal funds. The early 1980s has produced a rising indifference to the fiscal problems of declining central cities by state and particularly national government bodies. Black mayors can thus do little to alter the well-being of their constituents because they lack control over the economic resources needed to do the job.

Private capital can be induced to invest in America's aging cities if the terms are right: enter CBD renovation, convention centers, "favorable" tax climates, and the like. Leveraged by federal dollars, multibillion dollar urban renewal programs have transformed or are transforming downtown areas in cities as diverse as Boston and Pittsburgh. Urban renewal often removes "blight" from the periphery of the CBD, freeing potentially valuable property for use as infrastructure that complements CBD interests, and sites for private sector expansion, ranging from high-rise apartments to corporate office buildings. Blight typically consists of low-cost housing for blacks; it is replaced by parking facilities, sports stadiums, convention centers, freeway interchanges, and high-cost apartments. Urban renewal thus becomes urban removal, with the displaced minority population squeezed into a diminished stock of rental housing.[49]

Although urban renewal policies do indeed seem to be renovating downtown areas in many large cities, their political feasibility is increasingly being undermined by an obvious contradiction. How can black politicians be elected when they espouse CBD renovation projects, especially when these projects have traditionally destroyed black neighborhoods? How can scarce local government services be concentrated on downtown areas when the social needs of ghettos are so astoundingly high? Some ghetto blacks, of course, expect to benefit from the jobs generated by downtown expansion. Because these jobs are largely administrative, however, the highly educated segment of the labor force, managers and the professionals, are likely to benefit disproportionately from CBD job growth. Successful downtown renovation increasingly attracts young white professionals into inner-city neighborhoods, and a process of gentrification often results. Rents are invariably driven up in black neighborhoods adjacent to gentrified districts, further reducing the accessible housing supply for low-income blacks.

The resultant political unpopularity of urban renewal programs in black communities makes it difficult for black mayors to pursue the types of policies most apt to attract private capital to the central city. Equitable redistribution of city services and property tax burdens is similarly fraught with political dangers. Envision a mayor who successfully reallocates city services from the haves to the have-nots: educational resources are assigned to ghetto schools to bring them up to par with the city's best schools; police are transferred from the CBD to high-crime, inner-city neighborhoods, and so forth. Does the quality of life subsequently improve for the lower-income residents of this equitably governed metropolis? The answer is unclear. A city government that offers higher taxes and fewer services to the resident wealthy and local business interests is perceived as a threat to their well-being. If this threat appears to be more than transitory, the powerful and the prosperous will react in ways that may destroy much of the city's economic base. If local government does not cater to the interests of the business community, firms will cut back drastically on their local investment plans. Financial institutions, fearing a contraction in business activity, tighten up on their local lending activities. Firms that had contemplated moving job-generating activities into this locality will be inclined to locate in "friendlier" environs. Many higher-income residents will respond to service cuts and tax increases by moving to suburbia. Outward migration of both residents and economic activity, combined with tight local money markets, will generate declining property values. Declining property values create a need for higher local taxes and/or cuts in services. The city economy spirals downward; local employment opportunities diminish. Thus, even in cities where blacks have achieved political power, improvement programs become hostages to the economic interests of the corporate elite.

10

The Economic Dynamics of
the Ghetto

THE URBAN GHETTO IS A DEPRESSED AND UNDERDEVELOPED ENCLAVE within a prosperous and progressive economy. It produces little that can be sold outside the ghetto other than low-wage labor. Underdevelopment is preserved by a continuous drain of income and resources that keeps the ghetto poor. The pool of low-wage labor is preserved by barriers that make exit difficult, while other social and economic forces provide recruits from outside the ghetto. These flows of income, resources, and people interact with conditions of poverty and underdevelopment in a system of circular causation that maintains the ghetto as a characteristic feature of the national economy.

The Drain of Resources

One of the most striking characteristics of the urban poverty area is a continual drain of resources out of the area and into other sectors of the economy. The drain includes savings, physical capital, human resources, and incomes. As a result, urban poverty areas are left without the most important resources needed for development and improvement, and the economic infrastructure of supporting institutions is seriously deficient.

The drain of resources can be seen most clearly in the process of transition as an area becomes part of the spreading urban ghetto. As migration and population growth widen the boundaries of the ghetto into neighboring parts of the city, middle-class whites move out. With them go most of the professional personnel who provide personal and business services. Doctors, dentists, lawyers, and accountants, as well as insurance agencies and related professions, leave and are not replaced.

Other human resources depart by way of the educational system and the high-wage economy. Drawn by opportunities outside the urban poverty area, many of the most intelligent, capable, and imaginative young people move into the progressive sectors where rewards are greater and opportunities are wider. This drain of human resources leaves the economy of the ghetto—whose chief resource is labor—without many of its best products.

One of the side effects of the well-intentioned efforts to enlarge educational and employment opportunities for blacks and other minority groups has been to starve the ghetto of some of its best minds and most capable people. The idea behind the opening of opportunities and the breaking down of barriers is to facilitate the exit of individuals from ghetto life and poverty. It is rooted in the belief that individual effort aided by removal of barriers plus support for education and training will solve the problem as a whole. No one should quarrel with those programs. But they are only part of a larger solution that must focus on the problem of the ghetto as a whole, and particularly on the processes by which ghettos are created and sustained. Programs that enable some individuals to escape the ghetto serve to preserve ghettoization for many more. The best and brightest are drawn out of the ghetto to serve themselves and contribute to the further advancement of the progressive sector of society outside the ghetto.

The drain of capital is equally striking. A substantial portion of the savings of the urban ghetto goes into financial institutions whose investment policies draw funds out of the area and into business loans, mortgages, and other investments elsewhere. Little comes back to support the ghetto economy or promote its development.[1] Even though the ownership of the original savings or thrift accounts remains with ghetto residents, the funds are generally used outside the ghetto.

Some effort has been made to establish black-owned financial institutions in inner-city areas. The purpose is to provide better financial services for the black community and the inner-city ghettos. Success has been limited. Sources of capital within the inner cities are poor because the inner cities are poor. The same is true for deposits. Most important, however, is the fact that economic gains are higher and risks are lower outside the ghetto, and the opening and widening of financial markets in recent years make it easier for funds to flow where returns are greatest. Black-owned financial institutions, as a group, are too small to reduce this outflow significantly.[2]

National banking policies have not been used to ease the drain of capital from the ghettos. The federal government has done a great deal to encourage banks to provide large loans to developing nations overseas in coordination with U.S. foreign policy objectives. The Federal Reserve System has moved to guarantee such loans, in cooperation with other central banks, the World Bank, and the International Monetary Fund. The result was a large flow of capital overseas, where many of the loans turned sour. No similar effort was made to direct the flow of capital into inner-city ghettos, where the risks were probably lower and the payoff higher (in hindsight). The contrast shows what the political and economic priorities were, however.

Probably the largest flow of capital out of the urban poverty area takes place in housing. Failure to maintain housing facilities enables the owner to withdraw his capital while he maintains his income. Ultimately, the property will be worthless simply because of wear and tear, but while it is being used up the owner takes out his capital and obtains a nice current income. Housing authorities in most major cities are aware of this process but have found no way to stop it. Its basic causes are overcrowding and very high rates of deterioration through overuse, together with the failure of most cities to develop effective methods of preventing neighborhood decay.[3]

Two aspects of the drain of capital out of housing should be noted. If one or two property owners take their capital out by refusing to replace depreciation, surrounding owners are forced to do likewise in self-protection. One deteriorated building draws down the value of surrounding property. One house broken up into small apartments and crowded with numerous families makes it difficult to sell or rent to single families next door. These "neighborhood effects" cause the drain of capital to cumulate and accelerate once it begins and are almost impossible to stop.[4]

The process of housing decay was particularly evident in the 1960s and early 1970s. Some inner-city areas took on the aspect of the bombed-out European cities of World War II. New York City's South Bronx was perhaps the most highly publicized example, but there were others as well. The deterioration of inner-city housing was one reason for the spread of ghettoization out of the inner city to peripheral suburbs in the 1970s.[5] There the process of deterioration continues.

Public housing is a special problem. Many public housing projects were relatively shabbily built, to reduce costs by getting the maximum number of units for the limited funds available. Supervision during the building process was often inadequate, which enabled builders to cut corners and enlarge their profits. Private lenders who provided funds were uninterested in the quality of construction because the bonds had government guarantees. Because of these problems, many public housing projects started life with a much shorter life expectancy than planned.

Once in use, the buildings deteriorated more rapidly than expected because of deficiencies in the building stage. Since rents were based on unrealistically low depreciation charges, the housing authorities did not have adequate funds for repairs, which were postponed in order to pay current operating and administrative costs and to make necessary payments of principal and interest on the bonded debt. Supervision was also slighted, which meant in large housing projects that poor residents, or even non-residents, could break into vacant units to steal plumbing fixtures and other saleable elements. These now unusable units reduced rental income still further, which led to further reduction in maintenance and acceleration of deterioration.

Much low-income housing was subject to this process of decay. In the case of the huge Pruitt-Igoe project in St. Louis, the entire complex was torn down within ten years of construction. Most public housing is not that bad, but in the ghettos the process of deterioration is similar to that of privately-owned rental housing.

Some ghetto rental housing is owned by ghetto residents them-selves. These properties are subject to the same economic forces that lead to housing deterioration generally in the ghettos, but in this case the capital drawn out through failure to maintain the property accrues to the ghetto entrepreneur rather than to an outsider.[6] In addition, families owning their own homes may find themselves locked into the ghetto because of income, age, or race. Their investment in property either deteriorates or its value rises much more slowly than that of families outside the ghetto. A white suburban family discovers that economic growth creates a windfall gain in the form of rising property values. The effect on the ghetto family may be just the opposite: its house, located in an urban ghetto, may well decline in value as the neighborhood deteriorates. At the very least, the windfall gains from growth in property values is considerably below that in the white suburbs.

Capital also flows out of urban poverty areas through public facil-ities. Local governments throughout the country have allowed their capital investments in poverty districts to fall by not replacing depre-ciation of buildings and other investments. Schools, libraries, and medical facilities deteriorate, parks run down, streets and curbs go unrepaired, and fire and police stations depreciate. In part, this process is attributable to the added strains that a denser population places on public facilities. In part, it is the result of the financial problems that prevent cities from increasing their expenditures for public services to meet expanding needs. It is also due to the traditional tendency of city governments to maintain facilities in the middle- and upper-income areas and to put the priorities of the slums last. Whatever the reason, the lack of adequate government investment in the inner city results in another drain of capital out of urban poverty areas.

The transition to an urban ghetto also features the loss of many organized institutions. Hospitals move out. Inner-city hospitals serve the poor almost exclusively; since medicaid pays only about 80 percent of the cost of treatment, these hospitals face permanent deficits. Suburban hospitals, on the other hand, serve a population covered heavily by Blue Cross-Blue Shield and other insurance programs that pay full costs. Churches and other organized community groups also depart. One of the striking characteristics of today's urban poverty area is a lack of those groups and associations which have traditionally provided a community with stability and order and with a sense of continuity and participation. This gap in social needs tends to be replaced by informal community groups. In the urban ghetto, however, much of this informal organization has been outside the law—juvenile gangs, for example. Lack of organized community groups, together with the strains inherent in poverty (including the breakdown of family structures brought on by poverty and the system of welfare payments), contribute to and intensify the isolation and anomie of ghetto life. These social and psychological problems of the urban ghetto add a further dimension to the urban and racial problem, but it is important to realize that they are related to the fundamental economic problems of the area and are not independent phenomena.

The Drain of Income

Income flows out of the urban poverty area in much the same way as capital and other resources. Ghetto residents buy goods produced elsewhere in stores owned and staffed by outsiders and services (utilities, government services, etc.) provided from outside the ghetto. The bulk of goods and services are imported. Internal flows of income that might support greater economic activity and higher incomes within the ghetto itself are largely absent. Rather, ghetto income flows support economic activity elsewhere.

No community is self-sufficient. The goods purchased in any community are imported, except for a very small proportion of local products. In this respect the urban poverty area is like any other. But in other communities a significant portion of the retail and wholesale trades are owned locally and most of the employees are local. The profits and wages earned by those people are spent locally and serve to help support the local community. A chain of spending and re-spending is set up which adds strength and variety to the local econ-omy. These internal income flows are of growing importance in con-temporary urban areas. Cities used to be noted for their export in-dustries, such as steel in Pittsburgh, automobiles in Detroit, whiskey in Peoria, meat products in Chicago, and so on. Those industries formed the "economic base" on which retail and service industries developed. Although the economic base industries are important, stu-dents of urban economics are beginning to recognize that a very large portion of the economy of any metropolitan area is self-sustaining. Each sector of the city's economy strengthens and supports the other sectors by means of the income flows that each generates. Cities still specialize in certain types of export products, but they are becoming increasingly general in their economic activities.[7]

The urban poverty area lacks the highly developed internal income flows that might lead to a viable economic pattern. Aside from the irregular economy and relatively small enterprises requiring little cap-ital, business enterprises in the area are not owned by ghetto residents. The incomes earned by the ghetto residents, predominantly from jobs outside the area, are spent in chain supermarkets, furniture and ap-pliance stores, and other enterprises whose ownership, management, and employees are almost always of non-ghetto origin. The profits and wages received by the outsiders do not come back into the ghetto to support other enterprises or employees. They flow, instead, into the economy of the progressive sector located elsewhere.

These patterns are exaggerated by the low incomes that prevail in the ghetto. Compared with the rest of the economy, relatively small amounts of ghetto incomes are spent on services. With a larger than usual amount spent on goods, the income drain created by those purchases in any community are proportionately larger for urban poverty areas than for others. Low incomes also mean that housing costs comprise a larger proportion of family budgets than elsewhere. For many ghetto families, the cost of housing ranges upward to 40 percent of family income, thereby transforming a significant portion of ghetto income into withdrawals of capital by owners of rental prop-erty.

These income flows help to explain why the welfare system is needed. It stabilizes the ghetto economy. Flows of income in the pri-vate sector are generally outward, requiring a compensating inward flow via the public economy. The outward flow of income also helps to explain why increased welfare payments may help the individuals or families who receive them, but have little or no impact on the ghetto economy as a whole. The bulk of the increased payments leaks out rapidly.[8]

Permanent Depression

A condition of permanent depression prevails in urban poverty areas. In the ghettos, unemployment remains high, even when the rest of the economy is prosperous, and at levels that would signal a serious depression if they were present in the economy as a whole.

The permanent depression of urban poverty areas was documented carefully for the first time in the mid–1960s. In 1968, the Department of Labor reported on a study of employment and unemployment conditions in America's urban slums.[9] Based on the March 1966 Current Population Survey, the study showed an overall unemployment rate of about 7.5 percent in the poorest 25 percent of all census tracts in American cities with over 250,000 population (selected on the basis of the 1960 census). The United States as a whole had a national unemployment rate of 3.8 percent in March 1966, just half that of the slums.

The nonwhite unemployment rate was even higher. Forty-two percent of the residents of these poor census tracts were nonwhite. Their unemployment rate was 9.4 percent—about two and one-half times the national average. Among nonwhite teenagers (fourteen to nineteen years of age) the unemployment rates were 31 percent for males and 46 percent for females.

This preliminary survey was followed by a more intensive study of urban slum areas in twelve major cities in November 1966. At a time when the national unemployment rate was 3.7 percent, the average unemployment rate in the slums was about 10 percent, or almost three times the national average. Conditions varied from one city slum to another, but all showed serious unemployment problems (table 10.1). The unemployment figures of table 10.1 include only those who were actively looking for work. They do not include those who should have been in the labor force but were not because they believed, rightly or wrongly, that they could not find a job (or for other reasons). This "nonparticipation rate" in urban poverty areas was 11 percent among men in the twenty to sixty-four age group, as compared with a 7 percent rate for men of that age in the economy as a whole.

The unemployment figures also excluded a substantial number of adult men that other statistical sources indicated should be part of

Table 10.1. Unemployment Rates in United States Urban Poverty Areas, 1966

Area	Unemployment as Percentage of Labor Force
Boston, Roxbury	6.9
Cleveland, Hough and surrounding neighborhood	15.6
Detroit, central Woodward area	10.1
Los Angeles, South Los Angeles	12.0
New Orleans, several contiguous areas	10.0
New York, Harlem	8.1
East Harlem	9.0
Bedford-Stuyvesant	6.2
Oakland, Bayside	13.0
Philadelphia, North Philadelphia	11.0
Phoenix, Salt River Bed area	13.2
St. Louis, north side	12.9
San Antonio, east and west sides	8.1
San Francisco, Mission-Fillmore area	11.1

Source: U.S. Department of Labor, "A Sharper Look at Unemployment in U.S. Cities and Slums" (Washington, D.C., 1968, Mimeographed).

the slum area population. The November 1966 survey failed to find between one-fifth and one-third of the adult men of the slum areas. This parallels the census experience with the undercount problem.[10]

Finally, the unemployment figures did not include persons who were working part-time but who would have preferred full-time jobs. The November 1966 survey showed that 6.9 percent of all employed persons in urban poverty areas fell into this category. The national figure was 2.3 percent.

These considerations indicate that the unemployment situation in the urban ghetto is worse than the figures reveal. In particular, the contrast with the rest of the economy was sharp enough so that national unemployment rates become meaningless in describing conditions in the slums. This does not mean that when unemployment rates decline in the national economy, the slums feel no impact. They do. The manpower resources of urban poverty areas are used by the larger economy, but they form a pool of workers that is always underutilized. Even when markets everywhere else are tight and inflationary pressures in the progressive sectors of the economy are pushing up prices, wages, profits, and interest rates, unemployment in the urban slums falls only to the levels that are characteristic of serious recessions in the economy as a whole. Charles Dickens' famous phrase "It was the best of times, it was the worst of times" applies to this situation with something of an ironic twist: when the first part applies to the rest of the economy, the second part describes the urban poverty area.

The Department of Labor abandoned its studies of subemployment in the urban ghettos, although it did design an employment survey for the 1970 census. These findings confirm the earlier ones. In 1970, when the national unemployment rate was 4.9 percent, the rate in central-city ghetto areas was 9.6 percent. But this includes only those seeking work; adding discouraged workers who would be seeking work if it were available brought the figure to 11 percent. Finally, adjusting the figures for those working part-time who would like to work full-time raised the proportion of subemployed to 13.3 percent of the labor force. After 1970, national unemployemnt rates rose to 7 percent and stayed there for several years. If the 1970 relationships continued to hold, the ghetto unemployment rate would have been about 14 percent, and the subemployment rate would have jumped to about 19 percent.

As a general rule, then, the ghetto unemployment rate is about double that of the economy as a whole and the ghetto subemployment rate is about two and a half times the national unemployment rate. In the absence of specific data on ghetto unemployment (estimates of unemployment rates in urban areas are no longer made by U.S. government agencies) those rules of thumb can be used to provide rough estimates of economic conditions in the urban ghettos. Thus, in January 1983, at the low point of the 1979 to 1983 recession-depression, the national unemployment rate was 10.4 percent. This meant that the ghetto unemployment rate was about 20 percent. When measured by racial-nationality segments, the unemployment rate for white adults was 8.2 percent, Hispanic adults 15.5 percent, and black adults 19.0 percent for the nation as a whole. Among youths, the white unemployment rate was 20.0 percent and for blacks a huge 45.7%.

Income Flows

We now know enough about economic conditions in the ghetto economy to sketch, in qualitative terms, the chief economic relationships between the ghetto and the outside economy.

Income flows into the ghetto in part as earned income. By far the largest source of earned income is employment in the low-wage industries, which is a fundamental cause, together with high unemployment rates, of the poverty of the ghetto subsystem. A fortunate few have been able to find better employment, but these are the ones who are able to move up and out. Transfer payments supplement earned income, primarily through the welfare system, food stamps, social security, and medicaid.

These income flows support three characteristic aspects of the ghetto economy that most clearly distinguish it from the rest of the economy: the private business sector, with its special "penny capitalism" aspects that derive from the low-income nature of its customers; the irregular economy; and the criminal sector, with its numbers gambling, loansharking, narcotics, prostitution, and theft. These three aspects of the ghetto economy intertwine and overlap.

Outward flows of income, capital, and human resources to the rest of the economy serve to keep the ghetto in a permanently underdeveloped state and feed the economic interests outside the ghetto that have developed around those income flows. Some of those outside interests are relatively narrow and special: the slumlord, the criminal overlord, and the owner of ghetto business enterprises. Others are broader. The entire economy outside of the ghetto benefits from the income, capital, and manpower resources that are drawn out, just as it benefits from a pool of low-wage labor that provides relatively low-cost services to those outside.

These economic relationships are sketched in figure 10.1. It shows in diagrammatic form the dynamics of ghetto income flows. Within the ghetto, an internal flow of spending is generated by ghetto business enterprises, the irregular economy, and criminal industries. This flow of spending is supplemented by income earned outside the ghetto

FIGURE 10.1. Ghetto income flows

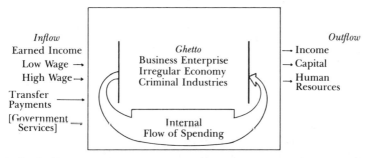

The level of income in the ghetto economy depends upon maintaining the inflow of income. Transfer payments play a crucial role, enabling society to maintain the ghetto at any level of relative poverty desired, thereby offsetting the outflows of resources and stabilizing both the ghetto subsystem *and* its place in the economy as a whole.

by ghetto residents, chiefly from low-wage employment but also from some relatively high-wage jobs in industrial cities like Detroit, Cleveland, or Pittsburgh. Labor is the ghetto's chief export. Earned income is supplemented by transfer payments and government services. These sources of income support the outflow of income and wealth to the larger economy outside the ghetto—the flows of income, capital, and human resources already described.

A study by Richard L. Schaffer of the Bedford-Stuyvesant ghetto in New York, then the nation's largest, confirmed the importance of the drain of income from the inner-city ghettos.[11] Schaffer used data on incomes in 1969 from the 1970 census, and a wide variety of other sources, to estimate income flows between the Bedford-Stuyvesant ghetto and the surrounding economy. Total income for the year was $852.7 million, from the sources shown in table 10.2.

The components of the adjusted gross income of individuals, shown in table 10.3, indicate the importance of outside earnings, primarily wages and salaries.

Schaffer compared his estimates for Bedford-Stuyvesant—largely black, 219,000 people, poor—with similar estimates for nearby Borough Park—largely white, 186,000 people, middle income. Borough Park, with a population about 85 percent as large had a total income 28 percent greater: Borough Park's adjusted gross income of individuals was more than double that of Bedford-Stuyvesant. Part of the difference between the two was made up by government services and

Table 10.2. Inflows of Income, Bedford-Stuyvesant Area, 1969
(in millions of dollars)

Income		Amount
Adjusted gross income of individuals		282.8
Sales by local firms to nonresidents		247.2
Government services		166.5
Transfer payments		121.7
Public Assistance	88.0	
Social Security	21.2	
Unemployment Compensation	8.0	
Worker's Compensation	4.5	
Extension of consumer credit		17.6
Policy game winnings		11.7
Business investment		5.2
Total		852.7

transfer payments. Bedford-Stuyvesant received $288.2 million from those sources, while Borough Park received $190.9 million.

The outflows of income from Bedford-Stuyvesant were estimated by Schaffer at $641.2 million, shown in table 10.4.

Comparing Bedford-Stuyvesant's total inflows and total outflows indicates a net favorable balance of payments of $212.4 million. This

Table 10.3. Adjusted Gross Income of Individuals, Bedford-Stuyvesant Area, 1969 *(in millions of dollars)*

Source of Income	Amount
Profits from local businesses received by resident owners	0.4
Profits from local multiple dwellings received by resident owners	6.6
Wages paid by local firms to local residents	44.5
Other earnings by local residents	231.8

Table 10.4. Outflows of Income, Bedford-Stuyvesant Area, 1969 *(in millions of dollars)*

Income		Amount
Personal taxes		51.5
Housing		80.1
Taxes	5.5	
Mortgage payments	9.7	
Operating expenses of resident owners	7.0	
Rental payments to outside owners	32.1	
Housing disinvestment	25.8	
Business		295.2
Taxes and social security payments	20.6	
Wages paid to nonresidents	54.3	
Other payments to outsiders	206.2	
Profits to outside owners	14.1	
Consumption		130.3
Payments to outside businesses	126.9	
Sales tax	3.4	
Savings		20.2
Repayment of consumer credit		16.2
Policy game payments		16.7
Narcotics		31.0
Total		641.2

sum contributed to the internal flow of payments and income within the area. It was not significantly different from Borough Park's favorable balance of $185.1 million, and was almost identical per person. But, when the total of government servies and transfer payments is deducted ($288.2 million), Bedford-Stuyvesant had a net payments deficit of $75.8 million, which is about 9 percent of the total flow. Borough Park's similar net deficit was only $5.8 million, and well within the range of estimating errors. In short, the middle-income Borough Park area was essentially self-sustaining, but Bedford-Stuyvesant was not. We will have more to say on this matter when we examine the key role of transfer payments in the ghetto economy.

Schaffer's study is the only comprehensive analysis of ghetto income flows. Some of its figures for individual income flows may well be rough estimates. In particular, the estimate of rental payments to outside owners of only $32.1 million seems too low. Its conclusions, however, are supported by less-detailed analyses of Newark by Frank G. Davis, of Harlem by Robert S. Browne, and of the Shaw-Cardozo area of Washington, D.C. by Earl Mellor.[12] A study of the Hough area in Cleveland, based on household expenditure diaries, documented the outflow of income from ordinary household spending. It showed that the "marginal propensity to spend" inside Hough was only 0.13. That is, of each additional dollar of family expenditures, only thirteen cents was spent within Hough.[13]

Population Flows

Every social system rejects individuals who do not meet the standards established for membership in the various subsystems that make up the larger social order. Rejection mechanisms are many and varied. For example, the requirements for acceptance into the northeastern suburbs of Detroit—one of the subsystems that make up the whole—include the income required to buy or rent an expensive home. Test scores and grades are important for admission to college. Certain requirements must be met to obtain a civil service job. Formal or informal restrictions keep some country clubs and fraternal organizations free of Jews and blacks. A middle-class pattern of behavior is necessary for acceptance in the typical suburban community. Examples can be multiplied, but the principle is clear: each of the subsystems into which the social system divides itself accepts or rejects individuals according to its own formal or informal criteria. One of the most unfortunate aspects of our society is that race is a major criterion for acceptance or rejection.

Rejection from one subsystem of the "desirable" sectors of society does not mean rejection from all, in most cases. The individual or family unable to find a place in one will usually find another. There may be frustrations and disappointments, but a place is usually found. Most people are not rejected out of the social system as a whole.

But some are. Dangerous or particularly bizarre behavior takes some people to mental hospitals. Crimes draw others to prisons. Others gravitate to the urban ghetto, often because of race, poor education, low skill, or lack of adaptability to the behavior pattern of the more successful sectors of the social order. Mental hospitals, jails, and slums are the chief depositories our society has created for those who cannot fit in or be fitted into the dominant way of life. They make up the subsystems into which society's rejects congregate.

An example will show how the mechanism works. The black share-cropper—poor, uneducated, unskilled, and employed in agriculture in the Mississippi delta region in 1950—was redundant there in 1955 after cotton picking was mechanized. He was rejected from the economic system in which he had formerly been able to subsist, even though he was at the bottom of the economic and social order. Cast out there, he made his way to the ghetto of a southern or a northern city. He moved to the place where other economic rejects also had moved. Partly by choice, and partly because there was no other place to go, he ended up in the urban ghetto.

Examination of the characteristics of ghetto residents indicates the chief factors that cause rejection from the progressive sector of the economy. (1) Race: blacks, Puerto Ricans, Mexican Americans and other minority groups. (2) Recent arrival: migrants from the rural South, Southwest, and Puerto Rico, as well as foreign countries. (3) Cultural differences: persons with a cultural background different from the white middle-class culture. (4) Low productivity: low earning power resulting from lack of skills, poor education, bad health, old age, and related factors. (5) Low income: inability to live in the style of the white middle class because of inadequate financial resources.

People rejected from the social-economic system are not scattered at random. They do not stay in the suburbs or in southern agriculture if they are caught up in the rejection mechanisms. They tend to collect or be collected at specific points in the system as a whole.

These residual subsystems are usually separated from the functioning central sectors of the social order by barriers of various types. Mental hospitals and prisons are walled or fenced, and entry is by a formal, legal process. The urban ghetto is different. There are no physical barriers between the ghetto and the rest of society, and no formal methods by which individuals are "committed" to life in the ghetto. The barriers are economic and social rather than physical, and the selection process is informal.

The barriers between the urban ghetto and the rest of the economic and social system do not cut off the ghetto completely. A substantial number of individuals move up and out into other sectors of society while others move down and into the ghetto. Individuals are always moving from one subsystem to another in our highly mobile society. The process is not that simple, however, and in the urban ghetto there exist three barriers that are insurmountable for most residents. (1) Mobility outward for many people is not based on merit, or even income, which often acts as a proxy for merit. Race is an important criterion for movement out. It is a barrier for blacks and Hispanics that is not present for whites. (2) The ghetto creates and fosters a way of life that makes it difficult for individuals to be accepted in other sectors of the economy and society. This includes such factors as work habits and attitudes toward work developed in the irregular economy and patterns of behavior fostered by the welfare economy. (3) The fact that the urban ghetto is a depository for people rejected from society influences the attitudes of the rest of society toward the ghetto. These attitudes are reflected in inadequate provision of public services, such as education and health, which tend to preserve ghettoization and reduce the upward mobility of ghetto residents. They also tend to reduce acceptance of blacks and other minority groups outside the ghetto.

The informal and unseen barriers show up in the economic statistics as inordinately high rates of unemployment, relatively low income levels, relatively low residential mobility, and many other distinctive features of the ghetto. The barriers tend to keep within the ghetto a large number of people whose native abilities and potential for development are largely wasted. This waste of human resources is particularly tragic in the case of young people whose chances in life are greatly diminished because of the ghetto environment in which they are born.

When the process of rejection from the larger economy takes place on a wider scale and at a faster pace than the movement up and out of the ghetto, the urban ghettos expand and grow, and conditions there deteriorate. This is exactly what happened in the 1950s and the 1960s. When the movements in and out are balanced, the size of the ghetto will depend on the pattern of population growth within the ghetto itself. Thus, three processes must be taken into account: the rate of population growth within the ghetto, the rate at which further rejects enter the ghetto from the wider society, and the rate at which people leave the ghetto.

FIGURE 10.2. The ghetto as a residual subsystem.

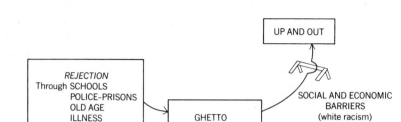

Circular Causation and Cumulative Effects

The condition of the ghetto economy is a classic example of circular causation in social processes.[14] The ghetto economy perpetuates its own poverty. Low incomes mean low levels of living. This style of life has obvious deficiencies: poor food, bad housing, poor health, and bad sanitation. These conditions lead back to low labor productivity and a perpetuation of low incomes.[15] The drain of resources out of urban poverty areas—manpower, capital, income—serves to reinforce the poverty. Social overhead capital is inadequate. The public services that might overcome part of the deficiencies in private incomes are insufficient. In particular, deficiencies in the educational system lead to inadequate training, low skill levels, and low productivity.

Employment patterns, especially in low-wage industries and the irregular economy, reinforce the pattern of poverty and create barriers to movement of workers into the high-wage sectors outside the urban poverty area. At the same time, those ghetto residents who do move up and out take with them much of the entrepreneurship that development of the ghetto economy would require.

Economic development is further retarded by ineffective instruments for local control: the destinies of urban poverty areas have been largely in the hands of outsiders. Weak political representation and control of local governments by an "establishment" power structure have kept the poor out of power. The result is a feeble infrastructure of voluntary organizations and a low level of popular participation in the decision-making process. This, in turn, retards the development of decision-making and entrepreneurial abilities. The dual lack of entrepreneurship and effective power means that decisions that affect the ghetto economy are made primarily by the outsiders who dominate the decision-making process.

One result has been that many policies and programs have hurt the ghetto rather than helped. Welfare payments have tended to weaken attachment to the labor market. Urban renewal has increased the overcrowding of housing rather than diminished it. Highway construction has had the same effect. Educational programs have been unable to prevent a serious deterioration of the schools. Even the benefits of low-cost housing have been relatively small compared with the incomes generated for non-ghetto residents.

In this context, the racial attitudes of whites and the long history of black repression take on key significance. Together they have kept the great majority of blacks in the ghetto, unable to move out of the vicious circle of self-generating poverty that prevails there.

The pattern of the ghetto economy, then, presents a series of self-reinforcing influences: (1) Poverty reinforces the conditions that lead to poverty. (2) Resources that might lead to betterment and development are drained out. (3) Lack of political power has brought public programs that are often harmful to the ghetto economy. (4) White attitudes toward race have kept most of the ghetto residents from moving out.

A social system in which a pattern of circular causation functions will generally reach an equilibrium in which causative factors balance each other. It may be a moving equilibrium if growth processes operate. If outside forces for growth or decay impinge on the equilibrium and if they set up secondary effects moving in the same direction, a self-sustaining process of change can be established, particularly if the social system can move beyond the threshold from which the old equilibrium can no longer be reestablished. These basic propositions embody the concept of cumulative effects: circular causation can lead to cumulative movements toward either growth or retrogression.

Economic growth is particularly difficult for the ghetto economy. Its weak infrastructure, lack of local initiative and entrepreneurship, and the shortage of capital make it difficult to generate a growth process. They create instead a self-generating poverty cycle. More important, the tendency for resources and income to drain out of the ghetto economy means that even if the forces of development were to appear, much of their strength would be dissipated before they had a significant impact on the ghetto itself. Any program or programs that seek to improve the economy of urban poverty areas must reverse the drain of skilled manpower, capital, and income if a cumulative process of growth is to be established.

Rather than growth, a cumulative process of retrogression has been the fate of urban poverty areas over the last thirty years. The key outside influence was the migration of the 1950s and the ensuing population explosion. These demographic changes both expanded the size of the problem and worsened the condition of a social and economic system already suffering from permanent depression and a self-reinforcing pattern of underdevelopment. Retrogressive forces intensified the poverty and accelerated the drain of resources. Only massive increases in public expenditure programs during the 1960s were able to stem the tide and recreate a temporary new equilibrium.

Conditions declined during the 1970s and early 1980s. National economic stagnation during the 1970s and two serious recessions doubled ghetto unemployment. Simultaneously, inflation eroded purchasing power: between 1973 and 1982 the purchasing power of the hourly minimum wage fell by 20 percent, in spite of an increase from $1.60 per hour to $3.35. Assistance programs were cut back by the federal government after 1980, as the Reagan administration shifted spending priorities to the military budget. During the 1970s, the income gap between white and black workers widened, as did the gap between low- and high-wage employment. With unemployment of black youths reaching 45 percent in early 1983, another lost generation is appearing in the cities. The inner-city ghettos are more deeply enmeshed than ever in the circular causation and cumulative effects of poverty and deprivation.

Policy Strategies

We have examined three aspects of the dynamics of the urban ghetto. First, the number of ghetto inhabitants is determined by the rate of ghetto population growth, the rate at which the larger society forces people into the ghetto, and the rate at which people move up and out. These flows move in response to economic forces, especially the level and growth of economic activity and the speed of technological change. The selection process by which the economy thrusts individuals into the ghetto has a large racial component, although factors such as education, training, and skill are also significant. The economy always tends to cast out those who are least able to produce. It is a grim proposition: the marketplace is not humane. Urban ghettos will continue to exist until a mechanism is devised that will stop the rejection process.

Second, levels of income within the ghetto, given the size of the population there, are determined by three income flows: internal income flows, transfer payments, and the outflow of income and wealth. These flows of people and income determine both the size of the ghetto and its level of well-being. Increased income flowing into the ghetto economy by means of larger transfer payments and improved government services can ease the poverty that prevails there, but can do little to change the systematic relationships that create the ghetto itself. Those programs are, at best, ameliorative. Some, however, serve to reinforce those aspects of the ghetto economy that perpetuate the status quo. We will have more to say on this topic in chapter 13.

Third, the ghetto has developed its own characteristic relationships within which its inhabitants function. We will look more closely at some of the economic relationships of this social system, particularly low-wage employment and the irregular economy, in the next chapter. More important, the process of circular causation with cumulative effects tends to preserve the ghetto in a relatively stable position from one generation to the next, even though size and income levels may change. In this context, programs designed to assist individuals through education and training, better housing, and improved health services, however desirable in themselves, will not have much impact on the fundamental processes at work that create and perpetuate the urban ghetto. If they are large enough and sustained long enough, such programs can make a contribution, but they are addressed to symptoms rather than causes. Helping individuals will not solve the problem as long as the social and economic processes that create the ghetto are left untouched.

11

Work and Wages in the Ghetto

THE GHETTO ECONOMY IS A WORLD APART. IT DIFFERS MARKEDLY FROM the rest of the economy in many ways. Its most distinguishing characteristics are relative poverty and backwardness. It lacks the resources and processes that bring advancement and relative affluence to the economy outside the ghetto. There are, of course, interactions by which the urban ghetto is influenced by economic activity in the rest of the nation. Prosperity in the national economy is reflected in economic improvements in the ghetto, an easing of the pressures of poverty. Bad times in the national economy bring economic disaster to the ghetto. Nevertheless, the ghetto economy has many of the characteristics of an economic enclave only partially and incompletely articulated with the world outside.

Sources of Income

The income of the urban poverty area comes from four major sources, only one of which is a viable and continuing link with the progressive economy outside the ghetto.

1. The high-wage progressive sectors of the economy provide employment for some. We can identify two chief patterns. (a) Em-

155

ployment in the high-wage manufacturing sector. In Detroit, for example, jobs in the automobile industry are held by a racially integrated workforce, many of whom live in the urban ghetto. The industry is very capital-intensive and oligopolistic and has a strong union; labor productivity is high and wages correspond. Detroit, however, is an exception in regard to the percentage of its ghetto residents who work in a high-wage industry. Most large cities have a much smaller portion of their central-city workforce in such industries. This sector of the economy, however, is declining in importance and the number of blue-collar jobs in unionized industries is shrinking.

(b) Employment in white-collar jobs in the government and service sectors of the economy. This sector of the economy has been expanding, opening up job opportunities for women in particular. Employment here is steadier than in the manufacturing sector, but salaries are lower. These sources of income support a middle and lower-middle income sector of the inner-city population that, in turn, provides the economic base for a more affluent professional and business class in the inner city. These groups tend to live in the outer areas of the inner-city racial ghetto and it is from this group that a movement into the suburbs develops.

2. The chief economic base of the urban poverty area is the more backward sector of the economy, characterized by low wages, relatively wide cyclical variations, and exposure to all the debilitating forces of competition. A large portion of the workers who are employed full-time in these industries earn wages at or below the poverty level. Many of the jobs in this secondary sector of the labor market are dead-end, sporadic, or temporary, and offer little opportunity for security or advancement. Jobs in this sector of the economy are increasing in numbers more rapidly than in the primary sector of the labor market, but the number of job-seekers in the secondary labor market has been rising even more rapidly. The result has been growing unemployment rates in the inner-city poverty areas and downward economic pressure on wage rates.

3. The low-wage economy is supplemented by an "irregular" economy, partly legal and partly illegal, which provides further income for the residents of urban poverty areas, largely through provision of services to other residents. The poor cannot afford to pay the high prices for services that prevail in the regular economy for, say, auto, appliance, or plumbing repairs. To meet

their needs, a substantial irregular economy has developed, much of which is "off the books" and unrecorded.

4. Income supplements from outside the urban poverty areas, some public and some private, provide the transfer payments without which the population could not survive. Welfare payments are probably the largest and certainly the most controversial of these transfers. The place of transfer payments in the ghetto economy will be examined in some detail in chapter 12.

Although these aspects of the ghetto economy can be readily identified, it is difficult to find carefully documented studies of them. Most economic data are reported on a national or statewide level. Labor market and employment data are usually not reported in ways that identify the residential location of workers. Since the necessary data are largely nonexistent, few studies of employment and incomes of inner-city poverty areas are available. Nevertheless, it is possible to look more closely at those topics.

The Working Poor

A large number of ghetto residents work in low-wage industries. The jobs may be in manufacturing, service industries or retail and wholesale trade. Their common characteristic is that many full-time employees who work steadily in these industries earn less than a poverty-level income. A job at the minimum wage of $3.35 per hour will bring in just $117.25 for a 35-hour work week, which is considered a full-time job. Even working steadily for fifty weeks a year, which is not characteristic of minumum wage jobs, would bring only $5862.50. Deductions for social security would reduce the take-home pay below that total unless the job were off the books in the irregular economy. There are not likely to be any other deductions, however, for few low-wage jobs include fringe benefits.

The preponderance of low-wage employment in the ghetto is shown by data for central Harlem for 1966.[1] Median family income was $3,907 as compared with $6,300 for the United States as a whole. The distribution of occupations, shown in table 11.1, demonstrates a heavy preponderance of low-skilled and low-wage occupations.

The survey did not break down the white-collar occupations into the two classifications of professional-managerial (mostly high-wage) and clerical-sales (mostly low-wage). An educated guess would allocate 20 percent of the white-collar employment, at the most, to the former category and 80 percent to the latter. Adding in the low-wage laborers

Table 11.1. Occupations of Employed
Persons, Central Harlem, November 1966

Occupation	Number	Percentage of total
White-collar	21,272	27.5
Blue-collar		
Craftsmen	4,642	6.0
Operatives	13,398	17.3
Laborers	11,718	15.1
Service	26,460	34.1
Total	77,490	100.0

and service workers would lead to the division between low- and high-wage employment shown in table 11.2. The calculation in the table is an estimate, of course, and is derived from only one central-city ghetto, although one of the largest. A rough approximation of about 70 percent of all ghetto employed working in the low-wage sector is consistent with other general descriptions. One would not be surprised if the figure were as high as 75 percent, but would be surprised if it were lower than 66 percent.

The garment industry in New York City is an example of the low-wage sector of the economy. Garment manufacturing in New York is an old industry. In the nineteenth and early twentieth centuries it used the low-wage labor of immigrants from Europe fresh off the ships that brought them to this country. Women and children were an important part of the workforce and the aptly named sweatshop was the typical locus of production. The situation began to change in the 1920s with the rise of union organization and the beginnings of state regulation of working conditions for women and minors. By the late 1930s, most of the sweatshops were gone, the industry was largely unionized, wages had risen (but were still relatively low), and working conditions had improved.

After World War II, however, the situation began to change. Low-wage labor overseas began to compete with domestic labor, and immigration from Puerto Rico provided a large source of low-wage labor outside the unionized garment worker group. The low-wage sweatshop—illegal now—reappeared in New York City, along with a shift of production to foreign centers. The industry is highly competitive, production units are small, and relatively little capital is required to start production. An illegal sweatshop can be established with as little

Table 11.2. Estimated Low-wage and High-wage Employment, Central Harlem, November 1966

	Number	Percentage of total
Low-wage employment	55,196	71.2
High-wage employment	22,294	28.8
Total	77,490	100.0

as $25,000 to $40,000. Furthermore technology makes it possible to separate one step in the production process from another, and the organization of the industry facilitates separation of production from marketing. An entrepreneur organizes design and cutting in New York, ships the unsewn parts to shops in the Caribbean by air freight where they are assembled by sewing machine operators earning wages equal to 10 to 20 percent of the official wage rates in New York, and then shipped back to New York for finishing and packaging. A tariff is paid only on the value added by low-paid foreign labor.

Large supplies of low-wage labor are available overseas for the more highly labor-intensive parts of the manufacturing process. For example, a free trade zone in the Dominican Republic allows duty-free imports of materials and duty-free export of goods processed there. In 1978, the hourly wage rate in the free zone was 34 cents per hour as compared with a U.S. minimum wage at that time of $2.90 and a $4.00 average hourly wage in the regular garment industry in New York. High unemployment rates in the Dominican Republic keep wages low, as do the armed guards patrolling the zone to keep out union organizers.[2] This type of international labor competition forced much garment manufacturing overseas. Between 1950 and 1980, employment in the apparel and textile industry in New York City fell from 340,000 to 140,000, a loss of 200,000 jobs in thirty years.

In the 1970s, however, manufacturing jobs in the clothing industry returned to New York City. There were between 3,000 and 4,500 illegal garment manufacturing sweatshops in New York City in 1981, employing some 50,000 to 70,000 persons. Most employees were women, and many were illegal immigrants from Latin America and Asia. Wages in the sweatshops averaged $1.75 per hour, in contrast to $4.58 in the regular apparel industry in New York City and $4.35 in the United States as a whole. This compares with $1.10 in Singapore, 96 cents in Hong Kong, 56 cents in Taiwan and 86 cents in Brazil— average hourly wages in the apparel industry.[3] Clothing manufacture is once again a major source of employment in New York City, and growing, but at low-wage rates and with working conditions that had gone out of existence almost half a century earlier.

We do not look to the low-wage industries for examples of progress and affluence. Typically, the individual enterprise is small, requiring relatively little capital investment, the technology is labor-intensive, and both labor productivity and profits are low. Workers are subject to the wage squeeze characteristic of labor-intensive, highly competitive industries. Sales in these industries are generally quite sensitive to prices, which means that even if competition were reduced, firms would have little chance of improving their revenues through price increases. Since profits are low, little is done in research or product development, which reinforces the technological backwardness of the industry.

The low-wage industries may well be subject to greater fluctuations than other sectors of the economy when aggregate demand falls. We know that labor turnover rates are high, which means that the incidence of unemployment in the labor force in also high. The bulk of the workforce is poorly educated with few job skills. Finally, a large proportion of the jobs are dead ends: there are not many higher-paying jobs that worker can qualify for by his or her daily work on the job. Workers who start out in the low-wage sector of the economy tend to stay there rather than move into similar jobs in the high-wage sector, although more studies of this phenomenon are needed to determine how strong a tendency this is.

These industries are part of the "unprotected" economy. For the most part, workers are not unionized. Employers are not protected by the oligopolistic industrial structure which shields such firms as General Motors Corporation and other industrial giants. Most protective legislation, such as the minimum wage, is only now being extended to low-wage jobs, and a large number are still not covered. Many federal programs which might have provided greater protection, such as the loan operations of the Small Business Administration, are inadequate. Workers are exposed to the "satanic mills" of supply and demand, which grind both workers and business firms exceedingly fine. The higher-income sectors of society have been protected while those needing it the most have gone exposed.

The low-wage labor force of the ghetto is preserved and reinforced by high rates of unemployment there. During the recession-depression from 1981 to 1982 when national unemployment rates rose to levels of 10 to 11 percent of the labor force, unemployment rates in the inner-city ghetto were doubled, reaching to 20 to 22 percent as measured by the U.S. Department of Labor. The employment picture for young people in the ghetto was far worse, with unemployment rates of 40 to 50 percent for persons under twenty-one years of age. The presence of these cadres of unemployed workers tends to keep wages low in those sectors of the labor market in which they compete. These are the low-wage industries and the menial occupations for which racial minorities are eligible.

Lack of union organization is another element that reinforces the low-wage pattern. The high-wage industries are largely unionized, and unions offer some degree of insulation against the pressures of supply and demand in the labor market. When a firm has a union contract that embodies an agreement on wages, the management has little to gain from replacing existing employees with new workers, for the new will have to be paid at the same wage rates as the old. Even during recessions most unions are able to effectively resist wage cuts, and many are able to achieve increases based on productivity gains; the recession of 1981–82 was an exception. Workers in the ghetto are less fortunate. Unemployment rates there are always high—double the national level even in the best of times—and wage rates are held down by the ability of the employer to replace workers at any time. There are few unions to protect low-wage workers from the impact of the market.

The presence of a large labor force employed in low-wage industries is of major significance to the larger metropolitan regions of which the ghetto is a part. The industries of any metropolitan area can be divided into three groups. One group comprises the "export" industries that provide the raison d'etre for the regional economy. They are oriented toward national and international markets, like automobiles in Detroit or steel in Pittsburgh, to cite two classic examples. A second group complements the first. These industries provide inputs for use by the "export" industries or use their outputs for further processing. Both groups, generally, are characterized by large firms, high wages, modern technology, and unionization in most parts of the country. The third group of industries supply the local economy with food, clothing, shelter, medical care, education, recreation, governmental services, and the like. Many are low-wage industries, and it is in this sector that most ghetto residents are employed.

An inherently exploitive relationship is established. Living costs in the whole metropolitan area are held down by the existence of low-wage service industries. Costs of production in the export industries and their complementary firms are lower because the services they buy are, in part, provided by a low-wage work force. All of the products and services on which the life of the community are based are available at prices that reflect the low wages paid to ghetto residents.

This economic relationship makes it difficult for any local government to take strong action to eliminate ghettos and the poverty found there. If one area made a serious effort along those lines, there would be an increase in the cost base of the area's export industries and their complements. Services would cost more, the cost of distribution would be higher, and governmental expenses would rise. Higher living costs would require higher wages in the export and complementary industries in order to attract and keep the necessary amounts of properly skilled labor. These higher costs (relative to other metropolitan areas) would result in slower economic growth and perhaps even retrogression if the cost effects were great enough. Low wages in service industries are as important to a city's export industries as are low taxes.

These effects would be felt particularly by real estate and commercial interests whose stake in local economic growth is greatest and who normally are influential in determining local governmental policies. It is in their interest, and in the interest of other elements in the local power structure, that the area should come last with the least effort to ameliorate or end the poverty inherent in low-wage industries.

There is a similar economic interest on the part of middle-income groups. If wages are raised in the low-wage industries, the cost of living will rise and the standard of living will fall. Many people are aware of this relationship, although it is usually expressed in some phrase such as, "Someone has to wash the dishes," or "Who will collect the trash?"

The basically exploitive nature of the urban ghetto is readily evident. It is easy to understand why there are strong economic and political barriers to its elimination. The structure of power is allied with those economic interests that have a vested interest in continued poverty. Unfortunately, those economic interests constitute a majority of those who vote.

There are large numbers of working poor in the United States. In 1977 almost 10 million workers had an hourly wage below $3.00. The minimum wage in that year was $2.25, and millions earned less. The Census Bureau identified nearly 5.3 million poor heads of households in 1977, of whom over 2.5 million were employed at some time during the year.[4] The occupations of those who were employed are shown in table 11.3.

Not all of the working poor were employed full-time. Table 11.4 shows that about one-half worked for forty weeks or more in 1977, and many held part-time jobs of less than thirty-five hours per week. Even full-time employment does not bring a decent income for the

Table 11.3. Occupations of Employed Poor Heads of Households, 1977

Occupation	Number of Persons
Professional and technical	83,000
Managers, officials, and proprietors	167,000
Clerical workers	197,000
Sales workers	111,000
Craftsmen and foremen	316,000
Operatives	509,000
Private household workers	99,000
Other service workers	446,000
Unskilled laborers	206,000
Farmers and farm managers	261,000
Farm laborers and foreman	149,000
Total	2,544,000

Source: Bradley R. Schiller, *The Economics of Poverty and Discrimination*, 3rd ed. (Englewood Cliffs, N.J.: Prentice-Hall, 1980), p. 69.

Table 11.4. Work Experience of Employed Poor Heads of Households, 1977

Weeks Worked	Full-Time (35 hrs. per week or more)	Part-Time (less than 35 hrs. per wk.)	Total	Percentage
50–52	850,000	190,000	1,040,000	40.9
40–49	200,000	43,000	243,000	9.6
27–39	240,000	80,000	320,000	12.6
14–26	325,000	134,000	459,000	18.0
1–13	284,000	197,000	481,000	18.9
Total	1,899,000	644,000	2,543,000	100.0

Source: Schiller, *The Economics of Poverty and Discrimination*, p. 69.

working poor. Of the 850,000 poor heads of households employed full-time for fifty weeks or more in 1977, almost 80 percent earned less than $6000 for the year and 28 percent earned less than $2000. Table 11.5 shows the full data. Reducing these figures to hourly wage rates, we find that no more than 4 percent of the working poor earned as much as $4.00 per hour. The majority earned from perhaps $1.25 to about $3.00 per hour. Many earned less than $1.25. Yet a head of

Table 11.5. Incomes of Full-Time Employed
Heads of Households, 1977

Total Income	Percentage of Full-Time Employed Heads of Households
Under $2,000	28
$2,000–3,999	24
$4,000–5,999	27
$6,000–7,999	16
$8,000 or more	5
Total	100

Source: Schiller, *The Economics of Poverty and Discrimination*, p. 68.

a family of four required a full-time job at $3.00 per hour in 1977 to reach the admittedly inadequate poverty line income of that year.

We can summarize. The working poor are found in a wide variety of occupational classifications, but many are either clerical, sales, service, or production workers, or unskilled laborers. About one-half are employed full-time or close to it. The other one-half work part-time, and intermittently. And the menial, low-wage jobs they hold or move in and out of are not the starting point of an upwardly mobile track that will ultimately get them out of the secondary labor market into the primary sector. The hardworking dishwasher or busboy or common laborer does not become a restaurant manager or construction foreman. He becomes only a hardworking dishwasher or busboy or common laborer.

The Irregular Economy

The urban ghetto supports an occupational structure and service economy that is quite unconventional and partly illegitimate. The need for it arises from the inability of residents to pay for the usual organized and commercially provided services of higher-income areas and from the lack of business enterprises which normally provide them. To compensate for this lack, the ghetto economy has developed an "irregular" economy characterized by informal work patterns that are often invisible to outside observers, a network of occupational skills unique to ghetto life but which have little significance for jobs outside the ghetto, and acquisition of skills and competencies by workers in nontraditional ways, making their use in the larger economy difficult if not impossible.

Louis A. Ferman has identified several occupational types in the irregular economy[5] *The artist.* Entertainers, humorists, painters, and craftsmen. *The hustler.* The supersalesman who often operates on both sides of the law: for example, the "casket salesman" who retrieves coffins from the local cemetery, refurbishes them, and offers them for sale. *The fixer.* The expert who can repair cars, appliances, plumbing, or electrical wiring. *The information broker.* The individual who receives cash income in exchange for information. Sometimes the information concerns the availability of stolen merchandise, sometimes job opportunities, sometimes the details of the welfare system. *The product developer.* Products such as rum-raisin ice cream, sweet potato pie, and barbecued spareribs enjoy large sales in some ghettos. They are also produced there for sale by ghetto residents.

Some of these irregular occupations are practiced full-time, some part-time, some almost as hobbies. They all fill needs not served through regular economic channels. Most are not illegal, although there is a substantial amount of illegal activity carried out by fences, thieves, bookies, narcotics pushers, pimps, and prostitutes.

Since there have been no systematic studies of the irregular economy, little is known about how closely people are tied to it or whether they move back and forth between the irregular and the regular work systems. Ferman noted five typical situations. (1) The worker holds a steady job in the regular economy but moonlights in the irregular economy to earn more, using the same skills used on his regular job. (2) The worker is sporadically employed in the regular economy, which he considers his chief employment, but works in the irregular economy when unemployed. (3) The worker shifts back and forth between the regular and irregular economies, depending on where he finds the best opportunities. (4) The worker is employed primarily in the irregular economy but ventures occasionally into a regular job. (5) The worker is wholly employed in the irregular economy and never works in a regular job.

The irregular economy has certain advantages over the regular economy. The worker is not accountable to any authority for his earnings, no records are kept, and taxes can be avoided. The work is individualistic in nature and can give the worker a sense of competence and control over his existence that a regular job may not provide. Entrepreneurship and risk give the activity some of the aspects of a game, yet the risks are usually not high. Finally, people who work either part- or full-time in the regular economy can supplement their incomes in the irregular economy, and vice versa.

The irregular economy has one major disadvantage, however. It encourages patterns of behavior and attitudes toward work which make it difficult for a worker accustomed to the irregularity, lax work standards, and high rate of turnover in the irregular economy to move easily into jobs in the regular economy, where work rules are more rigid, lost time and absenteeism are not tolerated to the same extent, and supervision is more rigorous. In some respects, work habits in the irregular economy are similar to those in the preindustrial work-force familiar to economic historians. Some of the same difficulties are found in adapting workers in the irregular economy to jobs in the mainstream of a modern industrial society.

However, the irregular economy does enable people to develop productive skills, entrepreneurship, and sales ability that could be put to use in more systematic ways for the economic development of the area. Its very existence indicates an unfortunate waste of ability and intelligence. Although the specific skills of the irregular economy may not be highly applicable in the regular economy, they indicate the presence of a high degree of initiative and entrepreneurship.

Crime in the Ghetto

If there is little information on the irregular economy, there is almost no data of a systematic nature on crime in the ghetto, for obvious reasons: criminals are even more reluctant to discuss their economic activities than the rich. However, we can piece together something of a picture from scattered sources.[6]

The ghetto is the home of organized crime that bleeds the poor of hundreds of millions of dollars annually. Four criminal industries are particularly important: numbers, loansharking, drugs, and prostitution. They comprise the bulk of that portion of the irregular economy outside the law.

The most lucrative is the numbers racket, or policy game, a form of gambling in which an individual bets on a three-digit number, with the winning number selected by chance—for example, the last three digits of the day's parimutuel receipts at a major racetrack. The payoff is very large, but the odds against winning are even larger. The operator does not have to be dishonest to realize large earnings as long as the odds are fixed at the proper level.

A high proportion of slum residents plays the policy game. The New York State Joint Legislative Committee on Crime estimated that, in 1968, the policy game was played by 75 percent of all adult and older teenage slum residents in New York City, who bet an average of $3.00 to $5.00 per week. In the three ghetto areas of Harlem,

South Bronx, and Bedford-Stuyvesant, some $150 million were spent on it annually, according to estimates made by city and state officials.

In order to operate the numbers racket, a network of organized crime permeates the entire ghetto. Hundreds of "runners" fan out into houses, apartments, stores, and factories to collect bets. The runners bring the bets and records to "controllers," usually store owners who collect the money, record the bets, and send the information to the "bank" or "office" via runners or pick-up men. The controller generally receives 35 percent of the bets brought in by his runners, who are usually paid a salary. The numbers banker gets the rest, out of which comes the day's payoff to winners. The controller is usually responsible for expenses, such as bail and legal fees for the participants who are arrested "in the line of duty," and payoffs to police. The overall profit margin of a numbers network is about 25 percent, after all costs. Most of the money does not stay in the ghetto. Although some of the runners and controllers may be residents of the ghetto, the men at the top generally are not. In New York City, for example, the numbers game employs many blacks and Hispanics, but the top management in 1970 was alleged to be the Mafia—some of whom had been driven from the city by the police and operated through lieutenants as absentee lords of the racket.

Loansharking is closely associated with numbers gambling. The numbers bank is a source of funds, and the network of runners provides a means of communication. There is also a network of loan sharks who haunt the street corners, stores, and work-places. Small loans are made at interest rates that range upward to 20 percent per week. Once a loan is made, usually for $10 to $25, little pressure for repayment is exercised as long as the interest is paid regularly. Ghetto residents are at the mercy of this system, for many of them need money before payday or the arrival of the welfare check. Their resources are often meager, and there are no other sources of loans. Lenders do not fear betrayal to the police because their customers have no other source to turn to in emergencies.

Narcotics is a much smaller but far more profitable segment of the criminal underworld. Based on estimates made by the New York State Joint Legislative Committee on Crime, the three major slum areas of New York City had between 12,000 and 24,000 drug addicts in 1968. The number has probably increased substantially owing to a major increase in drug use in the years since the black revolt of the mid–1960s. The average addict needed then about $30 a day for drugs, or about $10,000 a year. This would bring the gross revenue of the narcotics business in the three major ghettos to between $120 million and $250 million annually in 1968.

The figure is undoubtedly much larger today. In the late 1960s, police authorities believed that the business was controlled by the Mafia to an even greater extent than numbers and loansharking. With greatly intensified law enforcement drives against the traffic in drugs, however, the more risky parts of the business, importation and distribution, have been increasingly turned over to blacks, Hispanics, and Latin Americans eager for the high profits that can be gained. Control, financing, and the bulk of the profits remained within the established gangland structure, although by the early 1980s Colombians who controlled the manufacture and transportation of heroin may have taken over most wholesale drug operations in a number of eastern cities.

Narcotics are the source of two complementary industries, prostitution and the distribution of stolen goods. The narcotics addict must have a steady, high income. Unless he or she is part of the drug business itself, there is little opportunity to earn the money needed. Girls and women turn to prostitution and boys and men to stealing. Both provide the base for industries in which the workers earn enough to sustain their drug habit while others reap large profits.

The traffic in stolen goods is heavy. Most of the business is carried on through fences, who normally pay 20 percent of the wholesale value of the goods. An addict who needs $10,000 a year to support his habit has to steal $50,000 worth of saleable merchandise annually. On this basis, addicts of the three major New York City ghettos alone would have been responsible for the theft of some $300 to $500 million in 1968 if one-half of the cost of their drug habit were financed by stealing.

The goods move into a nationwide distribution network. They are sold to legitimate business firms in all parts of the country at two to three times the cost to the fence, which is still only 40 to 60 percent of the normal wholesale price. Much of this wholesale trade is said to be in the hands of the Mafia and represents its "legitimate" face. Even some of the retail outlets that deal in stolen goods at second- or third-hand have, it is believed, come under Mafia control.

The ghetto suffers most of all. Most of the narcotics addicts are slum-dwelling blacks and Hispanics. They steal from nearby sources, preying on their own neighborhoods. Ghetto business enterprise suffers heavily. According to several studies, robberies of stores in central-city commercial areas occur twice as frequently as in the suburbs, and armed robberies during business hours are four times as frequent. Enterprises lose as a result, pay higher insurance costs if insurance can be obtained, and pass on the higher costs to their customers. When special law enforcement and crime prevention programs are instituted in ghetto areas, the stealing is moved to surrounding parts of the city—which is the chief reason (rather than graft) that little is done about it. The political repercussions from non-ghetto areas make a hands-off containment policy the sensible policy for city governments.

Public opinion in the ghetto about the crime that preys upon its residents is mixed. On the one hand, there is strong support for action against the narcotics traffic because of its subversion of the young and its connection with prostitution, stealing, and armed robbery. On the other hand, there is a good deal of informal admiration for the successful hustler, who has power and money and who is able to meet the white, non-ghetto world on its own terms. This attitude is particularly strong among the young, for whom most other opportunities are highly restricted. In addition, the inability of law enforcement agencies to distinguish bweeen criminals and ordinary citizens—the source of much of the "harassment" of which blacks and Hispanics complain—makes many ghettoites leery of increased police action. Finally, the illegal industries permeate the lives of many ghettoites, providing important sources of excitement, entertainment, and emergency sources of funds. Crime is an integral part of the functioning economic system and will continue as long as the system remains.

A Separate World

The labor market of the inner-city ghetto is an integral part of the economy of our urban areas. It provides a low-wage workforce employed largely in the service industries, creating a low-cost base for export industries and their complements and for the living standards of middle- and upper-income groups. The low-wage system is preserved by high levels of unemployment which create continual pressures in the labor market to keep wages low.

The low-income population of the ghetto, in turn, supports an irregular economy that offers supplementary employment and income, but which functions in quite different ways from the economy outside the ghetto. The criminal industries are part of the irregular economy. By exploiting the ghetto, they drain off resources and help keep the ghetto poor. Crime contributes to the preservation of the ghetto, and thereby to the presence of a reservoir of low-wage labor.

This view of the ghetto economy differs from the conventional theory of modern economics, which tends to view the labor market as a unified whole, as a seamless web of economic relationships in which all the parts are closely articulated. In that scheme, low wages are the result of low productivity, and the poverty of the ghetto is the result of low levels of education and skill. The fact that the ghettos are heavily black and Hispanic is attributed in large part to racial attitudes of employers. The "seamless web" theory of labor markets focuses not on structural deficiencies in the organization of the economy, but on elimination of discrimination and improvement of the poor. These ideas are examined in the following chapter, and are shown to be seriously deficient. Rather, we find a labor market in which minorities are crowded into menial occupations. It shows how the structure of labor markets lies behind the low wages and lack of opportunity that are associated with the ghetto economy. If the analysis in these chapters is correct, the ghetto is indeed a separate world structured in such a way as to create an exploited class whose prospects are permanent poverty and continued exploitation.

12

Discrimination and Coerced Labor

THE CONVENTIONAL WISDOM AMONG ECONOMISTS EMPHASIZES TWO different approaches to racial discrimination and economic disparities between blacks and whites. One is an extension of utility theory and is closely associated with Gary S. Becker, whose book *The Economics of Discrimination*[1] has become a classic in economic analysis. The heart of Becker's theory is that individual employers and workers have a "taste for discrimination," which provides nonmonetary or psychic satisfactions from not employing or working beside black or other minority workers. The second approach has been developed out of work on human capital and stresses education, training, health, and other personal characteristics of low-income groups that are associated with poverty. In this theory, both black and white workers earn incomes determined by their productivity, but limited access to education and training keeps the productivity of black workers below that of white workers. The solution to the problem, in this view, is to improve the education and training of blacks.

Both of these theories of discrimination would solve the problem by changing people. Becker would change those who discriminate, while the human capital theorists would change those who are discriminated against to eliminate the poor education and low productivity associated with low incomes. Both theories have the comforting quality of drawing attention away from the institutionalized sources of the problem analyzed in this book. In these theories, people are the problem, not social and economic processes.

More radical analyses of discrimination emphasize the class structure of capitalist America as the source of the problem. Michael Reich and Paul A. Baran and Paul M. Sweezy argue that racial prejudices and discrimination are fostered both by market forces—whites and blacks competing for a limited number of jobs—and by deliberate actions of employers to create divisions and hostility among workers— preferential hiring of whites and use of black strikebreakers, for example.[2] In this view, discrimination in the workplace is a byproduct of the larger class conflict of a capitalist society.

A broader analysis has its roots in the classic study of the American racial problem by Gunnar Myrdal. Myrdal emphasized the self-reinforcing conditions of poverty and deprivation which keep blacks in a disadvantaged position. Blacks have high unemployment rates and low wages, are concentrated in menial occupations, obtain inferior educations, and have inadequate healthcare. All of these disadvantages reinforce each other and lead to perpetuation of black disadvantages in a vicious circle of poverty and lack of opportunity. In this view, the heritage of slavery is of major importance, for it imposed on blacks the original disadvantages from which they have been unable to recover.[3]

Lester C. Thurow combined the Becker and human capital theories with some elements of Myrdal's analysis. In *Poverty and Discrimination* (1969), he argued that whites, seeking to maximize their incomes and to maintain a social distance from blacks, use their control over economic resources to maintain a variety of forms of discrimination in employment, wages, occupational choice, investment in human capital, and so on. These types of discrimination interact with each other to keep blacks in an economically disadvantaged position. The legal system and government action are often used to reinforce discriminatory practices (the book was published before many of these practices were halted). Thurow argued, however, that if legal and government support for discrimination were ended, the chief remaining problems could be resolved by discontinuing discrimination in human capital. Education and training for blacks would lead to higher incomes for them and reduction or elimination of income differentials between blacks and whites. This, in turn, would reduce other forms of discrimination.[4] "Attacking human capital discrimination will not raise Negro incomes by itself, since wage, employment, and occupational discrimination also have to be eliminated, but eliminating human capital discrimination would make the enforcement of these other types difficult in the absence of government discrimination."[5]

Thurow put much less emphasis on human capital in a 1975 volume, *Generating Inequality*, where he developed a "job competition" explanation for the severe underrepresentation of blacks in the high-wage sector of the labor market.[6] He starts with the fact that most employees learn skills on the job. To minimize training costs, employers rank potential workers on the basis of their expected on-the-job training costs. Education is a common measure of a potential employee's ability to absorb the necessary job skills. "Through education one learns how to be trained or exhibits that one is trainable."[7] This of course supports the notion that improved education and training for blacks leads to greater job access. But more education by itself may not necessarily guarantee improved employment prospects, especially in times of labor surplus. Employee stability, educational credentials notwithstanding, may in the minds of employers be greater among whites than blacks. If higher black worker turnover leads the employer to believe that blacks are less likely than whites to complete the necessary period of on-the-job training, then whites will be the preferred applicants. Especially in cases where breaking in the new employee is costly, small differences in perceived worker stability may lead to racial discrimination in hiring. The training completion rate for blacks may be 80 percent versus 85 percent for whites; blacks may average seven years before quitting versus eight years for whites. In this situation, the employer hires whites if he can. In periods of labor shortage, however, the same employer may be faced with a shortage of ideally qualified white candidates. In this situation, the better-educated black job seeker may be hired rather than the less educated white—expected training costs may now be minimized by hiring the most qualified black worker. Thus, Thurow's job competition model does not postulate that blacks face rigid barriers in the primary job market. Job applicants are ranked according to numerous traits that are correlated in the employer's eyes with subsequent performance: education, race, sex, age, marital status, and past work history. The perceived greater instability of black applicants is weighed simultaneously with these other traits. As a result, better-educated blacks may have improved job access, and yet their race may still be an attribute that is weighed against them when hiring decisions are made. Thurow's job competition model is also consistent with the fact that black worker access to better paying primary sector jobs improves very dramatically in tight labor markets, such as that of the mid-to late 1960s.

A related argument considers the institutional structure of labor markets as the most important source of discrimination. According to this analysis, blacks and other minority groups are largely employed in the secondary labor market, where production is labor-intensive, employment is erratic, and productivity and wages are low. In contrast, the primary labor market, which features capital-intensive production, relatively stable employment, high productivity, and high wages and salaries, employs chiefly white workers. In this view, discrimination is the result primarily of the institutional structure of the economy.[8]

This chapter develops further the line of argument begun by Myrdal as extended by Thurow and the theory of segmented labor markets. The key point is that the dynamic forces which create urban ghettos also bring about a pattern of segmentation in the labor market in which minorities are crowded into low-wage occupations. Labor market "crowding" then serves to reinforce the economic processes responsible for the crowding, by sustaining a segment of the labor force with low productivity and poor skills that has few, if any, alternatives. Seen from this perspective, labor market crowding is simply a sophisticated form of coerced labor, other forms of which include slavery, serfdom, indentured labor, and various forms of sharecropping.

First, however, we take a closer look at Becker's "taste for discrimination" theory and the arguments of the human capital theorists.

The Taste for Discrimination

Becker's theory of discrimination fills a gap in the theory of the competitive market. In that theory, the interplay of individual consumers desiring to maximize their utility with producers seeking to maximize their gains brings a social optimum in which net benefits are maximized. Any departure of actual behavior from the assumptions about consumers or producers results in a less than optimum solution in which the social product is reduced. Some producers or consumers, or both, receive less than they would if the purely competitive market solution were achieved. Racial discrimination is excluded from this model by the assumptions made about individual behavior and by the driving forces of competition, which press economic units to maximize their net gains. Irrational behavior such as racial prejudice has no place in the race to optimize economic benefits.

Becker's contribution made a place for racial prejudice in this theoretic model. He postulated that participants in a transaction may have a taste for discrimination which influences their behavior along with the expected gains from the transaction. A white employer with a taste for discrimination against blacks will be willing to give up a certain amount of profit in order to hire white workers instead of blacks; a white employee with a taste for discrimination will be willing to take a somewhat lower wage in order to avoid working alongside blacks. The strength of the taste for discrimination can be measured by the amount of income each would be willing to forego in order to indulge his or her racist tendency.

This is the key to Becker's analysis. As a market imperfection, the taste for discrimination causes a reduced money income for the one who practices discriminaiton as well as for the person who is discriminated against. This conclusion is inherent in the theoretical base since it is assumed (advocates would say proven) that the competitive market results in maximum net gains for society. If that is true, any imperfection must be accompanied by losses that are shared to a greater or lesser degree by the participants in the market transactions.

Becker goes on to derive a series of theorems relating to discrimination. Discrimination will harm those discriminated against more than those who discriminate if the former are an economic minority supplying only a relatively small portion of the labor supply. The wages of workers who are the object of discrimination will be reduced while those workers who are not discriminated against will earn higher wages. However, employers will lose because they will have to pay more for the labor they hire. And if the minority workers attempt to retaliate against discrimination, they will lose more than will those who discriminate because, as a minority, they have little capital and weak bargaining power.

Market competition would work in the long run to reduce and possibly eliminate wage differentials between blacks and whites, even though it may not eliminate segregation on the job. Firms that hire low-wage blacks rather than higher-wage whites will have a competitive cost advantage that will enable them to grow more rapidly. Even if the taste for discrimination leads to separation of the races on the job, wage rates will tend to be equalized as the forces of competition take effect.

Becker did not carry his policy analysis beyond this point, but other conservatives have done so. Milton Friedman argued that persuasion rather than government intervention was the proper course. "In a society based on free discussion, the appropriate course is for me to seek to persuade them [those who have a taste for discrimination] that their tastes are bad and that they should change their views and their behavior, not to use coercive power to enforce my tastes and my attitudes on others."[9]

Friedman opposed government intervention on several grounds. It is a violation of the principle of freedom of contract. Business firms may lose sales if they are forced to hire blacks while their customers or other employees have a taste for discrimination. And once the principle is established, government intervention, voted by a majority, may be used to promote rather than to reduce discrimination. Leave the matter to market forces and persuasion.[10]

Setting aside its policy implications for the moment, there has been considerable criticism of Becker's theory. Becker argued that discrimination by whites left them worse off than if there were no discrimination, the difference being made up by the psychic income derived from discriminaiton and segregation. Anne O. Krueger was able to show that this conclusion was incorrect, that whites could gain economically as well as psychically from racial discrimination in the workplace. White workers, in particular, can gain from discrimination that reduces economic opportunities for blacks.[11]

Another problem with the theory is that economic competition does not seem to reduce differences in earned incomes. If we assume that the economy is largely competitive and that business firms are profit-oriented, why have discrimination and income differences based on race or sex remained? Employers with little or no taste for discrimination could be expected to hire low-wage workers and gain a competitive advantage over employers who discriminate and hire whites at higher wages. In the long run, the discriminating employers should be driven out of business by those who do not discriminate. In the process, the wages and salaries of blacks and other minority groups will rise. The theory of competition tells us that the differentials between white and black incomes should tend to disappear. Why has that not happened? One possibility, which is stressed by the human capital theory, is that the differences in incomes represent differences in productivity that result from differences in educational attainment.[12]

Kenneth J. Arrow made a more sophisticated use of productivity theory that roughly parallels parts of Thurow's job competition analysis. Even though blacks and whites may have equal innate characteristics, the past history of the two races may have caused whites to develop work habits and to acquire skills that give them greater productivity than blacks. Employers will then use skin color as a rough rule of thumb for hiring, as a cheap substitute for more costly information. This, in turn, will provide incentives for whites to acquire the needed work habits and skills, and to discourage blacks from doing so. Even employers without a taste for discrimination will act in this way.[13] Arrow adds two other factors that could prevent competitive adjustments from eliminating income differentials between white and black workers, the cost of hiring and firing, and the erroneous beliefs of employers. That is, discrimination itself can cause employers to adopt beliefs that justify their actions even though the beliefs are not congruent with reality.[14]

There are other possible reasons for the persistence of disparities in wages and salaries not attributable to differences in relevant economic characteristics of individuals or groups. Various forms of market control can make a difference, such as access to or control of capital, or the ability of unions or professional associations' to exclude individuals from access to jobs. Minimum wage legislation may cause the number of people seeking low-wage jobs to exceed the number of jobs, thereby enabling employers to indulge their taste for discrimination. Indeed, a general surplus of labor relative to job openings can have the same effect. Public policies that encourage location of firms in suburban areas, without provision of adequate public transportation facilities, can restrict access to jobs on the part of inner-city residents. Traditional patterns of access to jobs may leave some groups at the back of the line while others move to the front. To these so-called market imperfections can be added differences in access to information about job opportunities, and a desire on the part of some individuals for jobs that do not require continuous work or strict labor discipline, even at the cost of lower wages. All of these "market imperfections" could lead to wage and salary differentials, despite otherwise competitive adjustments.[15]

Finally, theorists in the Becker tradition can argue that the attitudes of white workers may affect the hiring policies of employers. If white workers have attitudes of malice or envy toward black workers, their attitudes can be transmitted to employers who will then act as if they had the same attitudes.[16] As Arrow points out, placating white workers may be necessary for profit maximization. Discriminatory attitudes, beliefs, and tastes, plus lack of accurate information about the productivity of individual workers and numerous market imperfections, account for the failure of market forces to eliminate income differentials between whites and blacks.

All of these efforts to explain why discrimination could be sustained in a competitive economy have a common deficiency. They are all short-run explanations, particularly those that rely on market imperfections. In the long run, smart entrepreneurs should take advantage of lower wages for blacks to make a profit for themselves, thereby reducing the black–white income differential and, in the end, eliminating it entirely.[17]

Human Capital

The theory of human capital attributes lower incomes for blacks to lower productivity caused by lesser amounts of human capital than whites. According to this analysis, all workers earn a wage or salary equal to their productivity at the margin. If a worker produces $10 worth of product each day, an employer would be unwilling to pay a daily wage of more than $10. On the other hand, if that worker were paid less than $10, a competitive employer would hire him away by offering more. In the competitive market, the forces of competition would assure the worker of a $10 daily wage, neither more nor less.

A worker's productivity is determined by three factors. First, the worker's native abilities. A more intelligent worker can do more complicated tasks and learn them more quickly than a less intelligent worker. Second, the amount and quality of physical capital at the worker's disposal. A worker with a bulldozer can move more dirt per hour than a worker with a shovel. Third, the amount and quality of the worker's education, training, and experience. This is the worker's human capital. More human capital enables a worker to produce more and therefore earn more, such as, for example, the knowledge of how to operate a bulldozer. In this theory, if native abilities are equal and the same capital equipment is used, productivity and earnings will vary with the quantity and quality of the human capital of workers.

Earnings are also affected by the ability of workers to move into job opportunities where the prospects for advancement are good. A worker who has little job mobility will be less able to transform his human capital into earnings than a worker with the opportunity to shift easily into another job. A closely related factor is the availability of on-the-job training. Some employers provide more extensive in-service training than others, and a worker's earnings are influenced by his or her ability to move into those sectors of the labor market where on-the-job training is offered. These qualifications modify the argument but do not change the basic theory: in a competitive labor market, differences in earnings are strongly related to differences in the quantity and quality of human capital.[18]

Empirical studies do not support the hypothesis that differences in human capital are a major cause of black–white earnings differentials. Most studies used years of education as a proxy for human capital, leaving aside the problem of quality of schooling and on-the-job training and experience. Stephan Michelson found that differences in years of schooling accounted for only about 6 to 9 percent of black–white earnings differentials. Otis Dudley Duncan could account for only 14 percent of black-white income differences through years of schooling. James D. Gwartney estimated that differences in productivity accounted for about two-thirds of the difference in incomes of black and white workers, but years of schooling were responsible for only about 21 percent of the gap. Approximately one-third of the gap was due to employment discrimination, according to Gwartney's study. Stanley H. Masters found that years of schooling could account for about 10 percent of the black–white earnings gap, and that discrimination against blacks seemed to be greater for blacks with more schooling. He also found that steadiness of employment was important: blacks with above-average education and steady jobs had a smaller income gap when compared with whites, but schooling still accounted for less than 20 percent of the gap.[19]

These findings are consistent with census data from the 1970s. For example, in 1977 black college graduates earned about as much ($12,649) as a white high school graduate, and a white high school dropout earned more ($9,735) than a black high school graduate ($9,147).[20] These data show clearly that years of schooling are associated with higher earnings for both blacks and whites, which tends to confirm the theory of human capital. But they also show that the theory of human capital can account for only a small portion of the black–white earnings differential.

The Crowding Hypothesis

Black workers have traditionally been restricted to low-wage occupations requiring relatively little skill. This pattern was changed, in part, by entry of a limited number of blacks into industrial employment, particularly during the two world wars, and by increased black employment in white-collar jobs during the 1950s and 1960s. But these breakthroughs into new sectors of the labor market were relatively limited. For the most part, blacks and other minority groups are found heavily in the secondary, rather than the primary, sector of the labor market.

The secondary sector of the labor market comprises both service and industrial occupations. The jobs are low-paid, relatively unskilled, and often unstable: employment is affected by seasonal and cyclical instability. Jobs are relatively labor-intensive, which means that worker productivity is low. Firms are often small and markets are competitive. These businesses tend to compete by "squeezing" labor. Most of the secondary labor market is not unionized.

When any minority group is crowded into a relatively small number of occupations, wage rates are depressed in those occupations because of the artificially increased supply of labor. Meanwhile, the supply of labor in other occupations is decreased, leading to wage rates somewhat higher than they would otherwise be in those occupations. Thus, workers in the white majority can benefit from the crowding of black workers into menial occupations. Analysis of this phenomenon was first developed in modern economics during the drive for women's rights in the period from 1890 to 1925 and culminated in Francis Y. Edgeworth's classic 1922 article on equal pay for men and women.[21]

To illustrate the hypothesis, we start with two occupations that require the same level of skills, and examine, first, the results in a color-blind economy and, second, the results in an economy with racial discrimination. In the color-blind economy, assuming competition in the labor market, the forces of supply and demand result in the same wage rate in the two occupations. Any wage differential will cause labor to shift from one to the other, since skill levels are the same, until wages are equalized. Furthermore, employers will hire workers in each occupation up to the point at which the amount added to total revenue by the additional worker is just equal to the wage paid (the theory of marginal productivity applies here). The results are shown in figure 12.1.

Now we close one occupation to blacks and force them into jobs in the other occupation, reserving the closed occupation for whites. Wage rates in the two occupations will differ, and the numbers employed will also shift. Wages fall in the occupation into which the minority group is crowded, as shown in figure 12.2. Meanwhile, wages rise in the occupation from which minorities are excluded, as shown in figure 12.3.

A number of corollary propositions follow from this analysis of crowding. First, total employment need not be reduced. Wages will fall in the crowded occupation until all those who are willing to work

FIGURE 12.1. Color-Blind economy: Two occupations with similar skill levels.

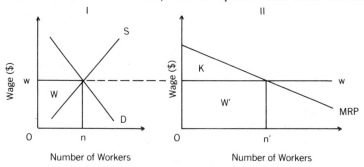

Wages in both occupations are the same, since skills are interchangeable. In Diagram I the wage in both occupations is determined by the interaction of demand and supply at level w, while n workers are employed. W is the total wage bill. Diagram II shows the individual employer hiring n' workers at wage w, given the marginal revenue product as shown by MRP. W' is the total wage bill of the individual employer, and K is the amount retained for payments to other factors of production, such as capital. (Marginal revenue product is the name given to the additional revenues obtained by adding one unit of a factor of production to a fixed amount of other factors, for example, adding an additional worker to the existing work force in a manufacturing plant.)

at those wages are employed. Similarly, the higher wage in the other occupation will clear the market and assure employment of all willing workers. These conclusions assume, however, that the level of aggregate demand is sustained at full-employment levels to assure jobs for the entire workforce. The white workers who earn higher wages need not fear unemployment as long as the national economy is healthy.

FIGURE 12.2. "Crowding" reduces wages rates in occupation A.

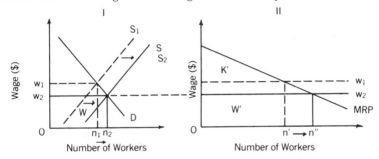

In Diagram I the increase in supply of labor in occupation A, due to "crowding," shifts the supply curve from S_1 to S_2, with demand conditions remaining unchanged. The wage falls from w_1 to w_2 and the number employed increases from n_1 to n_2. The total amount of wage paid (W) may or may not increase. In Diagram II the individual employer increases the number of workers he hires from n' to n'' (his wage bill, W', may or may not increase). However, the value of the marginal product has fallen, since w_2 is less than w_1. As we shall see, this indicates a misallocation of resources from society's point of view. In addition, the amount paid to other factors (K') rises.

FIGURE 12.3. "Crowding" of the minority in occupation A causes wages to rise in occupation B.

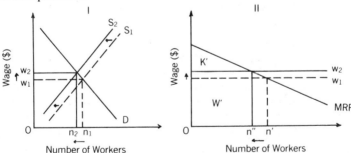

In Diagram I the decreased supply of workers in occupation B due to exclusion of blacks shifts the supply curve to the left of S_1 to S_2. With no change in demand the wage rate increases from w_1 to w_2 and employment falls from n_1 to n_2. These changes are reflected in Diagram II in individual employers' reordering of their activities. They hire fewer workers because of the higher wage rate (n' falls to n''). Labor productivity at the margin is higher than it was before (w_2 is greater than w_1). While the total wage bill (W') may or may not change, the amount paid to other factors of production (K') is reduced.

A more important corollary is the effect on work incentives among the minority group. Since wages in the crowded occupation will be abnormally low, the incentive to work (as against leisure time or ir-regular occupations) will be reduced. As a result, labor force partic-ipation rates among the minority group will be lower than among the majority, whose higher wages encourage a greater amount of work as compared to leisure. This expected result is consistent with the empirical finding that labor force participation rates are higher among whites than among blacks.

Related to this phenomenon is the movement of minority groups into criminal occupations. Low wages and exclusion from higher-wage occupations provide incentives to try for the rewards available from crime. This channeling of minorities into crime by economic forces has been characteristic of our history, attracting immigrant minorities from the Irish to Jews to Italians and now to blacks and Hispanics. The majority of any minority group have always been honest and law-abiding citizens, but there are strong economic incentives that draw a large proportion of minority groups into criminal activities.

Another result of crowding is payment of substandard wages to minority employees when they are able to get jobs in the higher-wage occupations. The alternative employment for a black engineer is a low-wage, menial occupation. He is willing, therefore, to accept less than the standard wage for engineers. Employers are aware of this situation, and enough of them take advantage of it to create the pattern of unequal wage rates for the same job between whites and blacks, men and women, and other groups subjected to crowding. In recent years there has been some modification of this unequal pay syndrome because of federal government pressure on firms produc-ing under government contract, but differential pay is still prevalent.

Crowding of minority groups into menial occupations brings about a noticeable misallocation of resources. Employment in the low-wage occupations is greater than it would be without crowding, while there is less employment in other occupations. This can be seen by referring back to figures 12.2 and 12.3. Lower wages in the crowded occupations result in more employment there. Higher wages in other occupations are accompanied by reduced employment in those jobs. At the same time, a larger total return to other factors of production (K in fig. 12.2) encourages expanded employment in the crowded occupations, while a smaller return to the other factors in the non-crowded oc-cupations (K in fig. 12.3) reduces employment there. The result is misallocation of all kinds of resources into the low-wage occupations and industries. Both labor and capital could be shifted to uses in which returns are higher. This is a loss that must be borne by everyone.

Although it is not obvious at first glance that overexpansion of low-wage industries and overemployment in low-wage occupations are harmful to the economy as a whole, that is, in fact, the case. Shifting a worker from an occupation in which he produces goods worth $3.50 per hour to one in which he produces $5.50 per hour brings a net benefit of $2.00 per hour to the economy as a whole.

Crowding should not bring the employer any special benefits or losses if competition prevails. Even though the firm pays low wages to some workers, competition will push his profits down to the normal level. Only if the employer is in a monopolistic position can he gain from crowding, and then only if he hires enough low-wage workers to more than offset the higher amounts he pays in other occupations.

The chief gainers from crowding are workers from the majority population. They earn more than they would if greater competition for jobs from minority groups were present. This has always been true and helps to explain why workers seek to maintain segregated occupational patterns.

The crowding hypothesis has been criticized on the same grounds as Becker's theory of discrimination: profit-seeking employers will hire low-wage workers from the secondary labor market to replace higher paid workers. This will reduce and ultimately eliminate the wage differential between the two. Empirical evidence does not support this criticism. The difference between wage rages in the primary and secondary sectors of the labor market has been widening during the 1970s. It tended to narrow in the 1950s and 1960s, when labor markets were relatively tight, but it widened when unemployment rates rose during the 1970s. There does not seem to be a consistent tendency for employers to substitute workers from the low-wage secondary sector of the labor market for higher paid primary workers.

There are good reasons why workers do not move readily from the secondary to the primary sectors of the labor market. Workers in the primary sector learn to work regular hours, report to work on time, take regular and specified work breaks, and respect the authority and discipline of the supervisor or the assembly line. By contrast, work in the secondary sector is often irregular, supervision is less rigorous, hours are less regular, and time requirements less strict. Workers who learn the more flexible routines of the secondary labor market need to learn new work habits and patterns of discipline when moving into the primary sector. During the transition period, their productivity is reduced and the employer's costs of training and supervision are increased. After the transition period, their productivity may be just as great as that of other workers, but we would expect more to drop out during the period of transition (which also adds to hiring costs) and that employers will have little incentive to hire them in the first place. These considerations help to explain why tight labor markets are a key condition for the movement of workers from the secondary to the primary sectors of the labor market.

A second factor is the relatively high degree of unionization in the primary labor market. The natural desire of labor unions to protect the jobs and wage rates of their members leads them to oppose the hiring of "substandard" workers—those willing to work for lower wages. An employer who insisted on doing so would arouse antagonism on the part of the existing workforce and the union leadership. They would be more difficult to deal with in collective bargaining. Employers, then, feel pressures from the existing work-force and its union representatives to hire new workers at wage rates equal to those paid to the existing workforce. An employer who did otherwise would face the prospect of heightened worker unrest and perhaps a costly strike. Even if a union were not present, such hiring policies could readily lead to unionization of employees. It is easier to continue hiring workers who are already in the primary workforce.

The hiring process itself adds to the barriers between the secondary and primary sectors of the labor market. The employer usually knows little about a prospective employee beyond age, sex, race, education, and what the employee or references can tell about experience in other jobs. These characteristics must be matched against the requirements of the job and the work habits required. If regular on-time attendance is mandatory and the employer's experience indicates that workers from the secondary sector of the labor market are a poor risk in that respect, those workers will be put near the bottom of the list of potential employees. Workers who have had jobs in which they learned the proper work habits will be placed nearer the top of the list. Thus, workers already in the primary sector of the labor market will tend to stay there and workers in the secondary sector will have difficulty in getting out. This "statistical discrimination," to use Thurow's phrase, causes the characteristics of a worker's peer group to determine the worker's employment prospects, rather than his or her individual characteristics.[22]

The process of being relegated to inferior secondary sector employment creates a self-fulfilling prophecy: rejection from better jobs leads to employment in the secondary labor market. Low-paying work that is unskilled and often unstable teaches employees bad work habits and negative attitudes toward employers; these traits in turn lead primary sector employers to view blacks as less reliable workers. Blacks thus treated are often less stable workers and their discriminatory treatment in the high-wage sectors may persist because actual labor market performance appears to confirm employer stereotypes.

Crowding and Economic Opportunity

Opening opportunities for blacks in higher-level occupations may appear to be the policy that would diminish and ultimately eliminate crowding, but that is not necessarily the case. In the 1960s, for example, under the impact of sustained economic growth, the civil rights movement, and government sponsored affirmative action hiring programs, there was a significant increase in the number of blacks in higher-level occupations. Between 1960 and 1969, the number of black men over twenty-five years of age in professional and technical occupations increased by 107 percent. In managerial occupations, the number increased by 117 percent. Other large increases occurred in employment as craftsmen (52 percent) and salesmen (42 percent). All of these percentage increases were greater than the percentage increase in black men over twenty-five years of age in the labor force as a whole. During the 1970s, in a stagnant economy and a changed political environment, these gains largely ceased. Blacks continued to move into higher level occupations, but at a rate about the same as the increase in the black population of working age. That is, the proportion of blacks in the primary sector of the labor force did not increase significantly. The bulk of the black population remained in the secondary labor market, crowded in the low-wage occupations.

It is quite possible for new opportunities to open for minority groups while the bulk of the minority remains crowded in menial occupations. Imagine a hypothetical urban metropolitan area in which 10 percent of the jobs are in low-wage occupations, 10 percent of the labor force is black, and all of the blacks are employed in the low-wage sector. It is a hypothetical situation of "perfect" crowding. Now let the local demand for labor expand at a given rate, say 5 percent annually, but the black population and workforce expands at a 10 percent annual rate while the white population grows by only 5 percent each year. Assuming no change in output per worker, we would expect several changes in the city's economy:

1. The overall unemployment rate will rise because overall population growth is more rapid than the rate of growth in the demand for labor. But the increase in unemployment will be concentrated very heavily among blacks. The black, low-wage sector of the economy grows at a 5 percent rate while the labor force crowded into that sector grows twice as rapidly. The white labor force, however, grows no more rapidly than the number of jobs in its sector of the workforce.

2. Simultaneously, employment in the low-wage sector will increase relative to employment in the high-wage sector. The high unemployment rate among blacks will push wages down in the low-wage sector, enabling employers to employ more workers there. This effect will mitigate the increase in black unemployment.

3. Some blacks may find employment in the white sector of the economy, even though the low-wage sector remains black. It is quite possible for blacks to move into such occupational categories as managerial, professional, technical, crafts, and sales without significantly modifying the process by which the bulk of the black labor force is crowded into menial occupations.

4. This movement of blacks into the high-wage sector will displace whites. White unemployment will rise and some whites will "skid" into low-wage jobs from which blacks will be "bumped" into unemployment or out of the labor force entirely. This process will increase the black-white antagonisms that are one of the underlying causes of crowding.

These expected effects of crowding are in general agreement with the historical record. As blacks moved north into urban areas from about 1910 to the present, the proportion of blacks in the workforce increased. This population movement, together with the process of crowding, led initially to a largely black labor force in the low-wage sector. This was followed by an upward shift in the unemployment rate for blacks as compared with whites, expansion of the low-wage sector itself, and a movement of some blacks into the high-wage sector, particularly during periods of tightness in the labor market. But this upward movement of some blacks was accompanied by ghettoization of most and an intensification of the economic conditions that sustain the urban ghetto and the process of crowding.

Lack of alternative opportunities is the chief economic factor that preserves the process of crowding. But simply opening opportunities for a portion of the crowded minority does not necessarily stop the process. Reality is far more complex. As we indicated in point 4, opportunities in the high-wage sector may even worsen the crowding process for others. Thus, hiring black college professors, for example, does not significantly modify the crowding of the bulk of the black labor force in low-wage occupations. Nor does the hiring of a woman corporate executive modify the process by which the secretarial and clerk jobs are reserved largely for women. More than affirmative action hiring procedures are needed.

Crowding and Coerced Labor

Crowding of blacks and other minority groups in low-wage occupations is a modern and sophisticated version of coerced labor. It is a phenomenon found throughout history. Slavery is its most obvious form. Labor is coerced by the law that declares slaves to be property, enabling owners to exploit them much as horses and cows are used to produce for humans. Serfdom, in its many forms of dependent peasantry, is another ancient form of coerced labor. The military draft is a contemporary form. The essential element in all types of coerced labor is exploitation of the worker, who receives less than he or she otherwise would if free to do something else.

For coerced labor to exist, alternative opportunities for the worker must be absent or substantially reduced. If the slave, serf, or draftee can evade the system, he or she cannot be coerced into accepting substandard pay. Thus, most systems of coerced labor use the power of the state, through its armies, police, and penal system, to limit the opportunities open to coerced labor and to force it to remain in its exploited condition.

But not always. The sharecropping and debt tenure system in the South after the Civil War (which remained strong through the 1940s—some remnants still survive today) was enforced by economic forces, legal constraints, and community pressures that were often more informal than formal. This is not the place for a history and analysis of the sharecropping and debt tenure system in the South, but the chief elements are important, because many blacks in this country came from that background. A sharecropper used the land owned by someone else, with the landlord often supplying seed and tools and sometimes living expenses. In return, the landlord received a share of the receipts after he was reimbursed for the cost of seed and sustenance. This system grew up after the Civil War when former slaveowners had land but no labor, while the former slaves had labor but no land. It was open to much abuse. The black farmer had little education, and the white landowner usually sold the crop and kept the books.

Simple sharecropping grew into a system of debt tenure. After a bad crop year the tenant might not have earned enough to carry him through the year to the next harvest and to provide seed for the next crop. Money for those purposes would have to be borrowed, either from the landlord or a storekeeper in town. Debt could then become a way of tying the tenant to the land. Debts had to be settled before a family was allowed to leave the land, and the debts had a habit of persisting from year to year. This happened throughout the rural South with poor whites as well as poor blacks—in much the same way as the Biblical Joseph was able to enslave the Egyptian peasantry for the pharaohs by using the stored surplus of seven fat years to make loans during the ensuing seven lean years.

Although sharecropping and debt tenure were used to tie labor to the land, lack of opportunity elsewhere was one of the chief reasons for the long retention of coerced labor in the South. Industry was slow in developing, poverty prevented acquisition of western land, and northern industry was surfeited with unskilled laborers from

Europe. Only with the cessation of immigration and the start of World War I did economic opportunity open the way to ending the coerced labor of the rural South. The black population of the South was able to migrate north to opportunity, and to the urban ghetto.

There a different form of coerced labor appeared. By excluding blacks from higher-paying occupations and crowding them into menial jobs, the pattern of exploitation was continued, but in a different form. The pattern can be found in southern cities as early as the 1890s when the great depression of that decade, particularly strong in agriculture, forced significant numbers of blacks off southern farms in spite of sharecropping and debt tenure. Moving into southern cities, they were met with an upsurge of Jim Crow legislation that imposed rigid segregation and largely eliminated their right to vote.[23] Concurrently, blacks were driven out of a number of urban occupations they had hitherto filled, such as the construction trades, longshoring, and barbering, and were crowded into the menial and low-wage occupations in which they are now found. When industry developed, blacks were largely excluded from the factory jobs except at the lowest custodial level. This happened, for example, in the steel industry in Birmingham and in textiles and furniture manufacturing in the Carolinas. Opportunities that might have broken the grip of sharecropping in the rural South more rapidly were closed off in the cities by restricting higher-paying jobs to whites and crowding blacks into a relatively few low-wage occupations.

Similar developments occurred in the North during and after the First World War. The black migration to northern cities led to the closing of some occupations to blacks in which they had already found a foothold and to their restriction to low-wage occupations. This form of economic exploitation was accompanied by residential segregation. Restrictive covenants in real estate deeds and residential zoning as means of excluding blacks from specific neighborhoods were first used on a large scale in the 1920s. Loss of the franchise and pervasive Jim Crow legislation were never a major feature of the northern reaction, but the results were similar. A pattern of coerced labor based on tradition, custom, and the attitudes of white workers and employers emerged, enforced in part by labor unions but more rigidly by customary practices in the labor market and the educational system.

White racism in unions, however, has also undermined the economic status of white workers. Utilizing blacks as strikebreakers helped companies break strikes and weaken unions quite often in the late nineteenth and early twentieth centuries. Since World War II, black–white worker antagonisms have severely weakened union organizing efforts in the southeastern United States. Failure to organize widely in the South meant that large union wage gains in the late

1940s and 1950s widened North–South wage differentials. This in turn encouraged some unionized industries to expand their southern manufacturing operations.[24] The resultant regional shift in manufacturing activity weakened the overall union movement and exacerbated unemployment among both white and black workers in heavily unionized regions.

At the root of the problem are the forces described in the last chapter that create and sustain the ghetto economy and its force of low-wage labor. Coercion of that portion of the labor force depends not on law, but is built into the structure and functioning of the economy as a whole. The form of coerced labor has changed, but coercion has persisted. The intensity of exploitation diminished but the fact remains that blacks have been kept in a disadvantaged position. They are no longer property. They are no longer held in thrall by a combination of economic circumstance and legal constraint. But they are oppressed by an economic system that relegates them largely to crowded occupations and low-wage jobs.

A variety of interconnected social and economic processes support the modern pattern of coerced labor. One factor is the historical legacy of much of the black population, which denied it the investment in education and work skills available to most whites. The human capital disadvantages of blacks are, in part, the result of generations of substandard education and lack of access to higher-skilled jobs. This process is still at work in the poverty areas of America's cities.

A second factor is racial prejudice and antagonism which historically has deprived blacks of equal opportunities. These white attitudes towards blacks are noticeably strong among low- and middle-income whites whose economic status is threatened as blacks seek to rise in the economic and social order. The most obvious manifestation of these white attitudes is the so-called "white flight" from central-city areas as blacks moved in.

A third factor is stressed in these chapters. The ghetto economy itself preserves and strengthens the existing economic status of the entire black community. The white community benefits from the low-wage labor that is the ghetto's chief export, and white workers benefit from the crowding of black workers in low-wage occupations. A self-sustaining economic process that benefits the white community, supported by the heritage of history and white attitudes, is the modern source of coerced black labor.

Some Conclusions

It is easy and comforting to attribute economic discrimination to faults in the people who discriminate and to those who are discriminated against. Remove prejudices (the taste for discrimination) by education, or counter its effects by legally mandated hiring policies. Promote the accumulation of human capital on the part of minority groups so that they can qualify for higher-level jobs. Change people to solve the problem. The implication is that there is nothing particularly wrong with the way the institutional structure of the economy functions.

These approaches to the problem are clearly inadequate. The theory of the taste for discrimination does not adequately account for the continuing economic disparities between blacks and whites. The theory of human capital can explain only a relatively small portion of those disparities. We must turn instead to an examination of the institutional structure of the economy, where we find two processes at work that enable us to understand the complex nature of the problem.

One is the ghetto itself. It is an integral part of the larger economy, providing a low-wage labor force which benefits the economy outside the ghetto. At the same time, social processes at work in the ghetto provide for its perpetuation, depriving the bulk of the low-wage labor force of the human capital and work habits necessary for success outside the ghetto in the more affluent sector of the economy.

The crowding of blacks and other minority groups in low-wage occupations is the second process at work. It has its roots in the same economic force that creates the ghetto: the benefit of whites. Self-perpetuating forces are also at work in the crowding process. Workers are crowded into occupations requiring little skill, and unemployment rates are high. Trapped in the secondary labor market, there is little incentive to acquire skills for which there is little use.

These institutional structures and the economic processes they embody interact with racial hostility and lack of human capital in a process of mutual causation. Ghettoization and labor market crowding are both causes and effects of racial antagonisms and lack of human capital on the part of blacks and other minority groups. Likewise, racial antagonisms and lack of human capital are at once causes and effects of ghettoization and labor market crowding. Yet the fundamental cause is economic: the white majority benefits.

13

The Welfare System and the
Ghetto Economy

FOUR INCOME TRANSFER PROGRAMS ARE PARTICULARLY IMPORTANT
for the ghetto economy. Two are cash programs designed specifically
to assist the poor, Aid to Families with Dependent Children (AFDC)
and Supplemental Security Income (SSI). Two involve payments in
kind, food stamps and medicaid. All four have means tests designed
to restrict benefits to the needy, as well as other qualifications that
must be met by recipients. There are, in addition, relatively small
specialized assistance programs: Emergency and General Assistance,
Housing Aids, Black Lung benefits, and Energy Assistance. The number and types of income transfers are complex, and their provisions,
eligibility standards, and exclusions are confusing. So we start with a
quick stroll through the welfare landscape to examine its chief con-
tours.

Aid to Families with Dependent Children

AFDC was established in 1935 as part of the Social Security Act. Until
1950, it provided assistance only to children whose parents were absent, disabled, or dead. In 1950, an amendment made possible payments to one parent as well, usually the mother. Additional amendments in 1961 allowed payments to some poor families with two parents and dependent children. These amendments greatly increased
the number of eligible recipients.

Some 80 percent of AFDC families were headed by women in 1980
and only 4 percent by men. Other relatives—grandparents, brothers

191

and sisters, aunts and uncles, cousins, etc.—headed the other 16 percent. About 20 percent of all AFDC families included a father, but in about two-thirds of those cases the father was disabled and a woman or other relative headed the family.[1]

Racial composition of the program has changed very little since 1970. As of 1977, 54 percent of the recipients were white (including Hispanics) and 43 percent were black. The remaining 3 percent were American Indians, Asians, and others.

The typical AFDC household is small. The average number of children in AFDC families was 2.2 in 1977, which is slightly larger than the national average. The difference is not statistically significant. Over three-fourths of all AFDC families (77 percent) lived in towns and cities in 1977, and about 20 percent lived in six large cities, New York, Philadelphia, Detroit, Chicago, Houston, and Los Angeles.[2]

There is a great deal of movement of households into and out of the AFDC program. In the late 1970s the average AFDC household received assistance for about thirty months.[3] About one-third are repeaters, and of the repeaters, some two-thirds received AFDC payments at least twice before.[4] Sporadic or part-time employment and/or low-wage jobs are characteristic of the AFDC population, and there is a significant group of people who move in and out of economic deprivation. Thus, a 1975 study showed that, in any single month, about 16 percent of AFDC mothers were employed and that, over a full year, some 25 to 30 percent would work. The employment, however, was primarily intermittent or seasonal, and was chiefly in the secondary sector of the labor market.[5]

Attempts have been made to reduce AFDC costs by moving heads of households or families into the labor market, but with little success. In 1972, recipients of AFDC were required to register for the new Work Incentive program (WIN). WIN provides both training and employment for adults in AFDC households to enable them to move out of the welfare system. Most AFDC family heads are exempt, including mothers who must care for children under six years of age; the aged, disabled, or sick; mothers whose husbands are in the WIN program; and those who do not live near a WIN project. Although WIN provides child care for an AFDC family head admitted to the program, such funds are very limited and have not been sufficient to allow many to enter. In addition, the number of job-training slots is small. The chief difficulty, in addition to the low skills of most AFDC mothers, is a lack of employment opportunities. There are few jobs to train AFDC mothers to fill without bumping someone else already in the labor market. Furthermore, the most likely positions are low-wage jobs in the secondary labor market, where employment is heavily intermittent and temporary. Finally, adequate child-care facilities are not available. Some four to seven million children would have to be cared for to enable all AFDC mothers to enter the labor force: the WIN program provides facilities for under 100,000 a year.[6]

Eligibility rules create disincentives for work under the AFDC program. Before 1969, payments were reduced by one dollar for each dollar earned—a 100 percent tax. Beginning in 1969, certain "income disregard" rules were adopted that reduced the effective tax to about 67 percent or less: the first $30 per month in earnings were disregarded, as well as 30 percent of any additional earnings, and all job-related expenses. The disregard rules were both eased and tightened in 1981: a standard deduction of $75 per month was allowed for work-related expenses, but the $30 plus one-third of earnings exemption was allowed only during the first four months of employment. The changes encourage both permanent jobs at low wages (the $75 expense allowance) and intermittent work at higher wages (the four-month limit)!

There are other anomalies in the rules. The income disregard provisions apply only to the unemployed who apply for AFDC. This encourages people to quit their jobs in order to obtain AFDC benefits. The 1981 amendments also reduce employment incentives because they leave working mothers with approximately the same income as nonworking mothers. In addition, some twenty-five states allow AFDC payments to families with a father, but eligibility is lost if the father works 100 hours a month or more. That is only twenty-five hours a week, which is not even a full-time job. The wonder is that the portion of AFDC mothers who work is as large as 25 to 30 percent.

AFDC has become large and expensive. In 1960, it assisted about 787,000 families per month for a total cost of a fraction above $1.0 billion. By 1980, it had grown to a program assisting over 3.7 million families per month at an annual cost of almost $12.5 billion.[7] As we shall point out later, this large-scale effort has made life more bearable for many of the poor and needy, but it has done little to remove the causes of poverty. Greater detail on the growth of the AFDC program is given later in this chapter and in table 13.1.

Supplemental Security Income

The federally administered Supplemental Security Income (SSI) program began in 1974, replacing older programs of aid to the blind and disabled and of assistance to needy aged persons. The program is designed to maintain incomes for eligible recipients at a specified amount each month. Keyed to the cost of living, that amount was $284.30 per month ($3,411.60 per year) for an individual in 1982, and $426.40 per month ($5116.80 per year) for a couple if both were eligible. If the individual or couple are living in a household headed

Table 13.1. Chief Transfer Payments to the Poor, 1960–1981
(in billions of dollars)

Year	AFDC	SSI*	PA	Food Stamps	Medicaid	Other Medical Assistance Programs	Total‡
1960	1.0	2.0	0.3	—	—	0.5	3.8
1961	1.2	1.9	0.4	—	—	0.6	4.1
1962	1.3	1.9	0.3	—†	—	0.8	4.3
1963	1.4	2.0	0.3	—	—	1.0	4.7
1964	1.5	2.1	0.3	—	—	1.2	5.1
1965	1.7	2.1	0.3	—	—	1.4	5.5
1966	1.9	2.2	0.3	—	0.4	1.0	5.8
1967	2.3	2.4	0.3	0.1	1.9	0.3	7.3
1968	2.8	2.4	0.4	0.2	3.2	0.2	9.3
1969	3.6	2.6	0.5	0.2	4.1	0.2	11.2
1970	4.9	3.0	0.6	0.6	5.0	0.1	14.1
1971	6.2	3.2	0.8	1.5	6.3	—	18.1
1972	6.9	3.4	0.8	1.8	6.3	—	19.2
1973	7.2	3.5	0.7	2.1	8.7	—	22.2
1974	7.9	5.2	0.9	2.7	10.0	—	26.7
1975	9.2	5.9	1.2	4.4	12.3	—	33.0
1976	10.1	6.1	1.3	5.3	14.1	—	37.0
1977	10.6	6.3	1.3	5.1	16.3	—	39.5
1978	10.7	6.6	1.3	5.2	18.0	—	41.7
1979	11.1	7.1	1.4	6.5	20.5	—	46.5
1980	12.5	7.9	1.6	8.7	23.3	—	54.0
1981	—	8.6	—	10.6	—	—	—

Source: *Social Security Bulletin, Annual Statistical Supplement, 1981,* pp. 78, 220, 225, 247–49; National Center for Social Statistics, *Medicaid: Selected Statistics, 1951–1969* (Washington, D.C.: Government Printing Office, 1970), p. 29.
*Aid to the blind and disabled plus old age assistance, 1960–1973; SSI from 1974.
†Less than $0.1 billion, 1962–1966.
‡Totals may differ from the sum of the columns because of rounding.

by someone else, the guaranteed level is reduced by one-third. The SSI program is designed to bring total income from other sources plus SSI payments up to the specified amounts. For example, if an elderly person has Social Security benefits of $150 per month, SSI will provide $154.30:

Social Security benefits	$150
less $20 per month exemption	− 20
	130
plus SSI benefits	+ 154.30
equals SSI standard	$284.30

This is a program for the truly poor. A single person is not eligible for SSI benefits if he or she has liquid assets of $1,500 or more. A couple is limited to under $2,250. Yet, in 1981, almost 4.5 million blind, disabled, or aged persons received benefits totaling $8.6 billion.[8]

Public Assistance and Other Programs

Two other cash payment programs for the poor can be lumped together under the general heading of Public Assistance (PA). They include Emergency Assistance and General Assistance. Emergency Assistance can be provided under the AFDC program, for a period up to thirty days to needy families with children. In 1980, some 49,000 families per month received Emergency Assistance. Expenditures for the year totaled a little over $113 million.[9] General Assistance, largely a state program, provides aid for the needy who do not qualify for help under the various federal programs. Eligibility and benefits vary widely. In 1980, only forty-one states had such programs, and a total of $1.4 billion was spent.[10]

There are two other assistance programs. Black Lung benefits serve a specialized group: former coal mine workers afflicted with black lung disease. Begun in 1970, it paid a little over $110 million in benefits to some 376,000 miners, widows, and dependents in 1981.[11] The other, Energy Assistance, is a new program begun in 1981 to assist low-income families to meet the cost of fuel to heat their homes. In its first year this program provided $1.7 billion to over 4.5 million households.[12]

Food Stamps

The earliest public programs to distribute food to the poor began in the 1930s during the Great Depression. The federal government bought surplus farm products to raise their prices, and gave the food to the needy in monthly distributions. By 1939 about 13 million people were benefiting from the program. In that year a food stamp program was substituted for direct distribution of commodities. But World War II eliminated food surpluses and the need for price supports for farm products. The food stamp program wound down and was eliminated in 1945.

After World War II, food assistance programs began once more. The national school lunch program was initiated in 1946. A program to assist the hungry overseas was started in 1954. Then, a new food stamp program was started in 1961 on a trial basis and was made permanent in 1964. The chief purpose of these postwar programs was to move surplus farm products off the market. Feeding the poor was a byproduct.

The situation changed in the 1960s with the civil rights movement and the national War on Poverty begun in 1964. Hunger emerged as a key issue after several congressional investigations were conducted in the mid-1960s, an important private investigation was published in 1968, and an influential television documentary was broadcast the same year.[13] The food stamp program, made permanent in 1964, began to expand. Growing slowly at first, it reached the $1 billion level in 1971, $5 billion in 1976, and $10 billion in 1981. The number of persons participating grew from 143,000 in 1962 to over 1 million in 1967, 10 million in 1972, 15 million in 1975, and over 21 million in 1980. By 1980, one person in ten in the United States was receiving food stamps, and the average "bonus" was $34.34 per month per person. The total amounts transferred to the poor under the food stamp program are shown in table 13.1.

The food stamp program is designed to help the needy obtain enough food for a nutritious diet. The present system, the result of 1977 and 1981 changes in the original legislation, provides food stamps to eligibile recipients whose net incomes are below 130 percent of the federally calculated poverty line. The amount obtainable is determined by a sliding scale keyed to individual or household incomes, and rises with increases in the consumer price index. In 1982, the maximum allowed for a family of four without any earned income was $233 per month, raised to $253 in 1983. The stamps can be used to purchase only food: tobacco, alcoholic beverages, soap, and other non-food items are excluded. Some elderly and disabled persons can use the stamps to buy prepared meals at approved non-profit centers. Eligibility requires that total disposable family assets be under $1,500 ($3,000 if the household has two or more members and one is sixty years of age or older).

The food stamp program has been successfully limited to those who are truly poor. In 1978, after the most recent reforms, 85 percent of all food stamp households had gross incomes of $6,000 or less, 60 percent had no liquid assets, 71 percent did not own a home, and 64 percent did not own a car. The recipients are very heavily the elderly, blind, disabled, AFDC mothers and their children, the unemployed, and low-income working families.[14] Yet some experts estimated in 1977 that only about one-half of those who could qualify were in the program.[15]

The food stamp program, along with the school lunch program, has significantly reduced hunger and malnutrition in the United States, according to a follow-up study by the Field Foundation in 1977. Nevertheless, inadequate food and nutrition were found frequently even in families receiving food stamps.[16] More recently, data from the National Center for Health Statistics show twice as much stunting of growth and two to three times the incidence of iron deficiency anemia among children from low-income families when compared with the general population.[17] Hunger and malnutrition persist. They are the result of poverty, and will continue to persist as long as we have an economy that generates poverty. The food stamp program, like AFDC, can make poverty more bearable and reduce its debilitating effects. But it treats symptoms, not causes.

Medicaid

The medicaid program, providing medical care for the needy, was started in 1966 under federal legislation of the previous year. It replaced several smaller medical care programs linked to welfare programs, the most important of which was the Kerr-Mills program for medical assistance to the aged, which was phased out in the period from 1966 to 1970.

Medicaid provides payment for medical care for persons eligible to receive cash payments under AFDC or SSI. Some states have more rigid standards than provided by federal law, and others allow broader coverage. Standards for eligibility include low income and limited additional resources, and vary among the states. State laws and regulations determine the scope of services covered. All states except Arizona have Medicaid programs, as well as Washington, D.C., Puerto Rico, the Virgin Islands, and Guam.

Like most programs to aid the needy, the number of persons receiving medicaid assistance increased rapidly in the late 1960s and early 1970s to reach a peak of 22.9 million in 1976 and 1977. There the number stabilized, and even fell slightly to 21.6 million in 1980. But costs continued to rise because of increases in the cost of medical care in the nation as a whole. In fifteen years the annual cost of medicaid rose from under half a billion dollars in 1966 to over $23.3 billion in 1980. The growth of medicaid costs has been more rapid than the cost of any other program of assistance to the poor.[18]

Despite its high and escalating cost, medicaid is plagued by serious problems. It does not cover all poor people. One study estimated that in 1975 some 8 to 10 million persons with incomes below the poverty line were not eligible for medicaid. Most of those excluded are single persons and families without children. Another study estimated that in 1976 only about one in four poor children in the southern states received medicaid. Within the program itself there has been a serious failure to identify and treat children who need medical treatment. Many states provide only small benefits, and numerous doctors and dentists refuse to treat medicaid patients. The program has also been plagued by fraud and profiteering on the part of some providers of medical services, particularly private clinics established primarily or solely to serve medicaid patients.[19]

Patterns of Growth in the Welfare System

The cost of transfer payments to the needy has grown steadily over the last twenty years. The total rose from under $4 billion in 1960 to about $54 billion in 1980. The figures for the chief programs are shown in table 13.1 and illustrated in figure 13.1.

As late as 1960, AFDC benefits were only $1 billion; SSI benefits to the blind, disabled, and needy aged persons were twice as great; and public assistance benefits were only about $300 million. During the early 1960s, these cash payments increased slowly each year. But the urban riots from 1964 to 1968 were quickly followed by increased money transfers to the poor. One of the reactions of the social order to those revolts was to alleviate tensions and reduce discontent by

FIGURE 13.1. Chief transfer payments to the poor, 1960-1981 *(in billions of dollars).*

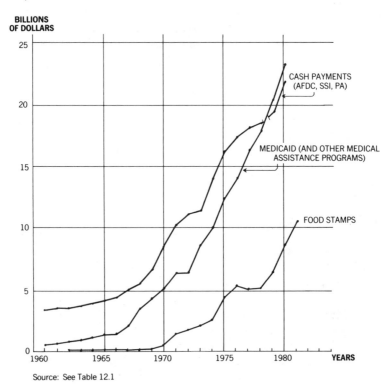

Source: See Table 12.1

admitting more persons to eligibility for AFDC and by raising payments.[20] Much of the campaign against poverty had the same effect. The welfare system first resisted the increased need: the great black migration of the first half of the 1950s brought almost no response, for total AFDC payments remained level until about 1956 or 1957. Then, reluctantly, the system began to accommodate itself to increased needs, with a steady increase in total payments to mid–1966. At that time the need to defuse the black revolt brought huge increases in welfare payments and the number of persons receiving benefits. However, by 1971 the administration of the welfare system began to clamp down and stopped the increase in the number of persons receiving AFDC benefits. Figure 13.2 shows the leveling off of AFDC recipients from 1971 through 1980. The cost of the program continued to rise, however, chiefly because of inflation.

The food stamp program, on the other hand, continued to grow

FIGURE 13.2. Number of persons receiving AFDC benefits and food stamps, 1960–1981. *(millions of persons)*

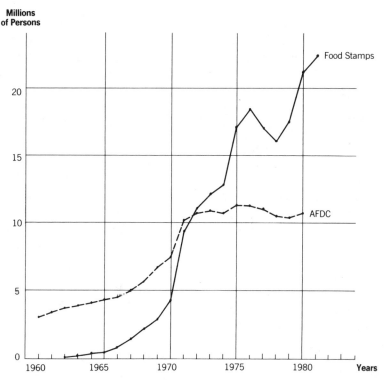

Source: *Social Security Bulletin, Annual Statistical Supplement, 1981,* pp. 78, 247

from the mid-1960s to the present in both number of persons served and total benefits. Its continued expansion was attributable to several factors. Knowledge of eligibility for the program continued to spread, and food prices rose rapidly during the 1970s. The most important factor, however, was that farm surpluses increased as well. The food stamp program is run by the Department of Agriculture, which also is responsible for maintaining the prices of agricultural products and incomes of farm enterprises. Its chief clients are agricultural interests. Any farm products distributed through the food stamp program make it easier to support farm prices and incomes, and actually save money in the price support program.

The situation is different with AFDC. The cost of that program is borne by the taxpayer directly without comparable savings in other parts of the federal budget. Furthermore, no strong political interest exists (other than the AFDC recipients) to push for expansion of the program. These considerations help explain why the number of AFDC recipients leveled off in 1971 while the number receiving food stamps continued to rise. There are good reasons why welfare programs will be limited in coverage and cost (a topic to be examined later in this chapter) but the distinction between the AFDC and food stamp programs helps us understand some of the political and economic factors involved.

Transfer Payments and Work Incentives

The present system of welfare payments can seriously erode work incentives. It also provides incentives to work "off the books" in the irregular economy, where there is no record of wages paid, and deductions for income taxes and Social Security benefits are not made.

Payments for child support plus food stamps bring many poor families up to or very close to the Census Bureau's poverty line income. For 1982, the poverty line income for an urban family of four was estimated at $9900. Although AFDC payment levels vary somewhat from state to state even with federal standards and guidelines, typically such a family will receive about $9,000, or 91 percent of the poverty line income, in cash payments from AFDC and payments in kind via food stamps and housing assistance.

A family of four in which one person works will have a higher income, but the difference is not great. Earned income is accompanied by reductions in AFDC payments and food stamp allotments. Thus, a family of four in which one person works full-time at the minimum wage of $3.35 per hour will have a total annual income before deductions of $11,000 (earned income, $6,700; AFDC payments, $3,300; food stamps, $1,000). The total will vary from state to state.[21]

The family with a low-wage, full-time worker obtains only about $2,000 more than the family receiving welfare payments and food stamps. That amounts to an effective hourly wage of just $1.00—a full-time job entails about 2,000 hours of work per year. In effect, the earned income of $6,700 is reduced to an increase in family income of only about $2,000, because of accompanying reductions in AFDC payments and food stamps.

If the earned income is concealed, AFDC payments and food stamps will not be reduced. Family income will be increased by the full amount of the earnings. An increase of $6,700 instead of $2,000, particularly for a poor family, is a powerful incentive to work "off the books" and to break the law on reporting income.

These general comparisons do not take into account differences among the various states, both in entitlements under the assistance programs and in the income needed. But specific instances bear out the general conclusions. A recent estimate of the income needed by a family of four in southeastern Michigan in 1982 was $754 per month.[22] A family of four receiving AFDC payments would receive an almost equal amount, $759. Cash received from AFDC would be $506, plus $253 in food stamps. The total is just large enough to meet the family's minimum needs.

Compare this with another family of four with an equal earned income. This would mean a full-time job at $4.75 per hour, providing a monthly income of $760. The family would be eligible for $115 in AFDC payments and $131 in food stamps, based on the sliding scales of payments related to income. The monthly family income would be $1,006. But—and this is the point—the increase in family income for the month over that of the welfare family would be only $247. Working 160 hours would bring in only $247, an hourly net pay of about $1.54. The $760 of earned income was accompanied by a reduction in public assistance of $513. This is equivalent to a marginal tax rate of 67.5 percent: 67.5 cents of every additional dollar is taken away. There is little incentive here for family members to work, unless, of course, they can earn money "off the books" in the irregular economy and keep the welfare authorities from finding out about it.

In another case, compare the family of four receiving only AFDC payments plus food stamps with a family of four in which one person has a full-time job at the minimum wage of $3.35 per hour. This family's monthly income would total $895: earned income [40 hours per week, 4 weeks, at $3.35 per hour] $536; AFDC payments, $274; food stamps, $85. In this case the additional income from a full-time job is only $136, or just 85 cents per hour. The effective marginal tax rate is about 75 percent. Thus, the lower the wage the higher is the effective marginal tax rate.

These examples are based on the specific payments schedules of one state. The amounts differ from state to state, but the principle is the same everywhere. With AFDC payments and food stamps as an alternative, the incentives to work are greatly reduced.

Finally, when there is a choice between a regular job and one in the irregular economy there are strong incentives to choose the irregular sector. Worker A who takes an unreported job ("off the books") at $2.00 per hour, which is well below the legal minimum wage of $3.35 per hour, needs to work only 124 hours a month to match the family income of worker B who has a full-time job at $4.75 per hour. Here is the comparison.

	A Full-time at $4.75 per Hour	B Unreported at $2.00 per Hour
Earned income	$760	$248
AFDC	115	506
Food stamps	131	253
Total	$1006	$1007
Hours worked	160	124

In the case of worker B, there are two illegal actions: the worker does not report his "off the books" income to the welfare authorities, and the employer is paying less than the legal minimum wage. Both have incentives to flout the law.

The medicaid program also discourages work. Most states have a cutoff point beyond which earnings result in loss of medicaid coverage. In some states the cutoff point is low enough to limit employment. Workers who are ill or have illness in the family may be better off not working, obtaining AFDC and food stamps, and remaining eligible for medicaid benefits. These effects are extremely difficult to measure, however. The logic of the program suggests that these difficulties are present, but we do not know how strongly they provide work disincentives or how many people are affected.

Welfare Dependency and Family Instability

Despite the relatively high turnover of AFDC recipients, there is reason to believe that transgenerational welfare dependency is a serious problem. Adults whose parents were on AFDC are the single group most likely to receive ADFC benefits. A 1967 study found that over 20 percent of AFDC mothers whose welfare history was known had received AFDC benefits as children. Other estimates are as high as 40 percent. Many AFDC mothers move in and out of the welfare net. A 1971 study showed that 18 percent of AFDC mothers received welfare for more than five consecutive years. An Illinois study showed that many AFDC mothers are on and off welfare an average of five times. Furthermore, AFDC mothers who were on welfare as children tend to remain on welfare longer, have more children by a larger number of fathers, drop out of school earlier, and have more delinquent children than the working needy or the transitional poor.[23] All of these data are probably low estimates, attributable to inadequate data collection, poor record keeping, name changes, movement within and among states, and the reluctance of recipients to reveal information.

The extent of welfare dependency should not be exaggerated, however. There is little evidence that a significant percentage of the children of welfare recipients remain on welfare as adults. Intergenerational welfare dependency is not significant. Poverty remains, and children of poor families are more likely to be poor than the children of non-poor families, but the poor circulate.[24]

A related issue is whether the availability of welfare benefits encourages the breakup of families. Two processes may be at work. One might be called "fiscal abandonment," in which the husband earning an inadequate low-wage income moves out of the household so that the wife can apply for AFDC payments to supplement the husband's earned income. The two, meanwhile, continue to see each other. The husband's abandonment of the family is only nominal and family ties continue.

Suppose, for instance, the husband has a low-wage job and earns $6000 a year. If he has a wife and two children, the family is not eligible for welfare payments in most states, although they may be eligible for food stamps. If he leaves the home, however, his wife and children will be eligible for AFDC payments of perhaps $5000 plus more food stamps and medicaid. The cash income of the family is now $11,000 and benefits in kind are considerably greater. The only additional costs are an inexpensive room for the husband rented nearby.

The second process of family breakup can be called the "poverty divorce." It occurs when the wife considers welfare payments an acceptable alternative to life with a low wage-earner husband whom she no longer cares for or whose behavior she no longer wishes to tolerate. She feels free to leave her husband or kick him out because she can go on AFDC with her children and not suffer much, if any, change in her standard of living.

Fiscal abandonment does not seem to be a significant cause of family breakup. A series of papers written for the Joint Economic Committee of the U.S. Congress found that the great bulk of AFDC families became one-parent families for reasons other than the availability of welfare; that an important cause of broken families was reduced income contributed by the father rather than the availability of welfare; and that no relationship existed between the availability of AFDC benefits and family instability.[25] Another study showed that at least 14 percent and perhaps as many as 28 percent of family breakups among a group of 500 New York City welfare mothers were influenced by the availability of welfare. In the great majority of these cases, however, it was a poverty divorce rather than fiscal abandonment. The relationship broke up because of problems with the husband: drug addiction, alcoholism, irresponsibility, quarreling and fighting, or physical abuse of the mother or children.[26] Family life at the poverty level suffers from serious problems that lead to family breakup, and welfare payments enable women to escape from intolerable situations.

Poverty is a terrible thing. About one-fourth of the U.S. population is permanently, intermittently, or temporarily poor. Permanent, hard-core poverty afflicts perhaps 4 to 5 percent of the total, intermittent poverty about twice that, probably 8 to 10 percent. We can not be more exact because of insufficient data—even these figures must be taken as informed estimates. The permanently poor are dependent on welfare because they are permanently poor, not because they are on welfare. Families break up not because welfare is available, but because they are poor. The welfare system helps the poor survive. It is not the cause of poverty. The sources of poverty are to be found in the economic system itself.

Welfare and Poverty

The Census Bureau provides estimates of the incidence of poverty. It calculates the proportion of the population receiving cash incomes below the annually estimated needs standard, the so-called "poverty line." These estimates are difficult to make. Income earned in the irregular economy or provided by relatives or friends is hard to document. Even if people were willing to make full disclosures to authorities or scholars—we know that they do not—memories are not always accurate. In addition, income is also received in kind rather than money, including assistance from relatives, in the form of food, clothing and housing, food stamps, and medical services provided through medicaid.

If these considerations suggest that the poverty line income is too high, others suggest it is too low. The census estimates are based on family budgets for 1958, when food costs represented about one-third of the budgets of poor families. The poverty line income was therefore calculated at three times the cost of the required amount of food. That method is still used. However, in the intervening years the cost of food has fallen to about one-fourth of poor family budgets: the price of food has risen less than other items in the budgets. On that basis, the estimated poverty line income is about 33 percent too low.

Nevertheless, the Census Bureau estimates of the incidence of poverty are a useful indicator of the extent of economic deprivation. They show a steady decline in the incidence of poverty from almost 23 percent of the population in 1960 to under 13 percent in 1968. For about twelve years, from 1968 through 1979, the incidence of poverty remained largely unchanged, fluctuating between 11 and 13 percent. This was a period of relative economic stagnation in the national economy, with high unemployment rates and high rates of inflation; transfer payments to the poor escalated rapidly. The incidence of poverty began to rise again in the late 1970s, breaking through the 13 percent level in 1980 and rising to 13.6 percent in 1981. This period was characterized by still worse national economic conditions plus cutbacks in programs designed to aid the poor. Figure 13.3 shows these trends.

Although the annual incidence of poverty as measured by the Census Bureau stabilized in the late 1960s in the range of 11 to 13 percent of the U.S. population, that figure does not tell the whole story. A continuing study of households receiving welfare payments by the University of Michigan Institute for Social Research showed that the welfare program was not reaching all of those in need. Thus, in 1978, when the Census Bureau incidence of poverty was 11.1 percent, only 8.1 percent of the population lived in households receiving some welfare income.[27]

Furthermore, in the ten years between 1969 and 1978, when the incidence of poverty stabilized at 11 to 13 percent of the population, fully 25.2 percent of the population received some welfare assistance in at least one year. Some 8.3 percent received assistance in at least five of the ten years, and 2 percent received assistance in all ten years.[28] Table 13.2 shows a further breakdown of the data.

We should not assume that everyone above the poverty line is doing well. Other methods of measuring poverty indicate a broad range of poor families above that line. For example, in 1968, the Census Bureau estimated the incidence of poverty at just under 13 percent; the incidence would have almost doubled to over 24 percent if a "minimum health and decency" level of income estimated by the United States Department of Labor had been used as the standard.

Other studies show a lower incidence of poverty. The University of Michigan study, which used the same poverty line as the Census Bureau, found the incidence of poverty since the late 1960s ranging from about 7 to 9.5 percent, with somewhat larger swings during business cycles than the Census Bureau estimated. The difference is attributable to more complete reporting of earned income in the Michigan study. The Michigan study also shows the importance of the standard of measurement. Increasing the poverty line income by only 25 percent more than doubled the incidence of poverty for the year 1978.

An interesting dynamic operates among the needy. A significant portion of the population, some 25 percent, experiences a period of need in which assistance is required. These people become needy for a variety of reasons—unemployment, illness, injury, or death of a wage earner, divorce, or abandonment—and need welfare to help support the household until its earned income is once more adequate.

FIGURE 13.3. Incidence of poverty, 1960–1981: percentage of U.S. population with incomes below poverty line.

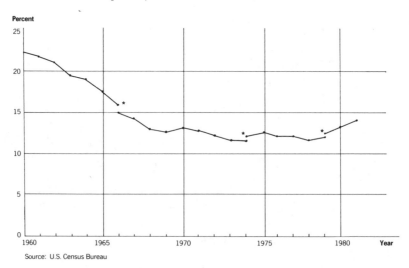

Source: U.S. Census Bureau

*Breaks are due to revised method of calculation

Table 13.2. U.S. Population Receiving
Welfare Assistance, 1969–1978 *(in percentage)*

Received no welfare		74.8
Received some welfare		25.2
In 1 to 2 years	12.3	
In 3 to 7 years	8.5	
In 8 to 10 years	4.4	

Source: Greg J. Duncan et al., *Years of Poverty, Years of Plenty* (Ann Arbor, Mich.: University of Michigan Institute for Social Research, 1984), p. 77.

For example, a family headed by a woman may be poor because of the absence of a spouse due to death or divorce. Remarriage, which brings an earner into the household, then removes the family from need. Occasional or temporary need of this sort affected over 12 percent of the population in the years from 1969 to 1978.

At the other extreme, there is a hard core of continuous poverty and permanent reliance on the welfare system for survival. This group included some 2 to 4 percent of the population. In between is a group that seems to move up and down, in some years off welfare and in other years on it. Need is not continuous in this group, but poverty is chronic. It comprised about 8 percent of the population in the years from 1969 to 1978. Poverty, then, is both a condition that affects a significant portion of the population at any time, and a process through which individuals and families pass. As a condition it is permanent, with the incidence of poverty rising or falling in response to economic conditions. As a process, however, it affects some persons temporarily, others chronically, and yet others permanently.

The welfare system performs two necessary functions. It is a resource available for those temporarily in need, and it provides a source of income for those who are chronically in need or permanently poor. With respect to the ghetto economy, however, the welfare system performs another function as well: it helps to stabilize the ghetto by providing a needed inflow of income.

The Economic Theory of Transfer Payments

Stabilization of the incidence of poverty in the late 1960s at some 11 to 13 percent of the U.S. population coincided with the end of the urban revolt of 1964 to 1968. This was soon followed by stabilization of the number of persons receiving AFDC payments. The urban ghettos then remained peaceful through the 1970s and into the 1980s. A new social and economic equilibrium had been established.

The ghetto economy requires a continuing inflow of income to balance the drain of resources and income out of the ghetto. The inflow is provided by the earned income of ghetto residents, chiefly from low-wage employment, supplemented by transfer payments, chiefly from the government. The level of life in the ghetto is determined by the equilibrium established by the inward and outward flows. An increase in transfer payments will raise living standards in the ghetto, but it will also bring an increase in the drain of resources and income until a new equilibrium is reached. When the two flows once more balance, the increase in ghetto income will stop.

A decrease in transfer payments, on the other hand, would set in motion a downward spiral of income and economic activity within the ghetto. As the downward spiral continues, the outflow of resources and income to the rest of the economy will diminish. Ultimately, the ghetto subsystem will be stabilized at a new lower level at which the inflows of income once more equal the outflow. At this lower equilibrium we would expect the ghetto economy to support a reduced retail trade and a smaller irregular economy, and higher rates of unemployment would prevail. The extent and depths of poverty would be greater.

Changes in the level of income transfers into the ghetto economy can have a significant effect on the size of the ghetto. An increase would enable a larger number of individuals and family units to subsist in the ghetto. This larger population would add to the demand for slum housing, with higher rents for existing housing within the ghetto and a geographical extension of the boundaries of the ghetto.[29] The outflow of income and physical capital into the hands of slumlords would increase as well. On the other hand, a decrease in income transfers would drive some ghetto residents out, perhaps to rural areas, and others would double up with relatives and form larger family units crowded into dwellings. The demand for slum housing would be reduced, the ghetto would become smaller, and the outflow of resources and income to slumlords would be less. Population densities would be greater, incomes per person lower, and the conditions of poverty intensified.

Increased transfer payments, then, can significantly affect the level of life of ghetto residents. But they also increase the economic drain of resources and income out of the ghetto. Property owners and business firms that profit from the ghetto enlarge their receipts and their numbers are increased. This will occur even if the ghetto population rises to absorb the increased flow of transfer payments without any increase in individual and family income.

It has sometimes been argued that the level of welfare payments depends strongly on the amount of unrest and disorder in the ghetto. Riots bring increased income transfers designed to dampen discontent and pacify the poor, according to this argument. The alternative to income transfers is larger expenditures for police and law enforcement to contain the outbreaks of violence and lawlessness generated by the poverty of the ghetto. Although this argument may be oversimplified, it calls attention to some of the important political and economic aspects of transfer payments.

An economically rational allocation of public funds to transfer payments into the ghetto would seek to achieve a cost-benefit equilibrium with two chief characteristics. The total amount of transfer payments to the ghetto plus the cost of police repression of ghetto violence tends toward the level at which the marginal cost to the taxpayer equals the marginal benefits in ghetto violence averted. Thus, if $1.00 spent on avoiding violence averts only 90 cents worth of destruction, it is not well spent. If it averts $1.10 worth of destruction there are net benefits to be obtained. The expenditure is optimized when the last dollar spent on elimination of violence averts just $1.00 worth of destruction. Thus, it is argued that an upsurge of ghetto unrest will bring forth, as an economically rational response, an increase in both transfer payments to the ghetto and expenditures for law enforcement.

There is also a tradeoff between the carrot and the stick in a rational allocation of public funds. The relative amounts allocated to transfer payments and law enforcement in the ghetto will tend toward the level at which the marginal benefits from the two types of spending are equalized. If a marginal dollar spent on transfer payments brings greater benefits in social stabilization than a marginal dollar spent on law enforcement, the marginal dollar will tend to be shifted from law enforcement to transfer payments until the marginal benefits are equalized. And vice versa if the imbalance is reversed.

There are, then, two equilibrium conditions for an economically rational allocation of resources for pacifying the ghetto. The total amount spent for that purpose will equalize the marginal cost of the tax money spent with the marginal benefits obtained in the form of violence avoidance: MC/tax = MB/police. Allocation of resources within that total for transfer payments and police protection will be determined by equalizing benefits at the margin for the two types of spending: MB/transfers = MB/police.

A "demonstration effect" is also present. The total amount spent on pacification of the ghetto can be reduced by violent repression of violence. If a ghetto riot is put down by violent police action against ghetto residents, including those not actively participating in the riot, ghetto residents will be shown that violent revolt has high personal costs. They will then be more willing to accept minimal transfer payments as an alternative to riots. On the other hand, if the velvet glove is used instead of the iron fist and transfer payments are increased as a substitute for police repression, ghetto residents will learn that riot brings monetary rewards. Astute use of the instruments of law and order can reduce the total spent on dampening ghetto unrest—in the short run, at least. The impact in the long run is more problematic.

These general rules should be modified by institutional factors. Transfer payments come largely from the federal budget and are financed primarily by progressive taxes. Police protection comes primarily from local and state taxes, and is financed primarily from regresive taxes at those levels. In addition, national norms for transfer payments are provided in federal legislation, while local conditions in the ghetto can vary widely. Finally, the political influence of local police forces and the welfare bureaucracy will differ from city to city and from state to state. These factors interfere with the pure economic rationality sketched above.

Larger political-economic forces are also at work. During the long period of prosperity and economic growth in the quarter-century post–World War II boom, when the urban ghetto and its dispossessed classes were developing in their modern form and scale, social policy tended to lag behind social changes. Political underrepresentation of the new socioeconomic formations contributed to their relative neglect. The riots of the mid to late 1960s were one result, triggering a substantial increase in transfer payments and police expenditures that reestablished relatively stable conditions in the ghetto. A catching-up process was at work.

On the other hand, during the period of relative stagnation in the late 1960s and 1970s, the relationship between the ghetto subsector and the rest of the economy shifted. With the rise of unemployment in the primary sector of the labor force, there was less need for a ghettoized, low-wage labor force to provide a downward pull on wage rates. In addition, an influx of low-wage immigrant labor, legal and illegal, from Asia, Mexico, Central America, and the Caribbean reduced the economic need to maintain a largely black, low-wage labor force in existing ghettos. At the same time, unemployment and economic insecurity among white workers at all levels (blue-collar, white-collar, pink-collar) heightened white-black antagonisms and brought political opposition to income transfers that benefited the poor. Those economic factors provided support for the political reaction of the Reagan administration in its effort to limit and reduce transfer payments to the poor.

Any assessment of the forces affecting the level and mix of expenditures to assist ghetto residents and maintain social stability must take into account both long-run forces and immediate reactions. For example, the public policy response to the riots of the 1960s was varied. Frances Fox Piven and Richard Cloward attribute the rapid expansion of AFDC caseloads from 1964 to "trouble in the streets, and trouble at the polls" from blacks. James Button points out that the response to the early riots brought relatively large increases in expenditures on the part of the Office Of Economic Opportunity, the Department of Housing and Urban Development, and the model cities program, but that the response to the later riots was substantially less. On the other hand, law enforcement efforts intensified between the earlier and later riots.[30] Button's findings suggest that, at the time of early riots, conditions in the ghettos had deteriorated because of neglect to a situation in which the marginal benefits from income transfers (in terms of social stability) were initially large. There had been, in other words, a non-policy of not-so-benign neglect. Once large increases in transfer payments began, however, their marginal benefits declined rapidly and led to a second phase in which they were equal to or lower than the marginal benefits from increased law enforcement.

One final element must be brought into the economic analysis of income transfers to the ghetto. One of the chief functions of the ghetto economy is to provide a source of low-wage labor. Transfer payments can interfere with this function, for they provide an alternative to income earned from work, particularly if the work is for low wages at a dirty or repetitious job. As we demonstrated earlier in this chapter, it is quite possible for a ghetto family to obtain transfer payments in money or kind that exceed the income that might be earned from full-time employment at the minimum wage. Work incentives can be seriously eroded if transfer payments are high. The tradeoff between transfer payments and work incentives helps to explain why the marginal benefits from transfer payments tend to decline and why increased expenditures on law enforcement become a more favored policy when transfer payments are relatively high. Stronger law enforcement does not erode work incentives.

There is a complex set of relationships that will, in the long run, affect the flow of transfer payments into the ghetto. One factor is the need of the modern economy for the supply of low-wage labor provided by the ghetto. Income transfers help to perpetuate ghetto conditions and the supply of labor it provides. A second factor is the need to keep the underclass peaceful. Income transfers plus law enforcement perform that function, with a tradeoff between the two that depends on marginal costs and benefits. A third factor is the political tolerance of taxpayers outside the ghetto for the expenditures necessary for social stability inside the ghetto. Finally, the estimated damage to work incentives must be considered. Income transfers plus expenditures for law and order must be high enough to preserve the ghetto and keep it peaceful, without significant political opposition from taxpayers or significant damage to work incentives. An uncertain and changing balance of marginal costs and benefits, both political and economic, will affect the outcome, and public policy may respond only after a considerable time lag. In any case, the policy mix will be couched in terms of liberal humanitarianism or conservative moral values that effectively channel debate away from the political and economic reality of a dispossessed economic underclass.

14

Business Enterprise in the
Urban Ghetto

THE STATE OF THE GHETTO BUSINESS COMMUNITY REFLECTS THE economic circumstances of its clientele. While the backward condition of most ghetto enterprises is symptomatic of more deeply rooted economic phenomena, these firms often exacerbate the poverty and underemployment problems of their customers. The retail districts of central-city ghettos outwardly appear to be like any retail district, except that they are shabbier and obviously cater to a low-income clientele. There are important differences, however, that are not apparent to the casual observer. Exploitive business practices are common, and the poorest customers often have few alternative sources of supply. Retail firms, particularly those selling consumer durables, prosper by providing easy credit, and by selling high-priced and inferior merchandise with high-pressure tactics. Door-to-door peddling is common in the ghetto.

Merchants cite the high costs and hazardous nature of conducting business in the inner city as justification for their pricing and credit policies. While this is undoubtedly true to some extent, it falls short of explaining such practices as selling goods on credit at exorbitant

interest rates. According to data assembled through the efforts of the
U.S. Senate Financial Institutions Subcommittee, the high credit costs
facing ghetto consumers are largely caused by factors other than default risks. More important than credit losses are high costs stemming
from the inefficient, costly selling practices utilized by inner-city merchants.[1] In an earlier classic study of Harlem retailing, *The Poor Pay
More: Consumer Practices of Low Income Families*, David Caplovitz
reached similar conclusions about ghetto retailing.[2] Efforts to reform
exploitive credit practices via truth in lending laws have simply encouraged merchants to include some of the credit costs in product
prices. Ghetto residents, because of their low and unstable incomes,
poor credit rating, and consequent inability to obtain credit from the
sources utilized by most Americans, often have no recourse but to
pay greater credit charges and higher prices for their goods. They
are "captive" buyers because they have limited options to transact
their business elsewhere. Sharp credit practices are often supplemented by use of law courts to get payment: repossession and garnishment of wages are devices used by furniture, appliance, and jew-
elry stores in particular. A history of wage garnishment, in turn, can
complicate job search efforts to ghetto dwellers since some employers
avoid hiring persons with such records. Ghetto merchants who provide credit do, nonetheless, perform a function, however imperfectly:
they permit the poor to buy durable goods that normal channels of
trade are unwilling to provide. The poor pay more, but they do obtain
goods that they would otherwise be unable to buy.

Black Business Enterprise

Black-owned firms were historically an obscure sector of the economy.
Nonetheless, in the 1960s, black businesses were thrust into the national spotlight, and "black capitalism" was viewed as a potential cure
for ghetto problems. The realities of black business ownership in
relation to the economic and social problems of decaying urban areas
made black capitalism an improbable vehicle for spurring ghetto economic development. However, numerous government programs were
initiated to promote black (and later, Hispanic) business expansion,
and these programs have continued to proliferate well into the 1980s.
By the 1980s, years of preferential treatment had succeeded in creating a subset of large-scale, black-owned firms in such fields as general
construction, manufacturing, and wholesaling. Roots of the black
business community, as well as its recent transformation into some
large-scale lines of business, are traced in the remainder of this
section.

Historical Background

Historically, black-owned businesses have been concentrated in several lines of small-scale retail and personal service enterprise. Some of the most common lines of black enterprise today coincide closely with those of the southern black business community before the Civil War. Since southern white entrepreneurs avoided businesses having a servile connotation, blacks had virtually no competition in certain fields. Personal service occupations were freely open to those who could obtain sufficient capital to establish a business. In many southern towns, they had near monopoly on cooking, cleaning and pressing, beauty parlor and barber shop operations, and shoeshining. After emancipation, black businesses failed to increase in size and scope, and late–nineteenth-century immigrants provided increasing competition in the personal service fields. Stagnation and outright decline in some lines of business characterized black enterprise until World War I. Events of that wartime era provided precedents for the renewed interest in black business development that materialized in the late 1960s.

The need for industrial workers during World War I produced the first large-scale black migration to the cities. A wave of race riots in Chicago, Washington, and other cities intensified urban blacks' racial consciousness. Capitalizing on a strong "buy black" sentiment and financing from high wartime incomes, black businesses formed in many lines of commerce and industry. By the 1920s, black businesses were common throughout the southern, eastern, and midwestern states.

Black retailers gained an advantage over their white competitors as a result of the "buy black" campaigns of the postwar decade, but they were hit harder by the Great Depression. White ghetto merchants had always enjoyed greater access to trade credit, and this frequently spelled the difference between survival and calamity. Black retailers failed in droves. Myrdal observed in 1944 that "the Negro businessman encounters greater difficulties than whites in securing credit. This is partially due to the marginal position of Negro business. It is also partly due to prejudicial opinions among whites concerning business ability and personal reliability of Negroes. In either case a vicious circle is in operation keeping Negro business down."[3]

Discrimination has played a major role in shaping the twentieth-century black business community.[4] Thus, the small number of black-owned construction companies is partially caused by the exclusion of blacks from most apprenticeship programs in the building trades. Discrimination in the labor market makes it difficult for blacks to accumulate the initial equity investment that business creation requires. Limited educational opportunities have undoubtedly handicapped black entrepreneurs in certain lines of business. Furthermore, educated blacks have traditionally avoided business as a career—73 percent of the black college graduates between 1912 and 1938 became either preachers or teachers.[5]

Government Promotes Minority-Owned Businesses

The vast publicity given to black economic development and "black capitalism" during the mid- to late 1960s was quite out of proportion to realistic prospects for alleviating ghetto problems via black business development. Adequate black business management expertise was largely lacking. Black-owned firms as a group had been stagnant for decades. Yet after 1965, federal dollars were increasingly available to assist black enterprise, and efforts to promote minority-owned businesses continue to be well funded. What response could be expected from a business community consisting chiefly of small-scale operations that employed a very small percentage of the black labor force, concentrated in comparatively few lines of activity that offered little potential for growth? As late as 1972, 65.2 percent of all black firms, as measured by the *1972 Survey of Minority-Owned Business Enterprises*, were concentrated in ten industry groups (table 14.1). These ten lines of enterprise accounted for over two-thirds of all paid employees working for black-owned businesses.

Among the ten key industry groupings, six suffered overall employment declines between 1972 and 1977, and only one field—business services—grew substantially (table 14.1). Despite recurring problems, promoting black business development has wide appeal across the political spectrum, as Republicans and Democrats alike have expanded procurement, financial, and managerial assistance programs for minority entrepreneurs. To some extent, the breadth of this appeal is itself at the root of program failures, because it reflects widely differing and sometimes inconsistent goals. For instance, on the one hand, most whites view the promotion of minority entrepreneurship as an effort to help industrious, ambitious minorities to start working their way upward in the American business system. On the other hand, many minority-group leaders stress independence from the dominant society as a principal goal. Former President Richard Nixon was roundly praised by black power advocates in 1968 when he stated that blacks must have "the economic power that comes from ownership, and the security and independence that comes from economic power."[6] Another goal with wide political appeal is to increase employment opportunities for minorities, particularly in ghetto areas of high un-

Table 14.1. Dominant Lines of Black Business Enterprise

| | 1977 | | 1972 | |
	Firms	Employees	Firms	Employees
Business services	15,461	18,502	10,472	11,797
Eating, drinking places	13,008	17,449	14,346	15,363
Special trade contractors	17,126	12,927	15,616	16,122
Auto dealers, gas stations	5,002	10,831	6,597	12,280
Personal services	35,035	9,328	34,693	10,889
Food stores	10,679	7,245	11,887	6,578
Insurance carriers	58	7,123	70	10,000 (est.)
Misc. retail	20,880	6,264	16,005	5,573
Trucking, warehousing	11,552	4,875	9,938	5,289
General building contractors	3,415	3,446	2,957	4,996
Total	132,216	97,990	122,581	98,887
Total as a percentage of all black firms	63.2*	62.9*	65.3*	67.2*

Source: U.S. Bureau of the Census, *1977 Survey of Minority-Owned Business Enterprises: Black* (Washington, D.C.: Government Printing Office, Dec. 1979).

*Firms in new industries not included in the 1972 survey totaled 21,944, with 8,312 paid employees, according to the 1977 survey. These new industries are entirely excluded from table 14.1. The 1972 data are taken from revised 1972 statistics that appeared in the 1977 survey; the summary statistics that were published in the original 1972 survey were incorrect by wide margins.

employment. A final purpose for encouraging minority business is to produce an expanding middle class to serve as a role model for ghetto youth.

The most fundamental conflict in goals concerns the question of who should be the target recipients—the most "deprived" minorities who (for that reason) need help most, or those who need help less but have better prospects for success. Contrasting these different kinds of potential beneficiaries highlights contrasting objectives: the first, to use aid to minority business as a kind of redistributive poverty program designed to help those who need help most; the second, to encourage success stories and role models and to create jobs.

These conflicting objectives run through various program initiatives, but as will become clear, some of these objectives are critically important while others are entirely inappropriate for assisting minority business.

The government programs have changed their emphasis in recent years. Until 1977, loans were the major component of the business promotion effort, although they peaked in terms of both numbers and dollar amount (constant dollars) in 1972 and 1973. From fiscal years 1969 through 1979, the Small Business Administration (SBA) approved over 65,000 loans to minority entrepreneurs for approximately $3 billion. SBA loan approvals to minorities declined from over 9,000 in 1972 to 5,975 in 1978 and 5,342 in 1979. In contrast to lagging loan approvals, federal government procurement contracts have been growing very rapidly in the late 1970s, exceeding $1 billion in fiscal year 1979. Total federal procurement from minority business reached $4.1 billion in 1981, and it is projected to continue to rise rapidly through 1985.[7] Minority-owned businesses stand to gain about $7 billion in contracts as a result of the Surface Transportation Assistance Act of 1982. An amendment to the final act, as signed by President Reagan, requires that at least 10 percent of all funds spent under the law must be awarded to minority firms. Expected spending under this law is approximately $70.1 billion through 1986.

Government Assistance to Minority-Owned Firms

Programs that provide long-term credit access on preferential terms to minority entrepreneurs have made a considerable impact on the size and scope of black businesses. But while they appear to be broadening the composition of the minority business community, they have also produced high rates of loan default and business failure. The inherent strengths and weaknesses of the SBA's loan programs can best be understood by examining their conception and administration.

In terms of numbers of businesses assisted, the largest has been the Economic Opportunity Loan (EOL) program. It is designed to help low-income entrepreneurs, both minority and nonminority, who operate very small businesses. Begun in 1965, the program was initially designed to assist only entrepreneurs living in poverty. The strict poverty criteria have been dropped, although the rules still require that loan applicants be "economically and socially disadvantaged." The EOL program has produced a high incidence of loan default, but this is perfectly consistent with its underlying ideology.

In terms of dollar volume, the largest loan program has been the one designated 7(a), which consists largely of bank loans guaranteed against default by the SBA. These loans are available to nonminority as well as minority applicants, although the latter are given more favorable terms. The 7(a) program has enabled thousands of minority enterprises to erode a tradition of financial discrimination by establishing banking ties. Unlike the EOL lending efforts, the 7(a) program targets its assistance to larger and more promising minority businesses.

The industrial composition of minority firms who borrow through the SBA differs sharply from the overall distribution of minority businesses because many loan recipients are moving into more capital-intensive, nontraditional fields. Loans to wholesaling and manu-facturing firms are much more numerous than loans to firms in such traditional enterprises as barber shops, food stores, and laun-dries.

The SBA has relied upon number of loan approvals to measure the success of its lending programs. One immediate problem with this method is that thousands of SBA-approved loans to minorities have never been disbursed—many people who plan to start a business quit before they begin. Many who do receive loans fail to establish or maintain viable operations and these people often default as they go out of business. Also, any measure of success must take into account the differences among programs.

To estimate success, a 1 percent sample was obtained from the SBA of all loans to minorities approved in fiscal years from 1972 to 1976 that had been disbursed as of February 1980. Between 8 and 9 percent of the loans approved have never been disbursed, and nondisbursal was highest in the EOL program.

A substantial number of SBA loan guarantees represent refinanc-ings of previous SBA-guaranteed loans. These must be excluded in order to isolate the actual number of businesses assisted, so that ac-curate failure rates may be established. Roughly 10 percent of loans to minorities are refinancings.

Using the 1 percent sample of SBA loans to minorities and adjusting for nondisbursal and the double counting inherent in including re-financing loans, approximately 42.6 percent of minority firms receiv-ing SBA loans between 1972 and 1976 had failed by spring 1980 (table 14.2). Failure rates were 26.4 percent and 53.3 percent, respectively, for 7(a) and EOL recipients.[8]

Clearly, an overall failure rate of 42.6 percent indicates that loan default and failure are serious problems for minority businesses. Moreover, they have helped erode the credibility of such programs.

Two things can be done to improve minority business loan pro-

Table 14.2. Repayment Status for Sampled Firms Receiving SBA 7(a) and EOL Loans During Fiscal Years 1972 Through 1976 *(in percentage)*

| | 7(a) | | EOL | | Total | |
	Success	*Failure*	*Success*	*Failure*	*Success*	*Failure*
Nonminority	79.8	20.2	56.2	43.8	78.7	21.3
Minority	73.6	26.4	46.7	53.3	57.4	42.6

Source: Author's estimates.

grams: (1) The SBA should seek to reduce the high default and failure rates that plague its minority lending efforts by placing greater emphasis on assisting economically viable concerns. (2) The EOL program should be completely abolished. Most recipients of EOL loans who establish successful businesses are not poverty cases, and could have qualified for SBA 7(a) loans. EOL loan recipients having incomes either below or slightly above the poverty threshold are almost invariably bad credit risks. If the SBA truly does lend in the spirit of the EOL program, then it can expect to experience phenomenal default rates—which indeed it does. In effect, the EOL program has too often served to perpetuate rather than to alleviate poverty among low-income minority entrepreneurs.

There is another ineffective SBA-connected loan program. The Minority Enterprise Small Business Investment Company project (MESBIC) was launched by the Office of Minority Business Enterprise in conjunction with the SBA. As privately owned and privately managed venture capital corporations, MESBICs are supposed to furnish four services to minority-owned firms. First, they provide venture capital by purchasing an equity interest in the business. Second, they provide long-term capital by lending funds (normally subordinated to other creditors) to the business, often with warrants permitting MESBIC to purchase an equity position. Third, they guarantee loans made by third parties. And, fourth, they provide general management and technical assistance.

Congress has given MESBICs the power to leverage their privately invested capital by selling long-term debentures and/or preferred stock to the SBA. For example, if they have $500,000 or more of capital and capital surplus, they may sell up to three times this sum in debentures to the SBA, priced at the cost of capital to the government.

MESBICs are in trouble. The most severe problems they face are those of undercapitalization and cash flow. These may simply be symptoms, however, of a more fundamental malaise: most are not able to cope successfully with the risks of financing small minority businesses. MESBICs often generate a negative cash flow because of the extended periods before equity investments start to yield dividends. To cope with cash-flow crises, they often avoid equity investments and turn, increasingly, to granting loans to minority firms. They fail, therefore, to provide the equity capital that is essential for minority business development. MESBIC debt clients are certainly not riskless firms, and the steady demands that loan repayments place on cash flow predictably push some of these firms into default. When loan losses occur, MESBICs have a capital-base erosion problem on top of their cash-flow difficulties. Virtually all successful SBA small business investment companies were initially capitalized at $1 million or more, and invested their funds in larger small businesses. Few MESBICs are capitalized at these levels. Facing investment losses, interest payments on borrowed funds, and operating expenses, MESBICs often quickly erode their inadequate capital resources. According to one report, 67 MESBICs with $52 million in funds ($23 million from the SBA) had investments in minority and disadvantaged small businesses totaling $17 million—less than one-third of the money available. Over 60 percent of MESBIC resources were held in risk-free liquid assets such as bank certificates of deposit, which paid rates of return exceeding the MESBIC cost of funds from their government borrowings.[9] Hence they have been, in many instances, engaging in riskless arbitrage operation whereby the SBA lends them money at a rate equal to the cost of funds to the federal treasury, and they in turn invest these funds in higher yielding yet very safe securities. While the minority community suffers from a severe lack of venture capital, MESBIC funds languish in bank accounts, certificates of deposit, and so forth.

There has proved to be another difficulty with MESBICs. While they have made few equity investments in minority businesses, there have been some large loans and equity investments in firms that are not owned by minorities, which is a direct violation of the law.

In recent years, procurement contracts have increased in importance as a component in the promotion effort, while loans have declined. A major element of the procurement approach is the 8(a) program, in which regular government contracts normally awarded through competitive bidding are reserved for firms owned by disadvantaged (overwhelmingly minority) businessmen. Since 1968, the SBA has awarded over 20,000 no-bid contracts under this program, worth over $4 billion. SBA-awarded 8(a) contracts have grown rapidly in the late 1970s, reaching $768 million in 1978 and $1.006 billion in 1979.[10]

Set-asides, as typified by the 1977 Public Works Employment Act which earmarked $400 million worth of local public works for minority enterprises, have real potential for assisting minority business because they are usually not targeted to the especially disadvantaged. In contrast, 8(a) procurement contracts are supposed to be awarded only to economically and socially handicapped minority entrepreneurs.

Much government procurement for minorities accrues to "salt-and-pepper" businesses. Nominally these firms are half-owned by minority entrepreneurs, but the de facto owners and controllers are not members of minority groups and are neither socially nor economically disadvantaged. It is common for contractors bidding for set-aside businesses to establish 50 percent partnerships with minority members in order to take advantage of the law. The minority partner typically has no voice in managing the business and the nonminority partner often has no intention of continuing the arrangement after completing the specific set-aside contract.

If procurement is to assist minorities in firms whose ownership is racially mixed, then minority members must have control over management, and a capital stake and earnings commensurate with their claimed proportion of ownership. The minority firm must perform significant work or services under the contract and not act merely as a funnel. In practice this is often not the case. Under set-aside contracts and subcontracts, minority suppliers often serve no useful commercial function, acting merely as an unnecessary intermediary between regular suppliers and the prime contractor or final customer. Studies by the General Accounting Office have repeatedly documented these abuses, which are accompanied by consistently weak SBA administration. Senator Lawton Chiles, who has conducted U.S. Senate investigations, estimates that as many as one-half of 8(a)'s contract firms have been controlled by whites and wealthy minority-group members who are statutorily ineligible for this assistance. After examining all participating 8(a) firms, the SBA's inspector general concluded in September 1979 that over 20 percent should not have been in the program.[11]

The Economic Development Administration has found that administering minority business sets-asides is expensive and time-consuming. When set-asides require a fixed percentage of funds to be targeted to minority firms, certain states have difficulty finding qualified local businesses. Vermont, for example, must use out-of-state minority firms extensively. The delays and added costs that result create havoc with tight deadlines and increase overall costs.

Some changes are clearly needed: Penalties, such as debarment from future federally funded contracts, should be imposed on contractors and suppliers who establish ineligible minority firms to circumvent the intent of minority procurement programs. The percentage of procurements reserved for set-aside programs should be flexible in order to reflect demographic realities. Value added rather than total sales should be the measure of a minority firm's input to procurement contracts. For wholesalers, markup on sales is a better measure of minority business involvement than total sales. This reform would reduce incentive for minority wholesalers to become unnecessary intermediaries between suppliers and customers.

Minority business set-asides are increasingly being utilized by local governments in the 1980s. Reflecting the growing political power of blacks and Hispanics in many central cities, set-asides and similar preferential programs for minority businesses have proliferated in recent years. A recent study sponsored by the U.S. Department of Commerce found that, of thirty-three major cities, only three—Boston, St. Louis, and San Francisco—had no major or significant programs for minority business development. Hartford, Connecticut, requires that corporations which receive tax abatements for local construction projects must earmark at least 10 percent of the construction dollars to minority contractors; furthermore, at least 15 percent of each contractor's labor force must be minority workers. New York, Chicago, Los Angeles, Philadelphia, Detroit, New Orleans, Dallas, and Minneapolis are among the large cities which have shown "major support for minority business development activities."[12]

Targeting corporate procurement dollars to minority firms became widespread in the 1970s, and it is often supplemented by more comprehensive assistance packages. Coca-Cola has selected twenty black wholesalers since late 1981 and it has directly lent $1.5 million to black entrepreneurs who were establishing new firms in that industry. Under the prodding of Reverend Jesse Jackson's PUSH, Heublein has agreed to increase the number of Kentucky Fried Chicken franchises owned by blacks from 7 to 112, and to provide $10 million in financing. Large corporations in the consumer products industries routinely target procurement dollars to minority firms, ad dollars to minority-owned publications and broadcasters, deposit dollars to minority-owned banks, etc. In addition to the obvious public relations value of such a strategy, it also provides insurance against criticism from activist civil rights groups such as PUSH.[13]

Minority Business Potential

History suggests that black entrepreneurship has been shaped by limited access to credit, limitations in educational and training opportunities, and prevailing attitudes about the roles that minorities should assume in society. These historical limitations have all been changing dramatically in the past two decades and the minority business community is now becoming more diverse. Aggregate figures on black-owned businesses understate this progress because they fail to identify two divergent trends: the absolute decline of many traditional lines of business, and real progress in emerging fields. While the total number of black businesses increased by approximately 11.5 percent between 1972 and 1977, the proportion of firms in food and personal service fields shrank from 32.5 to 28.1 percent. At the same time, the number of black business service firms grew from 1,303 to 2,440 and the jobs they provided increased by 56.8 percent, to 18,502. Wholesaling clearly exemplifies the differences between the emerging and traditional sectors. In 1960, there were practically no sizeable black-owned wholesale establishments. In 1977, there were 705 firms with 4,534 paid employees and sales exceeding $628 million.

In the late 1960s, when capital became more generally available, it was observed that black entrepreneurs frequently entered relatively capital-intensive fields and concentrated less on the traditional lines of black enterprise. The high rates of loan delinquency in government programs to finance minority enterprise do not change the conclusion that capital market access helps to alter the size and scope of the black business community. The social goals of the EOL program, the poor evaluation criteria used in screening black loan applicants, and the recessions of the 1970s and 1980s have all contributed to the high default rates that characterize the government's portfolio of loans to black entrepreneurs.[14]

At present, several major federal government loan and procurement programs are radically misdirected: promising minority firms are often ineligible for loans and procurement contracts, while eligible recipients of aid fail in droves. This absurd practice should be eliminated by abandoning the widespread ideological objective of targeting assistance to the economically and socially handicapped. The EOL loan and 8(a) procurement programs should be abolished. In contrast, the SBA 7(a) loan program has sought to improve capital market access for a more promising group of minority entrepreneurs. Recipients of these loans have created and expanded thousands of larger-scale minority-owned businesses in such nontraditional fields as business services, manufacturing, and wholesaling. Similarly, procurement resulting from set-asides such as 1977 Public Works Employment Act and the 1982 Surface Transportation Assistance Act can be highly beneficial. If procurement assistance is to serve as a viable program for minority business development, then it must seek to assist the stronger and better-managed minority firms.

Since the 1960s, the traditionally backward minority business community has started to diversify and expand in response to an influx of talent and capital. Opportunities created by set-asides, preferential procurement policies, and the like have induced better educated, younger minority entrepreneurs to create and expand firms in areas such as contracting and wholesaling. While the traditional minority business community consisted predominantly of very small firms serving a ghetto clientele, the lure of market opportunity in recent years has induced entrepreneurs to create larger firms that are oriented more toward a corporate and government clientele. A recent study of minority-owned firms who are listed in various government and corporate procurement directories revealed the following profile.

	1980 Median Annual Sales (in thousands of dollars)	Estimated Rate of Return on Net Investment (in percentage)	1980 Median Number of Employees
Construction	773.5	22.9	11.7
Manufacturing	1,079.9	22.0	25.0
Wholesale	1,220.4	15.3	10.6

These results are based upon a nationwide sample of 672 minority firms: black-owned businesses were predominant in the sample, Hispanic firms were a close second, and a few Oriental and American Indian firms were present.[15] The degree to which salt and pepper firms may be represented in this sample is unknown. The firms were mostly located in large cities, in or near areas where minority populations are concentrated. Businesses of this magnitude do have the potential to expand employment opportunities for local residents. As suppliers of goods and services to government units and corporations, they serve to attract funds that normally would not enter the ghetto economy. Although little is known at present about large-scale minority-owned firms, their contribution to the health of the ghetto economy appears to be small but positive.

Black-Owned Financial Institutions

Money too often passes through the ghetto economy "without lingering long enough to turn over several times and thereby generate incomes for other of the community's residents."[16] If the dollars that inner-city residents bring into their communities are spent several times within the community, then additional economic activity is generated that will tend to benefit other ghetto residents. Similarly, if the savings of black residents could be channeled via financial institutions to local borrowers, they would generate additional neighborhood economic activity. Developing black-owned financial institutions and other businesses is therefore advocated as a strategy for slowing the speed with which money flows out of the ghettos.

In black communities, financial institutions have traditionally done a minimal job of servicing the loan demands of local households and businesses. As the central-city areas in this country become increasingly populated by blacks and other minorities, local financial institutions have often preferred to lend money to developing areas. Limited access to the loan funds of existing financial intermediaries has been a major impetus for blacks to start their own banks and savings and loan associations.

The development of the financial sector of the economy typically stimulates economic growth by mobilizing savings that would otherwise be held as idle cash balances and by facilitating the allocation of funds to finance economic activity. Households, businesses, and local governments each depend upon the availability of such funds to finance economic functions beyond those supportable by their current internal capacity to raise funds. However, the mere existence of financial institutions provides no assurance that economically backward areas, such as inner-city black communities, will experience increased development by participating in the financial intermediation processes. Local savers undoubtedly enjoy the benefits of the safety and convenience that financial institutions provide, but local borrowers may not have access to the pool of community savings that financial intermediaries assemble.

Mere ignorance and or discriminatory attitudes are not solely responsible for the reluctance of financial institutions to serve the loan demands of inner-city black households and businesses. Ghettos may be risky places to lend money. Furthermore, in societies characterized by extreme local differences in economic activity, capital often migrates to the richer areas causing a "backwash" effect that may lessen investment in poorer localities. Myrdal has argued that in those economies characterized by uneven regional development, expansion in one area has backwash effects that may drain capital resources from other localities. According to Myrdal, increased demand in centers of expansion will spur investment, which in turn increases purchasing power and investment in a multiplier fashion. If rising savings lag behind investment, funds from outlying regions will tend to migrate to the expanding area in search of returns on capital that are high and secure. "The banking system, if not regulated to act differently, tends to become an instrument for siphoning off the savings from the poorer regions to the richer and more progressive ones."[17]

Black communities have been particularly incensed by the practice of red-lining, whereby lending institutions map older city districts off limits for loans and mortgages. When would-be property buyers are denied loans irrespective of income, older neighborhoods turn into newer slums.

Under the prodding of community groups in Chicago, the Federal

Home Loan Bank (FHLB) asked 180 area S & Ls to report the geographic locations (by zip codes) of their home mortgages and savings deposits. Though only 127 associations returned useful data, their responses clearly indicated that older Chicago neighborhoods were receiving far less for their deposit dollar in mortgage loans than the expanding suburban areas. The newer southwest and northwest areas of Chicago, which were predominantly white, were receiving, per savings deposit dollar, 4.5 times more in new mortgage loans than the red-lined, depressed, predominantly black areas of the city. Even these newer, more affluent areas were receiving new mortgage loans that were, relative to their aggregate savings deposits, disproportionately small in comparison to the loans extended to the outlying suburbs. Chicago's S & Ls were, collectively, serving as a mechanism for siphoning off the savings of Chicago residents to finance suburban housing. Although older parts of the city received the least in mortgage money for their deposit dollar, the FHLB survey indicates that the newer city neighborhoods were also net exporters of funds.[18]

The "efficient" allocation of mortgage money by a profit-maximizing financial intermediary often channels funds away from the central city to the expanding suburbs, where returns are attractive and loan risk is minimal. Inner-city disinvestment is the consequence, and the side effects are viewed by opponents of red-lining as a direct cause of deterioration in older neighborhoods. Beyond the obvious distributional consequences of S & L red-lining policies, the notion of market failure is relevant for judging the allocative efficiency of mortgage money utilization by the red-lining S & L. Neighborhood environment, a major determinant of property values, is considered a public good; when an S & L's lending policy contributes positively to the environment of an inner-city community, that S & L could not expect to capture most of the resultant benefits. When benefits cannot be captured, loans that carry a high social payoff may not be made, and resource misallocation is likely to occur.

Since blatant red-lining has been outlawed in recent years, it has become a matter of degree. Phase one entails increasing the difficulty of obtaining a home mortgage. For example, financial institutions demand high down payments, charge high interest rates, and write mortgages with maturities of less than twenty years, resulting in a decline in neighborhood property values. In phase two, conventional mortgages are cut off to a community. Prospective home buyers must find financial intermediaries that are willing to approve FHA-guaranteed mortgage loans.

With the disappearance of conventional mortgages, home improvement loans also start to dry up. Some FHA specialists, such as mortgage bankers, do not deal in home improvement loans. Certain banks or S & Ls that deal in FHA loans will not approve home improvement loans in neighborhoods that are red-lined from conventional mortgages. Since FHA mortgages are insured, the lending institutions holding these mortgages have no incentive to help the borrower keep up his property. Property in red-lined neighborhoods becomes increasingly unimproved and unrepaired. The self-fulfilling prophecy behind the logic of red-lining creates another deteriorating city neighborhood.

Most central-city S & Ls are vehicles for siphoning off city savings to finance suburban housing. Financial intermediaries have often served to channel savings toward areas where economic activity was expanding. In the era since World War II, outlying suburban areas have been expanding much more rapidly than the central cities; therefore, it is not surprising to observe that the savings of central-city residents have often been used to finance suburban construction. Mobility of capital is not, by itself, prima facie evidence of socially disruptive resource allocation. However, when housing segregation serves to limit the choice of residential location to the central city, America's urban black population has a vested interest in limiting capital mobility when it tends to undermine the quality of central-city life. When the flow of savings from the city to the suburb becomes a tidal wave, when the red-lining of neighborhoods by financial institutions becomes a causal factor in the deterioration of central-city neighborhoods, then the mobility of capital becomes a socially disruptive phenomenon for those whose lives are linked to the viability of the central city.

Black-owned banks and S & Ls can potentially reverse the ghetto savings drain by pooling and investing the savings of ghetto residents to finance local economic development. All of this sounds fine in theory, but what does the evidence indicate about its practical implementation? The black S & Ls do appear to be providing housing capital to their communities, in line with their stated role. They finance inner-city housing to a much greater extent than nonminority S & Ls that are located in central cities. The proportion of assets invested by black S & Ls in FHA and HUD (Housing and Urban Development) mortgages, particularly low-income HUD mortgages, averaged well over three times that of the white S & Ls. Evidence indicates, though, that black S & Ls experience relatively high costs in financing housing in their communities. Lower than average deposit accounts and loan sizes result in higher operating costs, per dollar of deposits, for the black S & Ls.[19] Relative to nonminority S & Ls, they also experience a higher proportion of foreclosed loans and bad debt losses. These problems are rooted in the lower and less stable incomes and high unemployment characterizing black communities. The result is relatively low profitability for the black S & Ls. Finally the black S & Ls as a group represent less than 1 percent of all U.S. S & Ls by number, and their asset holdings are under two-tenths of 1 percent of the industry totals. Their small numbers and their below-average profitability limit their total impact on ghetto housing markets and their potential for future expansion.

Black-owned banks have been growing in number much more rapidly than the black S & Ls. Most of the black banks have been chartered since 1963, and they break rather sharply into two groups: the older, conservative, predominantly southern banks and the newer, more aggressive, predominantly northern institutions. In some instances, aggregation of the older southern banks and the new black-owned institutions distorts the analysis of either type.

The recent record of black-owned banks has been mixed but their most severe problems appear to stem from start-up difficulties of very new banks. Difficulties ease measurably after several years of operations. The following sequence of events characterizes the early experiences of several black banks. While still learning basic operating procedures, they move aggressively into inner-city business lending. For example, Freedom National Bank in New York City (chartered in 1964) became the nation's largest lender to black-owned businesses, but it had little solid loan documentation and a weak collection system. When the inevitable retrenching came in the late 1960s, Freedom National had to write off over $900,000 in bad loans and the bank barely avoided bankruptcy and dissolution. The FDIC had to intervene in the affairs of the overextended Unity Bank of Roxbury, Massachusetts when its liberal business loan policy had driven it to the brink of insolvency after less than two years in business. In 1973, the Skyline National Bank of Denver (chartered in 1971) was transferred from black to white ownership and more than $700,000 in bad loans had to be written off.

After plunging into risky loans prior to learning basic banking operations, the affected banks find that they are losing money, having difficulty controlling their loan portfolio, and under pressure from bank regulatory authorities to mend their ways. They invariably retrench by switching from loans into such assets as government securities and sales of funds in the federal funds markets. In contrast, the more successful institutions moved gradually and cautiously into business lending as they acquired the expertise necessary to evaluate the credit worthiness of their particular business clientele.

Loan loss problems are not insurmountable barriers but they are very real constraints on the kinds of business financing that black banks can engage in profitably. No major barriers seem to stand in the path of black-owned banks who wish to finance local black entrepreneurs via such relatively low-risk vehicles as SBA guaranteed long-term loans. SBA loan guarantee programs proliferated in the 1970s and provided black bankers with the opportunity to make business loans (guaranteed against default risk by SBA) and protect their slim capital positions; in the event of default, SBA will absorb a minimum of 90% of the losses in loan principal. Another key role, encompassing the most traditional type of bank lending activity for black banks, entails servicing the working capital needs of existing community businesses whose viability is well established prior to loan approval. This short-term lending role is vital and it is being met quite inadequately by existing financial intermediaries. In this role, black banks would be only one piece in the financial infrastructure that is so essential to generating viable black business development. The long-term lending and financing of new businesses can best be handled on a large scale by government assumption of default risk via some vehicle like the SBA guarantee.

Black banks undoubtedly do face a loan demand function characterized by generally higher risk than that faced by nonminority banks. Because lower per capita income and less stable employment are characteristic of black communities, black banks may experience a high proportion of loan defaults relative to nonminority banks of comparable size. These phenomena are not necessarily severe problems for black banks because they can be offset by utilizing government loan default insurance programs, or by charging loan recipients rates of interest that compensate the banks for their risk. Available evidence clearly shows that newer black banks hold relatively far more FHA-HUD and VA insured home mortgages and SBA guaranteed commercial and industrial loans than do comparable nonminority banks.[20]

Problems facing black banks go beyond loan losses. They have lower average account sizes, more rapid deposit turnover, and, thus, higher personnel costs per deposit dollar relative to nonminority banks. As with loan losses, these problems are rooted in the nature of the communities served by the black-owned banks. Ghetto areas do offer some unique advantages, however, along with the burdens of loan risk and high operating costs. Often, the competition facing inner-city, black-owned banks is minimal. Thousands of residents in every big city ghetto are, after all, employed in high-wage sectors of the economy, and the pawnbrokers, ghetto merchants, and loan sharks offer banks very little competition for this market stratum. Chicago has proven to be an excellent market for black-owned banks. In the early 1960s, nine of the city's wards (each with an average population of 70,000) had no bank at all, while eleven wards had one bank each. By 1974, these same wards housed the nations's first, second, thirteenth, sixteenth, and seventeenth largest black banks. Although the evidence is not yet conclusive, it appears that those black banks that survive beyond the start-up phase of operations achieve operating costs that are only slightly above those of nonminority banks, and become increasingly active lenders within their communities.[21] Indeed, some of the most profitable banks are also the most aggressive lenders.

Some of the problems that characterize the operation of black financial institutions stem not from their institutional defects, but rather from the fact that these institutions are doing precisely what their proponents in the 1960s hoped they would do. They are collecting deposits from black community households and businesses, and they are channeling a substantial proportion of these funds back into these communities in the form of loans. These institutions mobilize the savings of a clientele whose incomes are, on the average, lower and less stable than those of nonminorities. If they are truly mobilizing the savings of their communities, black financial institutions will necessarily find that their mean deposit account sizes are well below the national averages for corresponding types of financial institutions. Smaller account size necessarily means more paperwork and extra teller labor time per deposit dollar, and this raises personnel expenses relative to deposits. While this represents "inefficiency" in a sense, it reflects, more accurately, the fact that the financial performance of black banks and S & Ls is affected by the economic characteristics of the markets they serve. If black financial institutions reported mean deposit sizes and personnel costs that were identical to the national averages, we would suspect that they were not serving the lower-income saver that typifies the inner-city population. If black financial institutions are truly serving their communities, then their financial performance should reflect the economic disparities that characterize black and white communities.

Community Development Corporations

It was in the 1960s, when violence and civil disorders erupted in south Los Angeles, Chicago's South Side, East Cleveland, and other black residential areas, that leaders from business, government, and academia began discussing black economic development. Among all of the ventures launched in that era, the community development corporations had the farthest reaching visions of ghetto uplifting. First, they were oriented toward improvement of the entire community. Individual gain was not dismissed as a motivating force, but it was quite secondary. Second, community development corporations acted as a channel by which capital, expert knowledge, and various kinds of federal assistance were drawn into the inner-city ghetto. This structure offered the potential for reversing the usual drain of resources out of the ghetto. Finally, none of the community development corporations were fully self-sustaining, and they flourished or died in direct proportion to the willingness of large corporations, foundations, and government agencies to finance their activities. By 1970, almost all major cities had one or more community development corporations, but their numbers declined in later years as their sponsors withdrew financial support.

The Bedford-Stuyvesant Restoration Project typified community development corporations of the 1960s. Its goals were far reaching and idealistic. The community it sought to restore was in dire straights. Today the Bedford-Stuyvesant Restoration Project stands as a monument to what the community development corporation can hope to achieve; it offers a valuable lesson in identifying the important components of a successful ghetto revitalization program.[22]

Early in 1966, the late Senator Robert Kennedy took a walking tour of Bedford-Stuyvesant. This section of Brooklyn occupies six square miles; if it were a city, it would rank, in terms of population, about even in size with Cincinnati, Ohio, Yet this "city" had no public hospital, no downtown shopping or commercial area, and only one public academic high school within its boundaries. There were rows of burned-out buildings, and abandoned cars rusting in the streets; the unemployment rate was close to 30 percent of the workforce. Senator Kennedy was appalled by what he saw. He responded by assisting in the establishment of two parallel nonprofit community development corporations. The Bedford-Stuyvesant Restoration Corporation was given primary responsibility for implementing restoration, and its board of directors consisted of community residents. Its sister corporation, the Bedford-Stuyvesant Development and Services Corporations, was (and is) made up of representatives from large corporations: IBM, Mobil Oil, Citibank, and the like. Their primary role was to encourage outside business investment in the area and generally to assist where needed.

By the late 1970s, community development corporations were declining overall but the Bedford-Stuyvesant Restoration Corporation was operating with a budget exceeding $50 million. Its economic development division (EDD) works on enlarging the community's economic base. By 1978, it had established or assisted over 125 business ventures and created over 3,300 new jobs. EDD has lent over $6.5 million in low-interest loans to encourage creation and expansion of businesses that are owned and operated by local residents. Its largest division is the physical development division (PDD), which seeks to renovate structurally sound buildings and to construct new buildings where renovation is not possible. Whenever feasible, the PDD hires local contractors, buys from local suppliers, and employs local labor. PDD has added nearly 800 new units and more than 900 rehabilitated units to the Bedford-Stuyvesant housing stock. PDD has also made over 1,100 mortgage loans totaling about $23 million, all to local residents. PDD has also played the role of developer in several major commercial and industrial building ventures, including an IBM plant and a commercial shopping center.

The Restoration Corporation's Nonprofit and Community Programs Division (CPD) operates, among other things, a 210-seat theater that makes off-off Broadway theater available to community residents and a seasonal employment program that has made cosmetic improvements to the exteriors of over 3,000 area homes. CPD, in addition, has placed over 8,000 local residents in jobs or training programs.

Restoration officers claim that no formula for success exists in running its programs, but certain necessary conditions for probable success are (1) the involvement of intelligent, well-trained, and highly motivated people. Restoration Corporation hires first-class staff and pays them competitive wages. (2) The board of directors members must be intelligent, responsible people chosen for the resources that they can bring into the organization, and for the amount of community support they have.

Today the Bedford-Stuyvesant Restoration Corporation is the country's largest community development corporation. It stands as a model of what such an organization can accomplish. Yet its achievements continue to be defined in the long-run by the willingness of its government and corporate sponsors to support its programs.

Barriers to Inner-City Development

While the development efforts discussed in this chapter have generated economic progress in many cities, it would take them at least a millennium or two to impact significantly the lives of most ghetto residents. Even in areas such as Bedford-Stuyvesant, all programs described at best directly touch the lives of less than 10 percent of the ghetto population. Less tangible, secondary effects—strengthening of the regional multiplier, for example—may indeed bring some benefit to most ghetto residents. Nonetheless, inner-city economic development efforts face some very real economic and political barriers.

The persistent drain of resources from the ghetto prevents the inner city from accumulating significant amounts of capital. Poor people do not generate, by themselves, large amounts of resources for economic growth. Public agencies and private sources have generated small flows of capital inward to the inner cities, but these flows, often mere tokens, have slowed in the 1980s. The lack of capital is the most important barrier to inner-city economic development. The internal ghetto market is weak due to the low incomes of its residents. The twin barriers of inadequate capital and poor markets could be overcome by economic development and assistance plans analogous to those applied to some of the developing countries abroad. Markets could be found outside of the ghetto, especially through government contracts, if capital was provided to supply resources for production.

A variety of government programs has sought to channel capital and procurement contracts to ghetto businesses. The record of the minority business loan programs is highly mixed, and loans from these sources have been declining in number since the early 1970s. Procurement contracts targeted for minority businesses have been growing rapidly in dollar volume in the 1980s, but a multitude of problems surrounding the awarding and administering of these contracts makes it difficult to judge their impact. Reforms in the administration of these contracts, as suggested earlier in this chapter, could assure that billions of procurement dollars enter the ghetto economy each year. Development of inner-city, minority-owned businesses could be aided greatly by this infusion of outside money. If they rely solely upon the limited ghetto market, black-owned firms as a group will lack the economic strength necessary to help alleviate inner-city problems.

The black-owned and controlled S & Ls and banks have helped to slow the drain of savings out of the ghetto. While they appear to be increasingly active lenders within the inner city, they are a small number of financial institutions and they are below average in profitability relative to their nonminority counterparts. The economic weakness of the markets they serve translates into high operating costs and above average loan losses. Like the nonfinancial minority businesses, their prospects for growth and profitability are limited if they rely solely upon the weak ghetto market.

Lack of capital, weak internal markets, and related problems—poor public services, a high incidence of economic crime, etc.—do not provide a favorable environment for the development of economic activity. Yet the most important barriers to inner-city development may be political rather than economic. Decisions about the use of public resources are made by people who live outside of the ghettos. In normal times, they prefer to ignore ghetto problems. When a group such as the Bedford-Stuyvesant Restoration Corporation succeeds in attracting outside resources, deterioration can be checked, jobs can be created. In the process, people subsisting on government transfers such as food stamps can, instead, become economically productive and self-sufficient. Community spirit can be improved and the restoration process can get underway. Such cases are the exception; neglect is the norm.

15

Can We Solve the Problem?

THE URBAN RACIAL PROBLEM IS DEEPLY ROOTED IN THE ECONOMIC structure of the United States. The problem is one of exploitation of racial minorities from which the white majority benefits in specific, material ways. This economic exploitation is strengthened and solidified by racial attitudes that identify the exploited minority, justify its exploitation, and provide a psychological rationale for those who benefit.

Whether white racism is the cause of economic exploitation, the result of it, or both, is immaterial. The two are intertwined and interrelated: racial attitudes help to justify and rationalize the white advantage, and the exploited position of blacks leads to conditions and relationships that generate white racist attitudes. Nevertheless, the fundamental problem is economic. The top dog position of whites helps to generate an ideology that sustains the underclass position of ghettoized blacks and Hispanics.

Yet individual acts of exploitation or overt discrimination are seldom necessary. The whole structure of the economic system crowds minorities into low-wage menial occupations and segregates them in the urban ghetto. The ghetto then becomes a source of low-wage labor. It is directly exploited by outside economic interests, and it provides a dumping ground for the human residuals created by economic change. These economic conditions are stabilized by transfer payments that preserve the ghetto in a poverty that recreates itself from generation to generation.

Solutions will have to break up the economic relationships on which exploitation is based. An underclass of low-wage workers will have to be admitted to the relative affluence of the rest of the society. The high rates of unemployment that preserve the low-wage system will have to be eliminated. These two propositions, plus full employment at a living wage, entail a substantial redistribution of income. If the bottom 20 percent of American families are to obtain a larger share of the good things in life, the upper 80 percent will have to share a small proportion of their affluence. This is the difficult decision we will have to make: strategies that ignore this fundamental proposition are destined to fail. The idea that both white and black can move together toward greater affluence through national economic betterment is a formula for preserving present economic relationships.

The Present Strategy

A coherent strategy for dealing with the urban racial problem has emerged in recent years. It consists of two interrelated sets of programs. One part is the equal opportunity program which seeks to open jobs and business opportunities to blacks and other minorities by eliminating barriers to employment and advancement. Special education, training, loan, and other opportunity-enhancing programs try to reduce the handicaps of blacks and other minorities, recognizing that they start from a disadvantaged position relative to whites.

These programs have had some success. Significant gains were made since their inception in the 1960s and many individuals benefited from them. Blacks, Hispanics, and other minority groups were able to move upward in government, the professions, educational institutions, and business enterprise. A number of relatively skilled jobs, both blue-collar and white-collar, were opened to blacks and other minorities.

The equal opportunity strategy focuses on the individual. It is based on the implicit assumption that one's position and rewards are the result of individual intelligence, ability, and effort. It assumes that if the race is fair the swift will win, that if the game is not fixed the best and brightest will do best. The name, equal opportunity, is quite apt: the program seeks to remove barriers and equate opportunities so that everyone will have an equal chance. It is in the American tradition of individual achievement.

This approach has serious limitations, however. It does nothing about the negative pressures that lead to labor market crowding. As we pointed out in chapter 12, opening opportunities in the primary sector of the labor market does not prevent crowding of minorities in the secondary sector. Expanded opportunities for some are quite consistent with restricted opportunities for most. Indeed, the era of widened opportunities was also one of a growing gap between the more and less fortunate. This is not to say that expanded opportunities are bad. They are clearly useful and important. But they are not enough.

In a subtle way, widened opportunities support the very economic processes that create and preserve the urban ghetto, the low-wage sector of the labor market, and poverty in America. They tend to draw intelligent and capable members of minority groups into the affluent mainstream, away from their fellows in the underclass. Some become fully committed to the ideology of individual achievement and exhort others to follow in their path.[1] Meanwhile, at the other end of the economic spectrum, those who remain caught in poverty and ghettoization are told, or believe, that the fault is theirs, that if they had the ability and initiative to seize opportunities, they too could have been affluent.

The ideology of individualism and its equal opportunity program achieve two things. They provide a rationale for not attacking the roots of the problem, and they divide minority groups into haves and have nots that correspond to a similar division in the political economy as a whole. Politically, they interfere with the united action of minority groups, which, as we shall see, is essential for effective remedial action. It is in this sense that equal opportunity progams are fundamentally supportive of the existing economic, political, and social order.

The second part of the present strategy is the income support programs, particularly AFDC and food stamps, that stabilize the urban ghetto. Together with subsidies for housing, medical care programs, and subsidized urban transportation, they make life in the inner city more bearable. These programs raise the incomes of the ghetto poor, and improve economic conditions in the inner city. But they preserve the problem instead of solving it.

First, transfers of real and money income to the ghetto come from taxpayers outside the ghetto who have a general interest in preserving the existence of a low-wage sector. Thus, transfers are maintained at a level no higher than the minimum amount necessary to preserve social and economic stability. This political reality condemns income transfers and subsidies to levels too low to bring fundamental changes in either income distribution patterns or the urban ghetto.

Second, the persistent flow of income and resources out of the ghetto continues. Higher incomes for the ghetto population mean an enlarged flow through the ghetto. The beneficiaries are not only ghetto residents, but those in strategic positions to benefit from the flow-through of income and resources. These beneficiaries are numerous: absentee landlords, managers and workers in the criminal industries, middle-income employees of the welfare bureaucracies and school systems, developers of low-income housing projects and the union members employed in the construction industries, and similarly situated people. One effect of a higher level of ghetto life sustained by income transfers and more public services is an enlarged group that benefits from the drain of income and that has a vested interest in continuing things as they are. The strategy of income support strengthens the economic position of those who live off the ghetto without removing the causes of ghettoization.

The present strategy is not all bad. Increased opportunities are clearly an improvement over the older pattern of highly restricted opportunities. Income support as a holding action to reduce human misery is clearly desirable. But these programs, by themselves, are inadequate. The next step is to move from amelioration to solution.

An Economic Program for Fundamental Change

Serious proposals for elimanating the urban ghetto must involve changes in the economic relationships that sustain the ghetto economy and preserve the low-wage labor force. These changes imply elimination of the poverty-ridden underclass that largely makes up the low-wage labor force. That can be done only if there is a significant shift in the distribution of income from the relatively affluent to the poor, not through transfer payments, but through the normal functioning of the economy. Put bluntly, the poor must earn a living wage if the urban ghetto is to be eliminated and America's economic underclass is to participate effectively in economic progress. This is the key to any real solution of the urban racial problem.

The means for achieving these changes are available. A group of programs and policies that build upon those that have already been tried and everyone is familiar with can be used. They attack the economic basis of the ghetto economy by concentrating on the employment problems and low-wage occupations that create its permanent depression and poverty.

Full Employment

The first requisite is full employment. A job for anyone wishing to work is necessary if the permanent depression of the ghetto economy is to be eliminated. Simply increasing aggregate demand by fiscal and monetary policies is not enough, for inflationary conditions will appear in the larger economy before the ghetto approaches full employment. Increases in aggregate demand will have to be supplemented by special employment programs that reach the ghetto un-employed. One possible approach could be the following.

1. Monetary and fiscal policies can be used to bring unemployment rates for the prime labor force—white men aged twenty-two to forty-four—down to the pure "frictional" unemployment rate of 1 to 1.5 percent. This criterion is used as a benchmark for full employment because inflationary increases in labor costs tend to begin when this prime labor force is fully employed.

2. At this point ghetto unemployment rates may still be as high as 6 to 7 percent or more. Special employment programs aimed at ghetto residents can then be used to bring ghetto unemployment rates down to levels prevailing in the rest of the economy.

A wide variety of employment programs could be used for this purpose. Public service employment, youth employment programs, or programs to encourage private employment of ghetto residents could be developed. The important point is that jobs should be made available by a combination of general prosperity and special employment programs focusing on the ghetto.

The only revolutionary aspect of these proposals for job creation is their magnitude. It may be neccessary to provide jobs for as many as 5 million persons, particularly if minimum wage rates are raised to levels that provide adequate support for a family. An employment program of that scope could be expensive. Suppose, for example, we were to employ 5 million persons at full-time jobs in public service employment at $5.00 per hour. The annual cost would be $50 billion. That total could be reduced by providing tax and other incentives to business enterprises for hiring some of the workers. And reduced costs for welfare and other social services to the poor, and for police protection, would chop off a significant part of the total, perhaps as much as half. Nevertheless, the potential annual cost of full employment for the ghettos would be high.

A Living Wage

The second requisite for fundamental change in the economics of the ghetto is employment at a living wage. With a poverty line of $9900 for a family of four in 1982, which is barely adequate and well below a minimum health and decency standard, a wage of $5 per hour will bring in $10,000 annually (40 hours per week, 50 weeks per year).

The standard for a revised and extended minimum wage law could be the wage that provides an income at or just above the poverty line for an urban family of four, indexed to consumer prices, when one member of the family is employed full-time. Coverage should be extended to all workers, and enforcement should be strengthened by stronger sanctions against employers who evade the law.

This is perhaps the most controversial part of the proposal set forth here, and the one most difficult for many to accept. It has tremendous implications for the entire economy. Before it is rejected out of hand, note this: Australian minimum wage legislation is written exactly the way that we propose here. Whatever may be the problems of the Australian economy, few experts attribute them to minimum wage legislation. A minimum wage is the quickest way to end the poverty and depressed conditions of the ghetto, with the proviso that it must be accompanied by a full employment program of the sort just described if it is to increase ghetto incomes adequately.

Part of the accepted folklore about the minimum wage is that it has adverse effects on employment. This folklore is supported by simplistic application of static economic theory. But the problem is intricate: higher costs to employers also mean increased aggregate demand when those who earn wages spend the money, and higher labor costs trigger increased use of capital equipment, with quite uncertain dynamic effects. The long-term effects of a higher minimum wage are not well understood, particularly when the circular flow of spending and the dynamics of economic growth are brought into the analysis.[2] Furthermore, the proposal made here does not stand alone, but is part of a larger program that would provide both jobs and training. If there are unemployment effects of a decent minimum wage, and that is problematic, they would be overcome by the job creation aspects of our program.

Nevertheless, caution should be observed. Increases in the minimum wage to the higher levels proposed here could be spread over a three- or five-year period. This would minimize its effect on unemployment and give employers time to adapt. Under ideal circumstances, changes in the minimum wage should be instituted during a period of recovery or economic expansion, in order to minimize any negative effects on the economy.[3]

With higher incomes from more jobs at higher wages, many of the other problems of the ghetto will be greatly reduced, and some may disappear entirely. Higher incomes will enable many of the poor to provide for their own transportation, either by public mass transit or by private cars. Cities may have to adjust by providing more extensive public transportation systems and more effective patterns of traffic control. But their revenue potential will also be increased because of higher incomes earned by their citizens. Higher incomes will enable ghettoites to move out of the ghetto if they wish (and if housing segregation is prevented), since they will be able to afford housing in other areas. Within the ghetto, effective demand for better housing will trigger a response from the housing industry. Strongly responsive to market demand, the industry can be expected to provide the better housing that buyers or renters could now afford. Many public services, including education, could be expanded and improved because of the higher revenues cities would obtain, for prosperous people create prosperous communities.

Business enterprise within the ghetto would be stimulated by the increase in purchasing power. With higher family incomes and greater financial stability, one could confidently predict a relative decline in the exploitive ghetto business community that stresses high prices and easy credit. A better climate for less exploitive business-consumer relationships would also result. The basis for ghetto-owned private, cooperative, or community business enterprises would be improved. Indeed, one could predict both a partial breakdown of the barriers between the ghetto and the rest of the economy and a stronger basis for economic development within the ghetto.

Training and Retraining

One way to minimize the unemployment effects of a decent minimum wage is to provide an extensive training program for workers in the secondary labor market. If higher productivity is needed to enable private firms to employ low-wage labor profitably, a portion of the gap can be overcome by training programs to make workers more efficient.

Efficient workers are only half of the story, however. Productivity is the joint outcome of human effort together with capital equipment. If workers must be paid higher wages, employers will invest in more capital to raise output per worker to levels that make it possible to pay the higher wages. For example, U.S. manufacturing firms that pay union wages here provide a substantially more capital-intensive plant within the United States than in their low-wage operations overseas. Low wages and labor-intensive production go together. As a general rule, the more capital-intensive the production process is, the greater the skill and training required of the worker. Compare the laborer who uses a shovel to the bulldozer operator, for example. An increased minimum wage will trigger more capital-intensive methods of production, which will require increased skill on the part of workers.

Training of workers, then, will be needed to facilitate and encourage the transition from low-wage, labor-intensive production and service jobs to higher-wage, more capital-intensive processes. One way to speed the transition is to provide training programs under public sponsorship to upgrade the general skills of the labor force and to provide specific skills needed by employers. The cost of training and placement is small compared with the cost of public service employment for workers displaced by technological change. To the extent that training for placement in private sector jobs can substitute for public jobs, the cost of a full employment program at a living wage can be greatly reduced.

Economic Opportunity

Unless attention is paid to the barriers that keep racial minority groups in urban ghettos, the program outlined here will have a limited impact. To some extent, those barriers can be weakened by geographical dispersion through integrated housing patterns in the suburbs. However, greater progress can be made by eliminating discrimination in employment, for it is there that the most important barriers to equality of opportunity are found. Far more than is now being done can be accomplished by extension of equal opportunity, affirmative action, and related employment programs, especially if they are coordinated with training and education and with public service employment.

For example, many local governments, government contractors, and public agencies have affirmative-action hiring programs in which specific jobs are designated as ones for which blacks or Hispanics will be hired. Some of these efforts to develop racial balance in employment have been relatively successful, especially when strong administrative pressures have been applied. The basic concept is that blacks and other minorities are hired at all skill levels in approximately the same proportion that they represent in the total labor force in the locality. This approach could well be extended by law to all private employers, not just government contractors. Private business firms could be required to develop affirmative-action hiring programs satisfactory to a human relations office in the local governmental unit, operating within federal guidelines and properly staffed for supervision and enforcement. In this way, the opportunity system could move beyond equal opportunity toward positive action that actively seeks out blacks and other minorities. The program has already been successfully tested on a limited scale. The time has come to apply it to the entire private and public sector.

Even this sort of action is bound to raise objections from members of the white majority on the grounds that it is essentially a thinly disguised quota system—which it is. The rationale for a general affirmative-action hiring program is that, up until now, an undisguised and open quota system has been operating in which the black quota in many occupations was zero or near zero. The result was the phenomenon of crowding discussed in chapter 12.

This proposal merely would raise the quota to a proportion approximating the nonwhite proportion of the labor force at all levels of employment and in all types of jobs. When combined with programs for full employment and manpower training, it could greatly diminish crowding and widen minority employment opportunities substantially.

Expanded opportunities for minorities is not sufficient by itself, however. Chapter 12 pointed out that blacks and other minorities can move into occupations formerly held by the white majority without significantly altering the crowding of large numbers of the minority into low-wage occupations. If that should occur, the problem will remain, while economic distinctions within the minority come to approximate those of the larger society. It is for this reason that affirmative-action hiring programs are at best a corollary to the more fundamental policy of achieving full employment at a living wage.

Economic Development

It is easier to take jobs to people rather than people to jobs, particularly in today's era of rapid communications and easy transfer of technology. But the inner city is not a favorable environment for economic development. Although it has a plentiful supply of labor, the internal market is weak. Poor people make poor customers and do not generate large amounts of capital for economic growth. Both markets and capital would have to be found outside the ghetto if a successful process of economic growth is to be started.

A proposal calling for the establishment of urban enterprise zones within the inner city would make a beginning. Enterprises locating within the zones would obtain tax reductions as an incentive to establish operations there and, presumably, would employ people from the inner city. Taxes, however, are one of the less important factors in location of enterprises, and the urban enterprise zones would have to compete with a variety of tax concessions that many states, counties, and cities offer in order to attract business firms. More is needed.

One promising approach would channel development capital into the inner city from private banks. Proposed in 1968 for New York City but never implemented, the plan would start with deposit of city-owned funds in local banks on the condition that the banks make loans to a group of development corporations within the inner city. The incentive to do so would be provided by the city funds that the banks would be able to use. Some of the development corporations would be devoted to attracting or starting new enterprises in the inner city. Others would provide loans or venture capital to private enterprises there. Included in this scheme is a guaranteed market for the new inner-city enterprises by purchases by the city government. For example, an enterprise might borrow from a development corporation to produce pencils for use in the city government and school system. The strategy is simple: enterprises providing inner-city jobs would obtain outside capital to produce for outside markets.[4]

Such a plan could also involve the federal government, which could also make deposits of federal funds tied to inner-city development loans by banks. The federal government could also contract to buy all or part of the output of the assisted enterprises. Another proposal would have a federal agency provide investment funds directly to enterprises, bypassing private banks. A national ghetto investment bank and a national ghetto credit corporation would provide both long- and short-term capital.[5]

Similarly, an internal flow of capital within the ghetto could be established through inner-city community banks. These financial institutions would obtain deposits from inner-city residents, and from outside as well, including workers in the enterprises it was helping to finance. The funds would be used to finance inner-city enterprises whose markets would be assured by government contracts. The purpose is to reduce the outward flow of inner-city savings to the economy outside the ghetto, and to use those savings for inner-city economic development.

A community bank could also contract with its enterprise clients to provide a variety of business services, such as record keeping and auditing, and business consulting services. The community bank would do more than merely provide capital. It would be a sheltering organization whose functions would include monitoring the performance of enterprises for which it provides capital, providing them with business services and expert advice, and assisting them when problems arise.[6]

Economic development within the inner-city ghetto must also address the problem of the outward drain of resources. The community bank is one device that could rechannel savings into economic development. Another proposal would use federal funds to establish a national ghetto development corporation to buy business enterprises already established in the inner city, including retail stores, that are owned outside the ghetto; sell them to ghetto residents, and assist in their development.[7] The new owners could be individuals, private business firms, worker-owned enterprises, or "community enterprises" owned by a substantial number of local residents, depending on the source of financing available.

The process of economic development in the urban ghetto requires changes in the flow of resources. Profits from inner-city enterprises and savings of ghetto residents need to find new channels that would direct them into inner-city development of viable producing enterprises. Capital needs to be brought in from outside as well, and markets must be found outside, if the enterprises are to remain viable. Together with a decent wage for the ghetto's chief resource, its labor, this strategy could both raise many in the ghetto out of poverty and start a self-generating process of economic development.

Transfer Payments

Not every family has a wage earner. The aged, the disabled, and broken families require assistance. With a stronger economic base, higher wages, reduced unemployment, and a process of economic development at work, the need for income supports such as AFDC, food stamps, public assistance, and medicaid should be substantially less. Significant reductions could be made in public funds to maintain the level of life in the ghetto.

Initially, these reductions in transfer payments to individuals would undoubtedly be less than the increase in public funds to provide resources for economic development. But as the process of economic expansion takes hold and becomes self-sustaining, the need for capital from public funds would diminish and end, while the need for transfer payments to individuals would decline more rapidly. Assistance to non-earners would certainly not be eliminated entirely, but it could be reduced substantially. An initial injection of investment capital for a decade or more could help bring about a permanent reduction in the population that requires public support.

Will continuation of transfer payments discourage employment? To some extent the employment disincentive of income supports is unavoidable. But it should be substantially reduced in an economy with high levels of employment and decent wages. Most Americans, whatever their racial or cultural background, are motivated by a desire to live well and to succeed as income earners. Not all are able to do so. Some become discouraged by repeated failures and rebuffs and effectively lose all or part of the desire to better themselves. But these economic failures are largely the result of an economic system that has a high incidence of unemployment and pays low wages in dead-end jobs for many workers. Discouragement is built into the system. An economy that sustains full employment and pays a living wage will be less frustrating and more encouraging. In such an economy a subsistence income will hardly beckon many people, when so much more can be gained by work.

A Digression: Broader Economic Policies and Inflation

One of the common objections to proposals of the sort suggested here, particularly increases in the minimum wage, is that they would be inflationary. Costs of production in the low-wage industries would rise, causing upward pressure on prices. If federal fiscal and monetary policies maintain aggregate demand at full-employment levels, the cost pressures could easily lead to price increases. The price increases would not only cancel out a large portion of the benefits from the higher minimum wage, but could also trigger demands for wage increases by other workers that, in turn, would push up prices in other sectors of the economy as well. An inflationary spiral could ensue.

There is some validity in this argument. At the very least, prices in the low-wage industries would undoubtedly be adjusted upward to compensate at least partly for the higher costs imposed by an increase in the minimum wage of the amounts proposed here. Whether an inflationary spiral would be established is another matter, for much depends upon the measures taken to avoid it.

First, special tax credits can be provided for business firms whose wage bill rises significantly because the minimum wage is increased. That fiscal device is widely used to encourage investment, to promote exploration for oil and gas, and generally to promote business enterprise. Here it would be used to ease the cost pressures on firms heavily affected by an increased minimum wage.

There is a second problem. The program envisaged here will enable the poor to earn a living wage, but middle- and upper-income groups will pay more for the products and services of the present low-wage industries. We envisage a significant shift of real income to the poor from others. At least partial compensation can be achieved by reduced personal income tax rates for low- and middle-income families. These are the groups that would be most heavily affected by higher minimum wages; the upper-middle (above $25,000 annual family income) and higher-income brackets could well absorb the higher costs. These changes in federal income tax rates would also have the effect of making the tax system as a whole somewhat more progressive.

Both of these adjustments in the tax system mean reduced government revenues, while programs of economic development for the inner-city ghetto imply increased government expenditures, at least initially. Together they would provide some of the economic stimulus

required to move the economy toward higher levels of aggregate
demand and reduced unemployment that would make possible higher
wages in the low-wage sector of the labor market and contribute to
the success of ghetto economic development.

The key issue is whether the U.S. economy, as it is structured now,
can sustain full employment levels of output without also generating
significant amounts of inflation. Many economists believe that it cannot, unless there is a workable and enforced policy to control wages,
profits, and prices. A comprehensive income policy, and possibly price
controls as well, may be the price of prosperity.

That is a larger issue, however. We are faced with a smaller one.
As the economy moves to generally higher levels of economic activity,
and the ghetto economy makes greater gains than other sectors, a
smaller proportion of the gains will accrue to the economy outside
the ghetto. If the economy as a whole does not expand, and the ghetto
is to benefit, the real costs will have to be borne by those outside the
ghetto. Those real costs may include higher prices for the products
and services of today's low-wage industries. They may also include a
shift in government fiscal priorities away from tax benefits to the
affluent and away from military and military-related spending. Economic programs to eliminate the urban ghetto mean a reordering of
priorities and a restructuring of economic benefits.

The Politics of Economic Change

The economic solutions to the urban racial problem presented here
can be accomplished without significant change in individual attitudes
toward persons of other races. Whites could continue to hate blacks,
and blacks could continue to hate whites, if they wish. They might
have to work together or live near each other because of changed
economic relationships, but there need not be any prior change in
individual racial attitudes for the program to succeed.

None of these programs or policies are new, and, taken indepen-
dently, none are revolutionary in either conception or impact. All
have been tried before, although on a much smaller scale than that
proposed here. Most are part of current programs and policies to a
greater or lesser extent. But their combined impact could shortly
eliminate the inner-city ghettos. The inner city would no longer be
the home of poverty; the low-wage industries would either have disappeared or would have been transformed into high-wage industries;
the low-wage work force would be working for higher wages in either
public or private employment; economic opportunities will have been

widened both through the economy as a whole and within the inner city itself.

Yet when the program proposed here is viewed as a whole, there is little cause for optimism. It envisages such large changes in the economic status quo that it could hardly be expected to obtain majority support at the present time. The political economy of the ghetto is one of a minority held in a dependent position by a majority that benefits economically from the minority's position. As long as the majority is satisfied with the status quo, no major changes can be expected.

One possible avenue of change is through political action by blacks and other minority groups. There has been an upsurge of political organization among blacks in American cities in the last fifteen years, one of the outcomes of the urban revolt of the 1960s. Several large cities, such as Detroit and Chicago, as well as a number of smaller cities, elected black mayors. Black political action has also had some conspicuous failures. New York City, for example, which has a large black population, did not have a single black in a major local government position in 1982. New York City also has a large Hispanic population, and rivalry between the two chief minority groups effectively neutralized the political influence of both. The large financial and real estate interests that provide the city's economic base effectively control city policies.

For the most part, inner-city ghettos lack the strong economic base from which political power might emerge. Even where blacks have achieved a strong political position public policies tend to be dominated by the existing economic pressure groups. Detroit is a good example. Public policies have been strongly oriented toward the interests of the automobile industry, a major employer, and a development program to make Detroit an important center for business services and finance, conventions and entertainment—sectors of the economy heavily weighted toward relatively low-wage service employment. Simply changing the locus of political power is not enough.

Development of political leadership, political cohesiveness, and local political control can make it possible to institute changes. But political action alone is not enough. The experience in New York city suggests that all minority groups must ally themselves politically in order not to dissipate their potential influence. The Detroit experience indicates that control of the economic base by industrial, financial, and real estate interests in the larger economy greatly limits and perhaps determines the direction of public policy. Political action must be combined with a coherent economic program. In particular, an economic program such as that suggested here is necessary, both to mobilize political support and solidarity within the inner-city ghetto and to build the economic foundations for political action.

Political action is limited, however. Economic and political gains for blacks and other minorities will come at the expense of other economic interest groups. In particular, lower-middle income whites may feel threatened as the present underclass moves up. A political backlash and heightened racial tensions or conflict are probable effects of economic and political gains by blacks and Hispanics. Indeed, economic gains for them are a threat to the existing economic and political power structure in general.

One is tempted to draw historical analogies. A traumatic social upheaval on the scale of the Civil War was required to break up the system of coerced labor embodied in slavery. The next pattern of coerced labor, sharecropping and debt tenure, was eliminated under the combined impact of three great social forces, the depression of the 1930s, the economic changes stimulated by World War II, and the technological transformation of southern agriculture. What will it take to eliminate the current pattern of coerced labor embodied in the ghetto economy? Will the majority of Americans willingly give up their favored economic position relative to the racial minorities of the urban ghetto? Probably not, unless they are forced to do so by a social upheaval that reorders basic economic relationships. In this sense, the urban ghettos represent a revolutionary core within American society whose presence will create continuing turmoil within the larger economic and social order.

Workable solutions to the problems of the inner-city ghettos may be quite feasible. One strategy was sketched here. But if the solutions do more than make cosmetic changes, if they get to the heart of the problem, they will challenge the existing pattern of economic relations. That challenge must inevitably arouse the strongest opposition from those who now hold economic and political power. The prospect is one of heightened economic, political, and racial conflict. In the end, the necessary changes will probably come as part of a more general crisis in the American political economy that breaks the existing pattern of economic relationships and makes possible some large changes in the processes that have created and preserved the inner-city ghettos. The immediate prospect is for maintenance of the status quo and continuing conflict.

Notes

Index

Notes

1. The Ghetto and the City

1. Joe T. Darden, "The Quality of Life in a Black Ghetto: A Geographic View," *Pennsylvania Geographer* 12, no. 3 (1974):3–8; Donald R. Deskins, Jr., "Residential Mobility of Negroes in Detroit, 1937–1965," University of Michigan, Department of Geography Geographical Publication no. 5 (Ann Arbor, Mich., 1972, mimeographed), chap. 4; Richard L. Morrill, "The Negro Ghetto: Problems and Alternatives," *Geographical Review* 55, no. 3 (1965):339–61; Harold M. Rose, "The Development of an Urban Subsystem: The Case of the Negro Ghetto," *Annals of the Association of American Geographers* (Mar. 1970):1–17; idem, "The Black Ghetto as a Territorial Entity," and Donald R. Deskins, Jr., "Interaction Patterns and the Spatial Form of the Ghetto" in Northwestern University Department of Geography Special Publication no. 3 (Evanston, Ill.: 1969); and Harold M. Rose, ed., *Geography of the Ghetto* (DeKalb: Northern Illinois Univ. Pr., 1972).

2. Some mass production–continuous flow industries had always been located in suburban industrial centers. The steel industry in the Pittsburgh area was a pre–World War I industrial development in the decentralization pattern. Steel brought its workforce to the industrial suburbs, into the steel towns. Some other large-product assembly industries followed the same pattern, the Pullman Company, for example, at Pullman, Ill.

3. Several books have partially closed the gap in American historical scholarship on racial attitudes, including C. Vann Woodward, *The Strange Career of Jim Crow* (New York: Oxford Univ. Pr., 1955); David B. Davis, *The Problem of Slavery in Western Culture* (Ithaca, N.Y.: Cornell Univ. Pr., 1965); Winthrop D. Jordan, *White Over Black: American Attitudes Toward the Negro, 1550–1812* (Chapel Hill: Univ. of North Carolina Pr., 1968);

253

George M. Fredrickson, *The Inner Civil War: Northern Intellectuals and the Crisis of the Union* (New York: Harper, 1965); idem, *The Black Image in the White Mind: The Debate on Afro-American Character and Destiny, 1817–1914* (New York: Harper, 1971); and Constance M. Green, *The Secret City: A History of Race Relations in the Nation's Capital* (Princeton, N.J.: Princeton Univ. Pr., 1967).

4. The evidence of multicultural diversity is to be found in work by social psychologists, including Ruby Jo Reeves Kennedy, "A Single or Triple Melting Pot?" *American Journal of Sociology* 58, no. 1 (1952):56–60; Will Herberg, *Protestant, Catholic, Jew: An Essay in American Religious Sociology* (Garden City, N.Y.: Doubleday, 1955); Gerhard E. Lenski, *The Religious Factor: A Sociological Study of Religion's Impact on Politics, Economics and Family Life* (Garden City, N.Y.: Doubleday, 1961); Edward O. Laumann, "The Social Structure of Religious and Ethnoreligious Groups in a Metropolitan Community: A Smallest Space Analysis," *American Sociological Review,* 34, no. 2 (1969):339–49. The leading historian of U.S. immigrants adopted the schema of four socioreligious categories in American society: Oscar Handlin, "Historical Perspectives on the American Ethnic Group," *Daedalus* 90 (Spring 1961):220–32. Continued development of multicultural diversity was predicted in Nathan Glazer and Daniel P. Moynihan, *Beyond the Melting Pot: The Negroes, Puerto Ricans, Jews, Italians and Irish of New York City* (Cambridge, Mass.: MIT Pr., 1963), which has been the most influential book in breaking down the old melting-pot thesis.

2. The Evolution of Urban Racial Segregation and Discrimination

1. C. Horace Hamilton, "The Negro Leaves the South," *Demography* 1, no. 1 (1964):273.
2. Allan Spear, *Black Chicago: The Making of a Negro Ghetto, 1890–1920* (Chicago: Univ. of Chicago Pr., 1967), pp. 29–31.
3. Robert Weaver, *The Negro Ghetto* (New York: Russell and Russell, 1948), pp. 11–16.
4. C. Vann Woodward, *The Strange Career of Jim Crow* (New York: Oxford Univ. Pr., 2nd rev. ed., 1966), pp. 44–51.
5. Carl Kelsey, "The Evolution of Negro Labor," *Annals of the American Academy of Political and Social Science* 21, no. 1 (1903):70.
6. Roger Ransom and Richard Sutch, *One Kind of Freedom* (New York: Cambridge Univ. Pr., 1977), p. 36.
7. Sterling Spero and Abram Harris, *The Black Worker: The Negro and the Labor Movement* (Port Washington, N.Y.: Kennikat Pr., 1966), pp. 160–161.
8. Woodward, *Strange Career,* p. 85.
9. Weaver, *The Negro Ghetto,* p. 15.

10. See chapter 11 in Spero and Harris, *Black Worker.*
11. St. Clair Drake and Horace Cayton, *Black Metropolis: A Study of Negro Life in a Northern City,* vol. 1 (New York: Harper, 1962), p. 304. Drake and Cayton's figures refer to Chicago only.
12. Spero and Harris, *Black Worker,* p. 273.
13. Ray Marshall, *The Negro and Organized Labor* (New York: John Wiley, 1965), p. 17.

3. The Emergence of Black Ghettos

1. Allan Spear, *Black Chicago: The Making of a Negro Ghetto, 1890–1920* (Chicago: Univ. of Chicago Pr., 1967), p. 131.
2. Chicago Commission on Race Relations, *The Negro in Chicago: A Study of Race Relations and a Race Riot* (Chicago: Univ. of Chicago Pr., 1922), p. 80.
3. St. Clair Drake and Horace Cayton, *Black Metropolis: A Study of Negro Life in a Northern City,* vol. 1 (New York: Harper, 1962), p. 59.
4. Arthur Ross, "The Negro in the American Economy," in *Employment, Race, and Poverty,* ed. Arthur Ross and Herbert Hill (New York: Harcourt, 1967), p. 13.
5. Robert Weaver, *The Negro Ghetto* (New York: Russell and Russell, 1948), p. 29.
6. Drake and Cayton, *Black Metropolis,* vol. 1, p. 64.
7. Weaver, *The Negro Ghetto,* pp. 36–37.
8. John Bracey, August Meier, and Elliott Rudwick, "Introduction," in *The Rise of the Ghetto,* ed. John Bracey, August Meier, and Elliott Rudwick (Belmont, Cal.: Wadsworth, 1970), p. 4.
9. Joseph Pierce, *Negro Business and Business Education* (New York: Harper, 1947), p. 24.
10. Ross, *Employment, Race, and Poverty,* pp. 14–15.
11. Chicago Commission on Race Relations, *The Negro in Chicago,* pp. 98–102.
12. Spear, *Black Chicago,* p. 155. For example, the Chicago Telephone Company was one of the city's largest employers of females. Yet it did not employ black females—not even as temporary workers.
13. See chap. 4 in Sam Bass Warner, *The Urban Wilderness* (New York: Harper, 1972), for a detailed discussion of this urban growth pattern.
14. In Charleston, South Carolina, for example, detailed data document very little housing segregation as late as 1930. In general, pre-1940 data on the degree of housing segregation in various cities are unavailable. Average levels of segregation were still slightly lower in southern than in northern cities in 1940, but this difference disappeared by 1960. See Karl Taeuber and Alma Taeuber, *Negroes in Cities* (Chicago: Aldine, 1965), pp. 43–55.
15. Drake and Cayton, *Black Metropolis,* vol. 1, p. 74.

4. Ghetto Life During the Great Depression

1. Arthur Ross, "The Negro in the American Economy," in *Employment, Race, and Poverty*, ed. Arthur Ross and Herbert Hill (New York: Harcourt, 1967), p. 15. According to Ross, the proportion of black workers in the manufacturing labor force fell from 7.3 percent in 1930 to 5.1 percent in 1940. Numbers of blacks employed in manufacturing, mechanical, and mining occupations fell from 1,100,000 in 1930 to 738,000 in 1940. These losses were concentrated in northern industrial cities rather than in southern urban areas.
2. Robert Weaver, *The Negro Ghetto* (New York: Russell and Russell, 1948), p. 52.
3. Arthur Schlesinger, Jr., *The Age of Roosevelt: The Crisis of the Old Order*, vol. 1 (Boston: Houghton, 1957), p. 249.
4. Ibid., p. 250.
5. Edith Abbott, *The Tenements of Chicago: 1908–1935* (New York: Arno Pr. and the *New York Times*, 1970), p. 250.
6. Schlesinger, Jr., *Old Order*, pp. 248-54, provides a good journalistic account of these conditions.
7. Abbott, *Tenements*, p. 442.
8. Ibid., p. 442.
9. Ibid., p. 454.
10. Arthur Schlesinger, Jr., *The Age of Roosevelt: The Coming of the New Deal*, vol. 2 (Boston: Houghton, 1957), p. 264.
11. Ibid., p. 273.
12. Weaver, *The Negro Ghetto*, p. 53. These figures include emergency workers on government payrolls.
13. Gunnar Myrdal, *An American Dilemma* (New York: Harper, 1944), pp. 255–59.
14. Robert Weaver, *Negro Labor: A National Problem* (New York: Harcourt, 1946), p. 12.
15. Federal Housing Administration, *Underwriting Manual*, 1939, sections 932 and 935; cited in Weaver, *The Negro Ghetto*, p. 72.

5. The World War II Interlude

1. Robert Weaver, *Negro Labor: A National Problem* (New York: Harcourt, 1946), pp. 18–20.
2. Gunnar Myrdal, *An American Dilemma* (New York: Harper, 1962), p. 410.
3. Weaver, *Negro Labor*, p. 137.
4. Ibid., p. 88.
5. Ibid., p. 86.
6. Ibid., p. 81.
7. Black gains were particularly prevalent in the durable goods industries. Employment in manufacturing grew by 7.3 million between 1940 and late 1943, and four-fifths of this increase was for production workers

in durable goods industries; see Charles Killingsworth, *Jobs and Incomes for Negroes* (Ann Arbor, Mich.: University of Michigan Institute of Labor and Industrial Relations, 1968). p. 35.

8. Weaver, *Negro Labor,* p. 91.

9. C. Horace Hamilton, "The Negro Leaves the South," *Demography* 1, no. 1 (1964):276.

10. Robert Weaver, *The Negro Ghetto* (New York: Russell and Russell, 1948), p. 87.

11. Ibid., p. 94.

6. The Collapse of Traditional Southern Agriculture

1. C. Horace Hamilton, "The Negro Leaves the South," *Demography* 1, no. 1 (1964):276.

2. Soil erosion was a particularly severe problem throughout the South. By 1933, over 50 percent of all U.S. severely eroded farming areas mapped by the Soil Erosion Service were in the South. See Carter Goodrich et al., *Migration and Economic Opportunity* (Philadelphia: Univ. of Pennsylvania Pr., 1936), pp. 125–26.

3. Gunnar Myrdal, *An American Dilemma* (New York: Harper, 1962), p. 242.

4. Ibid., p. 247.

5. Arthur Raper, *Preface to Peasantry* (Chapel Hill: Univ. of North Carolina Pr., 1936), p. 161.

6. Charles Johnson, Edwin Embree, and W. W. Alexander, *The Collapse of Cotton Tenancy* (Chapel Hill: Univ. of North Carolina Pr., 1935), p. 17.

7. Raper, *Preface to Peasantry,* p. 202.

8. Johnson, Embree, and Alexander, *The Collapse of Cotton Tenancy,* p. 12.

9. Edwin Nourse, Joseph Davis, and John Black, *Three Years of the Agricultural Adjustment Administration* (Washington, D.C.: Brookings Institution, 1937), p. 342.

10. C. Horace Hamilton, "The Social Effects of Recent Trends in the Mechanization of Agriculture," *Rural Sociology* 4, no. 1 (1939):3.

11. Myrdal, *An American Dilemma,* p. 1248.

12. Richard Day, "The Economics of Technological Change and the Demise of the Sharecropper," *American Economic Review* 57, no. 3, (1967):427–28.

13. Thomas Woofter, *Negro Migration* (New York: AMS Pr., 1971), p. 147.

14. Raper, *Preface to Peasantry,* p. 306.

15. Timothy Bates, "The Impact of Multinational Corporations on Power Relations in South Africa," *Review of Black Political Economy* 12, no. 2 (1983):135–36.

16. Raper, *Preface to Peasantry,* p. 343.

17. Day, "Technological Change," p. 442.

18. Francis Fox Piven and Richard A. Cloward, *Regulating the Poor: The Functions of Public Welfare.* (New York: Pantheon, 1971), p. 206.

7. Organized Labor and Black Workers

1. Irving Howe and B. J. Widick, *The UAW and Walter Reuther* (New York: Random House, 1949), pp. 216–17. Frank Winn, "Labor Tackles the Race Question," *Antioch Review* 3, no. 3 (1943):349.

2. Horace Cayton and George Mitchell, *Black Workers and the New Unions* (Westport, Conn.: Negro Universities Pr., 1970), p. x.

3. Sterling Spero and Abram Harris, *The Black Worker: The Negro and the Labor Movement* (Port Washington, N.Y.: Kennikot Pr., 1966), pp. 59–60.

4. Ray Marshall, *The Negro and Organized Labor* (New York: John Wiley, 1965), pp. 28–29.

5. Many AFL unions did nothing to alter their racist practices during this period. See Herbert Hill, "The Racial Practices of Organized Labor— The Age of Gompers and After," in *Employment, Race, and Poverty*, ed. Arthur Ross and Herbert Hill (New York: Harcourt, 1967), pp. 394–97.

6. Robert Weaver, *Negro Labor: A National Problem* (New York: Harcourt, 1946), p. 267.

7. Ray Marshall, *Labor in the South* (Cambridge, Mass: Harvard Univ. Pr., 1967), p. 246.

8. Cited in E. Franklin Frazier, *The Negro in the United States* (New York: Macmillan, 1957), p. 619.

9. Seymour Wolfbein, "Postwar Trends in Negro Employment," *Monthly Labor Review* 65, no. 6 (1947):665.

10. Cited in Philip Foner, *Organized Labor and the Black Worker, 1619–1973* (New York: Praeger, 1974), p. 268.

11. Joseph Rayback, *A History of American Labor* (New York: Free Pr., 1966), p. 367.

12. Marshall, *The Negro and Organized Labor*, p. 42.

13. For example, in a pamphlet circulated among black workers, the AFL claimed that: "Out of 36 (CIO) International Unions, 21 are dominated by leaders who follow the Communist Party line. It is a well-known fact that Moscow has given orders to its American Fifth Columnists to give special attention to spreading unrest and dissension among American Negroes. If you fall for this you are Dictator Joe Stalin's prize suckers" (cited in ibid., p. 44).

14. Ibid.

15. Sumner Rosen, "The CIO Era, 1935–1955," in *The Negro and the American Labor Movement*, ed. Julius Jacobson (Garden City, N.Y.: Anchor Books, 1968), p. 196.

16. Cited in Marshall, *The Negro and Organized Labor*, p. 47.

17. Ray Marshall, "Unions and the Negro Community," *Industrial and Labor Relations Review* 17, no. 1 (1964):183.

18. Herbert Hill, "Racial Practices of Organized Labor," p. 396.

19. Marshall, "Unions and the Negro Community," pp. 187–88.

20. "Carey Quits Post on AFL-CIO Unit," *New York Times*, 12 Apr. 1957, p. 52.

21. Marshall, *The Negro and Organized Labor,* p. 68.
22. Ibid., p. 41.
23. Howe and Widick, *The UAW and Walter Reuther,* p. 219.
24. Frank Adams, *Unearthing Seeds of Fire: The Idea of Highlander* (Winston-Salem, N.C.: John F. Blair, 1975), pp. 72–73
25. Ibid., p. 122.

8. Changing Economic Base of Metropolitan Areas

1. Industry statistics utilized in chapter 8 have been collected from the following standard metropolitan statistical areas (SMSAs): *Snowbelt SMSAs* (26 total) Illinois: Chicago, Peoria; Maryland: Baltimore; Michigan: Detroit, Flint, Grand Rapids, Lansing; Missouri: Kansas City, St. Louis; Ohio: Cleveland, Cincinnati, Columbus, Dayton, Toledo, Akron, Canton, Youngston-Warren; Pennsylvania: Allentown-Bethlehem-Easton, Erie, Harrisburg, Johnstown, Lancaster, Philadelphia, Pittsburgh, Reading, York.

   Sunbelt SMSAs (23 total) Alabama: Birmingham, Mobile; Arizona: Phoenix, Tucson; Colorado: Denver; Georgia: Atlanta, Augusta; Kansas: Wichita; Louisiana: Baton Rouge, New Orleans, Shreveport; North Carolina: Charlotte, Greensboro-Winston Salem-High Point; Oklahoma: Oklahoma City, Tulsa; Texas: Austin, Corpus Christi, Dallas-Fort Worth, El Paso, Houston, San Antonio; Virginia: Norfolk-Portsmouth, Richmond.

   Criteria for SMSA selection were, primarily, population in the 1950 census, and secondarily, data completeness. SMSAs having fewer than 100,000 residents in 1950 typically had incomplete census data on industries; therefore all SMSAs with fewer than 100,000 residents in 1950 were dropped from the sample utilized in this study. Two SMSAs with more than 100,000 residents were eliminated because of missing data: Lorain-Elyria, Ohio, and Beaumont-Port Arthur-Orange, Texas. SMSAs with multiple central cities often had incomplete census data on industries when one or more of the central cities had a small population.

   Selection of states for inclusion in this study depended upon SMSA presence, strong industrial orientation for snowbelt states, and absence of major idiosyncracies that might make a state quite unique from its neighbors (for example, Florida).
2. See, for example, chapter 3 in Edward Banfield, *The Unheavenly City* (Boston: Little, 1970).
3. For an elaboration, see chap. 10 in this volume.
4. See, for example, James Smith and Finis Welch, "Black-White Male Wage Ratios: 1960–1970," *American Economic Review* 67, no. 3 (1977):323–25.
5. John Kain, "The Distribution and Movement of Jobs and Industry," in *Essays on Urban Spatial Structure,* ed. John Kain (Cambridge: Ballinger, 1976), pp. 79–114.

6. Ibid., pp. 79–91.
7. Their stated aim is to accelerate the rate of capital formation in private industry. Furthermore, investment tax credit provisions are designed to promote new plant construction whereas, previously, renovation of existing plants had been encouraged.
8. Sam Bass Warner, *The Urban Wilderness* (New York: Harper, 1972), pp. 101–4.
9. Alfred Chandler, *Strategy and Structure* (New York: Doubleday, 1961), pp. 21–23.
10. The logic of locating headquarters in CBDs is explained in Benjamin Chinitz, "The Economy of the Central City: An Appraisal," in *The Urban Economy*, ed. Harold Hochman (New York: Norton, 1976), pp. 118–30.
11. For an elaboration on this theme, see Stephen Hymer, "The Evolution of the Corporation," in *The Capitalist System*, ed. Richard Edwards, Michael Reich, and Thomas Weisskopf (Englewood Cliffs, N.J.: Prentice-Hall, 1978), pp. 122–24.
12. Ibid., pp. 123–24.
13. Jonathan Kesselman, Samuel Williamson, and Ernst Berndt, "Tax Credits for Employment Rather than Investment," *American Economic Review* 67, no. 3 (1977):345.
14. James O'Connor extends this line of analysis by arguing that "monopoly sector" growth may be directly responsible for rising government welfare expenditures. See James O'Connor, *The Fiscal Crisis of the State* (New York: St. Martin's, 1973), pp. 159–62.
15. Exploitation is defined as occurring when the benefits which central-city governments provide to nonresidents are not fully offset by such direct means as user charges and nonresident payroll taxes, and by such indirect effects as the scale economies which centrally located activities can achieve precisely because of the existence of a wider metropolitan market. See Bennett Harrison, *Urban Economic Development* (Washington, D.C.: Urban Institute, 1974), pp. 114–16, for evidence on this.
16. This theme is elaborated upon in Timothy Bates, *Economic Man as Politician: Neoclassical and Marxist Theories of Government Behavior* (Morristown, N.J.: General Learning Pr., 1976), p. 28.
17. George Sternlieb, "The City as Sandbox," *Public Interest* 25 (Fall 1977):14–21.
18. John Kain, "Distribution and Movement," p. 80.
19. Data inconsistency or unavailability plagued the other nine central cities and those consisted chiefly of smaller cities. Three of the five missing snowbelt cities were small Pennsylvania central cities.
20. Charlotte Freeman, *The Occupational Patterns of Urban Employment Change, 1955–1967* (Washington, D.C.: Urban Institute, 1970), p. 7.
21. Katharine Bradbury, Anthony Downs, and Kenneth Small, *Urban Decline and the Future of American Cities* (Washington, D.C.: Brookings Institution, 1982), p. 75.

9. Black Economic Well-Being Since the 1950s

1. The increasing incidence of two-earner families among whites is partially responsible for the downward trend in relative black family incomes. See Charles Brown, "The Federal Attack on Labor Market Discrimination: The Mouse That Roared?" National Bureau of Economic Research Working Paper no. 669 (Cambridge, Mass., Apr., 1981) pp. 2–14, for a discussion of this question.
2. John Reid, "Black America in the 1980s," *Population Bulletin* 37, no. 5:24–25.
3. Cited in Christopher Jencks, "Discrimination and Thomas Sowell," *New York Review of Books* 3 Mar. 1983, p. 36.
4. Occupational figures were taken from U.S. Bureau of the Census, *Current Population Reports*, ser. P-60, 132, table 55 (Washington, D.C.: Government Printing Office, July 1982), pp. 192–99. These figures refer to persons eighteen years of age and older as of Mar. 1981; occupation was recorded for all who worked during the 1980 calendar year.
5. Results of this Gallup poll were cited in "Black Statistics: A Look at the Figures on Social Change," *Focus* (Spring 1981):1. A good overview of the employment gains of better-educated blacks appears in Richard Freeman, *Black Elite: The New Market for Qualified Black Americans* (New York: McGraw, 1976), chaps. 6 and 9.
6. National Urban League report, *The State of Black America 1980*, cited in ibid., p. 4.
7. U.S. Bureau of the Census, *Current Population Reports*, ser. P-60, no. 137, table 16 (Washington, D.C.: Government Printing Office, Mar. 1983), pp. 43–46.
8. See, for example, Richard Freeman, "Black Economic Progress Since 1964: Who Has Gained and Why" in *Studies in Labor Markets* ed. Sherwin Rosen (Cambridge, Mass.: National Bureau of Economic Research, 1981), pp. 247–94.
9. Regional breakdowns of relative income trends over time must be done with caution because of incomparability problems between the two groupings, "nonwhite" and "black." Nonwhite and black are often used interchangeably as groupings for describing black income trends; this procedure is invalid when applied to the western united states because trends in nonwhite incomes differ sharply from black income trends. This bias rises due to rapid income gains realized by the sizeable Oriental population that resides in the West. Smaller Oriental populations in other regions of the united states decrease this bias substantially.
10. Studies showing substantial progress in black economic well-being typically focus upon wage and salary earnings only. This approach further distorts trends in *overall* black status, particularly among males, because it neglects the high and rising incidence of zero-wage and salary earners which is much higher than the incidence of black zero-income earners. See, for example, James Smith and Finis Welch, "Race Differences in

Earnings: A Survey and New Evidence," in *Current Issues in Urban Economics*, ed. Peter Mieszkowski and Mahlon Straszheim (Baltimore: Johns Hopkins Univ. Pr., 1979), pp. 40-69.

Severe biases arising in relative income studies that exclude the zero-income (or wage) individuals are analyzed in William Darity "Illusions of Black Economic Progress," *Review of Black Political Economy* 10, no. 4 (1980):153–67, and Charles Brown, "Black-White Earnings Ratios Since the Civil Rights Act of 1964: The Importance of Labor Market Drop-outs," National Bureau of Economic Research Working Paper no. 617 (Cambridge, Mass.: National Bureau of Economic Research, Jan. 1981).

11. Michael Reich, *Racial Inequality* (Princeton, N.J.: Princeton Univ. Pr., 1981), p. 65. By 1970, the proportion of southern blacks residing in urban areas had risen to 67.4 percent.

12. Sar Levitan, William Johnson, and Robert Taggert, *Still A Dream: The Changing Status of Blacks Since 1960* (Cambridge, Mass: Harvard Univ. Pr., 1975), p. 24.

13. Ibid., p. 26.

14. Improved social security disability benefits have contributed to falling labor force participation rates among black males 45 and older. Older people who have not yet reached retirement age opt for these benefits because they are poor and unhealthy—not because they are black—according to a study by Donald Parsons, "Racial Trends in Male Labor Force Participation," *American Economic Review* 70, no. 5 (1980):912–14. Blacks disproportionately are recipients of disability benefits. Parsons found, however, that black-white differences in the incidence of benefit recipients were eliminated when health and economic circumstances were controlled for.

15. Before 1970, black teenage labor force participation rates were falling nationally but this was caused largely by the shift out of southern agricultural work. In nonsouthern areas, participation rates were stable between 1950 and 1970, although unemployment rates were rising. See John Cogan, "The Decline in Black Teenage Employment: 1950–1970," *American Economic Review* 72, no. 4 (1982):621–35.

16. Michael J. Piore, *Birds of Passage* (Cambridge: Cambridge Univ. Pr., 1979), pp. 79–80, 162–63.

17. Reid, "Black America in the 1980s," p. 16.

18. Ibid., p. 21.

19. Ibid., pp. 11–12.

20. Arthur Ross, "The Negro in the American Economy," in *Employment, Race, and Poverty*, ed. Arthur Ross and Herbert Hill (New York: Harcourt, 1967), p. 30.

21. Alan Batchelder, "Decline in the Relative Income of Negro Men," *Quarterly Journal of Economics* 78, no. 4, (1964):525–48.

22. In the Chicago SMSA, for example, white-collar jobs in manufacturing increased from 1950 to 1960, while production jobs decreased in number; on balance, total manufacturing employment declined by approximately three thousand. Black employment in manufacturing de-

clined by about two thousand between 1950 and 1960 in the Chicago SMSA. See John Kain and John Quigley, *Housing Markets and Racial Discrimination: A Microeconomic Analysis* (New York: National Bureau of Economic Research, 1975), p. 89.

23. See Walter Butcher, "Productivity, Technology and Employment in U.S. Agriculture," in *The Employment Impact of Technology Change, Appendix, Vol. II, Technology and the American Economy,* Report of the National Commission on Technology, Automation, and Economic Progress (Washington, D.C. Government Printing Office, 1966), pp. 135–52.

24. Evidence on this issue is highly conflicting but it points, on balance, to limited suburban job access for the younger and poorer (least mobile) ghetto residents. See Mahlon Straszheim, "Discrimination and Transportation Accessibility in Urban Labor Markets for Black Workers," University of Maryland Project on the Economics of Discrimination (College Park, Md.: Mimeograph, 1979), pp. 10–15, for a good summary of the controversy surrounding this issue.

25. See Batchelder, "Decline in Relative Income," p. 544. A more comprehensive survey known as the "Wirtz Survey" revealed shockingly high rates of ghetto subemployment in 1966. This survey is discussed in Francis Fox Piven and Richard A. Cloward, *Regulating the Poor: The Functions of Public Welfare* (New York: Pantheon, 1971), pp. 215–17.

26. James Geschwender, *Class, Race, and Worker Insurgency* (Cambridge: Cambridge Univ. Pr., 1977), pp. 32–34.

27. Ibid., pp. 41–42.

28. U.S. Bureau of the Census, *Census of Manufacturers 1967,* vol. 3, *Area Statistics* Part 2, Nebraska-Wyoming, (Washington, D.C.: Government Printing Office, 1971), pp. 36–37.

29. Bennett Harrison and Edward Hill, "The Changing Structure of Jobs in Older and Younger Cities," Joint Center for Urban Studies of MIT and Harvard University Working Paper no. 58 (Cambridge, Mass.: Joint Center for Urban Studies of MIT and Harvard University, Mar. 1979), p. 21.

30. Occupation data cited in this section have been calculated from the public use samples of the U.S. Census of Population.

31. Harrison, "Changing Structure," pp. 12–19.

32. Brown, "Federal Attack," p. 9.

33. Levitan, Johnson, and Taggert, "Still a Dream," p. 272.

34. Peter Eisinger, "The Economic Conditions of Black Employment in Municipal Bureaucracies," Institute for Research on Poverty Discussion Paper no. 661-81 (Madison, Wis.: Institute for Research on Poverty, 1981), p. 16.

35. Geschwender, *Class, Race, and Worker Insurgency,* p. 43.

36. Mark Dodosh, "Auto Industry's Moves Jolt Many in Midwest and More Jolts Loom," *Wall Street Journal,* 26 May 1981, p. 1.

37. Barry Bluestone and Bennett Harrison, *The Deindustrialization of America* (New York: Basic Books, 1982), pp. 69–71.

38. Ibid., p. 57.

39. U.S. Bureau of the Census, *Advance Estimates of Social, Economic, and Housing Characteristics—Supplementary Report: Counties and Selected Places* (by state), ser. PHC80-S2 (Washington, D.C.: Government Printing Office, 1983).
40. Harrison and Hill, "Changing Structure," pp. 16–32.
41. "America Rushes to High Tech for Growth," *Business Week* 28 Mar. 1983, p. 86.
42. Total manufacturing employment declined from 26,382,000 in Jan. 1979 to 23,133,000 in Jan. 1983. The emerging consensus on this decline is summarized by Audrey Freeman, senior research associate at the Conference Board: "Employment is going to recover somewhat among production workers, simply because output is going to rise again, but I don't think it will ever reach its former level," in Henry Myers, "Recession Ripples: Economists Say Slump Hastened Some Trends but Spawned Very Few," *Wall Street Journal,* 25 May 1983, p. 1.
43. Harrison and Hill, "Changing Structure," pp. 20–26.
44. Reich, *Racial Inequality,* p. 30.
45. Harry Braverman, *Labor and Monopoly Capital* (New York: Monthly Review Pr., 1974), chap. 15.
46. This is documented in Robert Mare and Christopher Winship, "Racial Socioeconomic Convergence and the Paradox of Black Youth Joblessness: Enrollment, Enlistment, and Employment, 1964–1981," University of Chicago Economics Research Center Discussion Paper 83-14, (Chicago, July 1983).
47. Timothy Schellhardt, "North Central U.S. Surpasses South in Black Poverty Rate," *Wall Street Journal* 9 Aug. 1983, p. 35.
48. Richard Child Hill, "Fiscal Collapse and Political Struggle in Decaying Central cities in the United States," in *Marxism and the Metropolis,* ed. William Tabb and Larry Sawers (New York: Oxford Univ. Pr., 1978), pp. 226–28.
49. For an excellent case study of this phenomenon, see Chester Hartman and Rob Kessler, "The Illusion and Reality of Urban Renewal: San Francisco's Yerba Buena Center," in *Marxism and the Metropolis,* ed. William Tabb and Larry Sawers (New York: Oxford Univ. Pr., 1978), pp. 153–78.

10. The Economic Dynamics of the Ghetto

1. Very little is known about the details of these financial flows. The now prohibited practice of red-lining by many banks and insurance companies effectively prevented funds from moving into the ghetto economy. Attempts have been made by several banks and insurance companies to redirect the flow of some of these funds back into the urban ghetto.
2. On the problems of black-owned financial institutions, see Timothy

Bates and William Bradford, *Financing Black Economic Development* (New York: Academic Press, 1979), chaps. 2–6.

3. On the problems of slum housing, see Alvin L. Schorr, *Slums and Social Insecurity* (Washington, D.C.: U.S. Department of Health, Education, and Welfare, 1963), and Bernard J. Frieden, "Housing and National Urban Goals: Old Policies and New Realities," in *The Metropolitan Enigma* (Washington, D.C.: U.S. Chamber of Commerce, 1967), pp. 148–91.

4. See Chester Rapkin, *The Real Estate Market in an Urban Renewal Area* (New York: City Planning Commission, 1959), for a careful analysis and case study of the cumulative deterioration of housing. This process seems to have accelerated substantially in the early 1970s, particularly in the core area of large cities like New York, Philadelphia, Baltimore, Detroit, Chicago, and St. Louis. On these developments, see "Federal Housing Abandonment Blights Inner Cities," *New York Times*, 13 Jan. 1972, pp. 1, 28; Michael A. Stegman, *Housing Investment in the Inner City* (Cambridge, Mass.: MIT Pr., 1972); George Sternlieb, *The Tenement Landlord* (New Brunswick, N.J.: Transaction Pr., 1973); and George Sternlieb and Robert W. Burchell, *Residential Abandonment: The Tenement Landlord Revisited* (New Brunswick, N.J.: Transaction Pr., 1973).

5. On the migration of blacks to the suburbs, see *Blacks on the Move: A Decade of Demographic Change* (Washington, D.C.: Joint Center for Political Studies, 1982); W. P. Hare et al., "Black Migration in the 1970s," *Focus* 10, no. 4 (1982):3–4.

6. Property ownership by ghetto residents was studied by Michael Zweig, "The Dialectics of Black Capitalism," *Review of Black Political Economy* 3, no. 3 (1972);25–37, and 4, no. 1 (1972):42–57. See also Thomas Vietorisz and Bennett Harrison, *The Economic Development of Harlem* (New York: Praeger, 1970).

7. See Wilbur R. Thompson, "International and External Factors in the Development of Urban Economies," in *Issues in Urban Economics*, ed. Harvey S. Perloff and Lowden Wingo, Jr. (Baltimore: Johns Hopkins Univ. Pr., 1965), pp. 43–62.

8. See chap. 13 for a detailed discussion of the stabilizing role of welfare payments.

9. U.S. Department of Labor, "A Sharper Look at Unemployment in U.S. Cities and Slums" (Washington, D.C., 1968, Mimeographed).

10. One result of the census undercount of men in the slums is a serious political underrepresentation of slum areas. Election districts are based on census counts of population. The undercount means that the slum constituency is underrepresented at the local, state, and national level.

11. Richard L. Schaffer, *Income Flows in Urban Poverty Areas: A Comparison of the Community Income Accounts of Bedford-Stuyvesant and Borough Park* (Lexington, Mass.: Lexington Books, 1973).

12. Frank G. Davis, *The Economics of Black Community Development: An Analysis and Program for Autonomous Growth and Development* (Chicago: Markham, 1972); Robert S. Browne, "Cash Flows in a Ghetto Community,"

Review of Black Political Economy 1, no. 3 (1971):28–39; Earl Mellor, "Costs and Benefits of Public Goods and Expenditures for a Ghetto: A Case Study," in *Transfers in an Urbanized Society*, ed. Kenneth E. Boulding et al. (Belmont, Cal.: Wadsworth, 1972).

13. William H. Oakland, Frederick T., Sparrow, and H. Louis Stettler, III, "Ghetto Multipliers: A Case Study of Hough," *Journal of Regional Science* 11, no. 3 (1971):337–45.

14. See Gunnar Myrdal, *Asian Drama*, vol. 3 (New York: Random House, 1968), app. 2, especially sections 2, 4, 5, and 8–11.

15. Pedro Belli, "The Economic Implications of Malnutrition: The Dismal Science Revisited," *Economic Development and Cultural Change* 20, no. 1 (1971):1–23, provides a detailed review of empirical studies on the relationship between malnutrition, health, and intelligence that shows the process of circular causation at work. See also Irving Leveson, Boris Ullman, and Gregory Wassall, "Effects of Health on Education and Productivity," *Inquiry* 6, no. 4 (1969):3–11, and Danny M. Leipziger, ed., *Basic Needs and Development* (Cambridge, Mass.: Oelgeschlager, Gunn, and Hain, 1981).

11. Work and Wages in the Ghetto

1. U.S. Department of Labor, "Sub-Employment in the Slums of New York" (Washington, D.C., 1968, Mimeographed).

2. Michael Flannery, "America's Sweatshops in the Sun," *American Federalist* 85, no. 5 (1978):16–20.

3. Rinker, Buck, "The New Sweatshops: A Penny for Your Collar," *New York* 12, no. 9 (1979):40–46; Robert Ross and Kent Trachte, "Global Cities and Global Classes: The Peripheralization of Labor in New York City," *Review* 6, no. 3 (1983):393–431; North American Congress of Latin America, "Capital's Flight: The Apparel Industry Moves South," *Latin America and Empire Report* 11, no. 3 (1977):1–33.

4. Bradley R. Schiller, *The Economics of Poverty and Discrimination*, 3rd ed. (Englewood Cliffs, N.J.: Prentice-Hall, 1980), chap. 5.

5. Louis A. Ferman, "The Irregular Economy: Informal Work Patterns in the Urban Ghetto" (Ann Arbor, Mich.: University of Michigan Institute of Labor and Industrial Relations, n.d., Mimeographed). Descriptions of life-styles based on the irregular economy can be found in Elliott Liebow, *Tally's Corner, A Study of Street Corner Men* (Boston: Little, Brown, 1967); Claude Brown, *Manchild in the Promised Land* (New York: Macmillan, 1965); Oscar Lewis, *La Vida* (New York: Random House, 1965); Piri Thomas, *Down These Mean Streets* (New York: Knopf, 1967); Malcom X, *Autobiography* (New York: Grove Pr., 1965); and Herbert Gans, *The Urban Villagers* (New York: Free Pr., 1962). See also William McCord et al., *Life Styles in the Black Ghetto* (New York: Norton, 1969), and Lee Rainwater, *Behind Ghetto Walls* (Chicago: Aldine, 1971).

6. A series of articles in the *New York Times* in 1970 provides some insight

into the numbers game and the drug traffic: "Cubans Here Are Ending Mafia's Monopoly of Numbers Racket," 22 Feb. 1970, p. 36; "Heroin Traffickers Here Tell How $219 Million Trade Works," 20 Apr. 1970, pp. 1, 36; "Organized Crime in City Robs Black Slums of Millions," 27 Sept. 1970, pp. 1, 85; "Numbers Called Harlem's Balm," 1 Mar. 1971, pp. 1, 44; and Fred J. Cook, "The Black Mafia Moves into the Numbers Racket," *New York Times Magazine*, 4 Apr. 1971, p. 26ff. The reports of the New York State Legislature Committee on Crime provide a great deal of information on organized crime in the urban ghettos. Although these references primarily pertain to the New York City ghettos, the situation is similar in the ghettos of other major cities. Dominance of the heroin traffic by Colombians was documented recently in the *Wall Street Journal:* Stanley Penn, "Cocaine Cowboys: Colombia's Syndicates Prove to Be Tough Foe for U.S. Agents," 5 Apr. 1983, pp. 1, 16. See also Bruce Bullington, *Heroin Use in the Barrio* (Lexington, Mass.: Lexington Books, 1977) and Samuel L. Myers, "The Economics of Crime in the Urban Ghetto," *Review of Black Political Economy* 9, no. 1 (1978): 43–59.

12. Discrimination and Coerced Labor

1. Gary S. Becker, *The Economics of Discrimination* (Chicago: Univ. of Chicago Pr., 1957).
2. Michael Reich, *Racial Inequality* (Princeton, N.J.: Princeton Univ. Pr., 1981); Paul A. Baran and Paul M. Sweezy, *Monopoly Capital* (New York: Monthly Review Pr., 1966), chap. 9.
3. Gunnar Myrdal, *An American Dilemma* (New York: Harper, 1944).
4. Lester C. Thurow, *Poverty and Discrimination* (Washington, D.C.: Brookings Institution, 1969).
5. Ibid., p. 138.
6. Lester C. Thurow, *Generaitng Inequality: Mechanisms of Distribution in the American Economy* (New York: Basic Books, 1975).
7. Ibid., p. 88.
8. Charles C. Killingsworth, *Jobs and Incomes for Negroes* (Ann Arbor, Mich.: University of Michigan Institute of Labor and Industrial Relations, 1968); Peter Doeringer and Michael J. Piore, *Internal Labor Markets and Manpower Analysis* (Lexington, Mass.: Lexington Books, 1971), chaps. 7, 8; David M. Gordon, *Theories of Poverty and Unemployment* (Lexington, Mass.: Lexington Books, 1972); Michael J. Piore, "Fragments of a 'Sociological' Theory of Wages," *American Economic Review* 63, no. 2 (1973):377–84; idem, "Notes for a Theory of Labor Market Stratification," Massachusetts Institute of Technology Department of Economics Discussion Paper 95 (Cambridge, Mass.: MIT, 1972); Michael Reich, David M. Gordon, and Richard C. Edwards, "A Theory of Labor Market Segmentation," *American Economic Review* 63, no. 2 (1973):359–65; idem, *Labor Market Segmentation* (Lexington,

Mass.: Lexington Books, 1974); Thomas Vietorisz and Bennett Harrison, "Labor Market Segmentation: Positive Feedback and Divergent Development," *American Economic Review* 63, no. 2 (1973):366–76.

9. Milton Friedman, *Capitalism and Freedom* (Chicago: Univ. of Chicago Pr., 1962), p. 111.

10. Ibid., pp. 112–14.

11. Anne O. Krueger, "The Economics of Discrimination," *Journal of Political Economy* 71, no. 5 (1963):481–86.

12. Finis Welch, "Labor Market Discrimination in the Rural South," *Journal of Political Economy* 75, no. 3 (1967):225–40.

13. Kenneth J. Arrow, "Models of Job Discrimination" in *Racial Discrimination in Economic Life,* ed. Anthony H. Pascal (Lexington, Mass.: Lexington Books, 1972), pp. 83–102.

14. Kenneth J. Arrow, "The Theory of Discrimination" in *Discrimination in Labor Markets,* ed. Orley Ashenfelter and Albert Rees (Princeton, N.J.: Princeton Univ. Pr., 1973), pp. 3–33.

15. Joseph E. Stiglitz, "Approaches to the Economics of Discrimination," *American Economic Review* 63, no. 2 (1973):287–95.

16. Marcus Alexis, "The Political Economy of Labor Market Discrimination: Synthesis and Exploration" in *Patterns of Discrimination,* ed. Ann R. Horowitz and George M. von Furstenberg, vol. 2 (Lexington, Mass.: Lexington Books, 1974), pp. 63–84.

17. W. H. Hutt, *The Economics of the Colour Bar* (London: Institute of Economic Affairs, 1964), forcefully presents the argument that, in the long run, the competitive economy is color-blind.

18. The theory of human capital stems from Theodore W. Schultz, "Investment in Human Capital," *American Economic Review* 51, no. 1 (1961):1–17. It was systematized by Gary S. Becker in *Human Capital: A Theoretical and Empirical Analysis, with Special Reference to Education* (New York: National Bureau of Economic Research, 1964). Brief summaries are presented in Burton A. Weisbrod, "Investing in Human Capital," *Journal of Human Resources* 1, no. 1 (1967):5–21, and Lester C. Thurow, *Poverty and Discrimination* (Washington, D.C.: Brookings Institution, 1969), chap. 5.

19. Stephan Michelson, "Incomes of Racial Minorities" (Ph.D. diss., Stanford University, 1968); Otis Dudley Duncan, "Inheritance of Poverty or Inheritance of Race," in *On Understanding Poverty,* ed. Daniel P. Moynihan (New York: Basic Books, 1968); Otis Dudley Duncan, "Ability and Achievement," *Eugenics Quarterly* 15 (Mar. 1968); James D. Gwartney, "Discrimination and Income Differentials," *American Economic Review* 60, no. 3 (1970):396–408; Stanley H. Masters, *Black-White Income Differentials: Empirical Studies and Policy Implications* (New York: Academic Pr., 1975), chap. 5.

20. These figures are taken from Bradley R. Schiller, *The Economics of Poverty and Discrimination,* 3rd ed. (Englewood Cliffs, N.J.: Prentice-Hall, 1980), p. 118.

21. Francis Y. Edgeworth, "Equal Pay to Men and Women for Equal Work,"

Economic Journal 31 (Dec. 1922):431–57. Edgeworth's analysis built on the work of Millicent Fawcett, including "The Position of Women in Economic Life," in *After-War Problems*, ed. W. H. Dawson (London: Allen and Unwin, 1917), pp. 191–215, and "Equal Pay for Equal Work," *Economic Journal* 28, (Mar. 1918):1–6. Taussig's concept of noncompeting groups is somewhat similar. See Frank W. Taussig, *Principles of Economics*, vol. 2 (New York: Macmillan, 1946), pp. 234–45; and Norval D. Glenn, "Occupational Benefits to Whites from the Subordination of Negroes," *American Sociological Review* 28, no. 3 (1963):443–48. Barbara Bergmann developed the crowding hypothesis in "Effect on White Incomes of Discrimination in Employment," *Journal of Political Economy* 29, no. 2 (1971):294–313.
22. Lester C. Thurow, *Generating Inequality*, pp. 170–77.
23. C. Vann Woodward, *The Strange Career of Jim Crow* (New York: Oxford Univ. Pr., 1955), is the standard treatment of the rapid spread of Jim Crow laws and disfranchisement of blacks during the 1890s in the South. Woodward, however, failed to note the importance of the black migration to cities and gave inadequate attention to the changes in occupations and economic opportunity that occurred.
24. Reich, *Racial Inequality*, pp. 268–304.

13. The Welfare System and the Ghetto Economy

1. *Social Security Bulletin* 44, no. 3 (1981):56.
2. Social Security Administration, *Aid to Families with Dependent Children: 1977 Recipient Characteristics Study* (Washington, D.C.: Government Printing Office, 1980), pp. 1–3.
3. Ibid.
4. Sar Levitan, Martin Rein, and David Warwick, *Work and Welfare Go Together* (Baltimore: Johns Hopkins Univ. Pr., 1972), p. 50.
5. U.S. Congress, Joint Economic Committee, Subcommittee on Fiscal Policy, *Public Welfare and Work Incentives in Theory and Practice* (Washington, D.C.: Government Printing Office, 1974), p. 13.
6. Harrell R. Rodgers, Jr., *The Cost of Human Neglect: America's Welfare Failure* (Armonk, N.Y.: M.E. Sharpe, 1982), pp. 81, 192.
7. *Social Security Bulletin, Annual Statistical Supplement, 1981* (Washington, D.C.: Government Printing Office, 1982), p. 247.
8. Ibid., pp. 224–25.
9. Ibid., p. 247.
10. Ibid., p. 249.
11. Ibid., p. 245.
12. Ibid., pp. 242–44.
13. U.S. Senate, Select Committee on Nutrition and Human Needs, *Legislative History of the Select Committee on Nutrition and Human Needs* (Washington, D.C.: Government Printing Office, 1976); Nick Kotz, *Hunger in America: The Federal Response* (Chicago: Field Foundation, 1979);

Citizens' Board of Inquiry into Hunger and Malnutrition in the United States, *Hunger, USA,* (Boston: Beacon, 1968). *Legislative History,* cited above, includes a wide variety of documents and reports from non-governmental as well as governmental sources related to the anti-hunger campaign.

14. "Food Stamp Costs Head for $10 Billion Mark," *Congressional Quarterly Weekly Reports,* 26 Jan. 1980, p. 192.

15. Kathryn W. Gest, "Major Food Stamp Overhaul Nears Approval," *Congressional Quarterly Weekly Reports,* 6 Aug. 1977, p. 1642.

16. Kotz, *Hunger in America.*

17. Matthew D. Slater, "Going Hungry on Food Stamps," *Social Policy* Jan.-Feb. 1981, pp. 18–24; Elin Schoen, "Once Again, Hunger Troubles America," *New York Times Magazine,* 2 Jan. 1983, pp. 21–23.

18. *Social Security Bulletin, Annual Statistical Supplement, 1981,* pp. 220-21.

19. U.S. Congress, Congressional Budget Office, *Catastrophic Health Insurance* (Washington, D.C.: Government Printing Office, 1977); National Council of Organizations for Children and Youth, *America's Children 1976* (Washington, D.C.: Government Printing Office, 1976), pp. 44–46; U.S. Congress, House, Subcommittee on Oversight and Investigation, *Department of Health, Education and Welfare's Administration of Health Programs: Shortchanging Children* (Washington, D.C.: Government Printing Office, 1976); and U.S. Congress, House, *Hearings Before the Subcommittee on Health, July 1976* (Washington, D.C.: Government Printing Office, 1976), pp. 172–75. For a more recent evaluation, see Edith M. Davis, Michael L. Millman and Associates, *Health Care for the Urban Poor: Lessons for Policy* (Totowa, N.J.: Littlefield, Adams, 1982).

20. See Frances Fox Piven and Richard A. Cloward, *Regulating the Poor: The Functions of Public Welfare* (New York: Pantheon, 1971), chaps. 6–10, for a detailed analysis of the welfare "explosion" of the 1960s as a response to the urban revolt. A more orthodox view of the increase in welfare payments was expressed by David M. Gordon, "Income and Welfare in New York City," *The Public Interest,* 16 (Summer 1969): 64–88. "One can easily argue that the cause of the welfare 'crisis' is simply the widespread poverty in the city—not chiseling or welfare rights organizations or liberal administrative practices," (ibid., p. 87).

21. The foregoing estimates were based on federal guidelines for AFDC payments and food stamp allotments as they existed in January 1983.

22. "Michigan Standard of Need/Position Paper," (Lansing, Mich.: Michigan County Social Services Association, 9 Feb. 1983).

23. Morley D. Glicken, "Transgenerational Welfare Dependency," *Journal of Contemporary Studies* 10, no. 3 (1981):31–32.

24. Martha S. Hill and Michael Ponza, "Poverty and Welfare Dependence across Generations," *Economic Outlook USA* 4, no. 3 (1983):61–64.

25. U.S. Congress, Joint Economic Committee, Subcommittee on Fiscal Policy, *The Family, Poverty and Welfare Programs: Factors Influencing Family Stability,* Studies in Public Welfare, Paper no. 12 (Washington, D.C.: Government Printing Office, 1973).

26. Blanche Bernstein and William Meezan, *The Impact of Welfare on Family Stability* (New York: New School for Social Research, Center for New York City Affairs, 1975).
27. Greg L. Duncan et al. *Years of Poverty, Years of Plenty: The Changing Economic Fortunes of American Workers and Families* (Ann Arbor, Mich.: University of Michigan Institute for Social Research, 1983), p. 75.
28. Ibid., pp. 74–77.
29. Richard F. Muth, *Cities and Housing: The Spatial Pattern of Urban Residential Land Use* (Chicago: Univ. of Chicago Pr., 1969), pp. 14, 115–35, 241–83. The idea that AFDC payments provide a public subsidy to owners of slum properties is argued in Alice R. McCabe, "Forty Forgotten Families," *Public Welfare* 24, no. 2 (1966):159–71.
30. Piven and Cloward, *Regulating the Poor;* James Button, *Black Violence: Political Impact of the 1960s Riots* (Princeton, N.J.: Princeton Univ. Pr., 1978).

14. Business Enterprise in the Urban Ghetto

1. John Dominguez, *Capital Flows in Minority Areas* (Lexington, Mass.: Lexington Books, 1976), pp. 31–32.
2. The book was published by the Free Pr. in 1967.
3. Gunnar Myrdal, *Economic Theory and Underdeveloped Regions* (London: Gerald Duckworth, 1957), p. 308.
4. Timothy Bates, *Black Capitalism: A Quantitative Analysis* (New York: Praeger, 1973), chap. 2.
5. A. Holsey, "Seventy-Five Years of Negro Business," *The Crisis* (July 1938):241–42.
6. Cited in John McClaughry, "Black Ownership and National Politics," in *Black Economic Development,* ed. G. Douglas Pugh and William F. Haddad (Englewood Cliffs, N.J.: Prentice-Hall, 1969), p. 38.
7. *Guide to Federal Minority Enterprise and Related Assistance Programs, 1982* (Washington, D.C.: U.S. Department of Commerce Minority Business Development Agency), pp. 25–29.
8. Timothy Bates, "Effectiveness of the Small Business Administration in Financing Minority Business," *Review of Black Political Economy* 11, no. 1 (1981):326–34.
9. Timothy Bates and William Bradford, *Financing Black Economic Development* (New York: Academic Pr., 1979), pp. 139–40.
10. Timothy Bates, "Black Entrepreneurship and Government Programs," *Journal of Contemporary Studies* 4, no. 4 (1981):67–69.
11. Ibid., p. 68.
12. National Institute of Government Purchasing, "Minority Business Participation in State and Local Governments," unpublished manuscript, pp. 3–10.
13. Johnnie Roberts, "Threatening Boycotts, Jesse Jackson's PUSH Wins Gains for Blacks, *Wall Street Journal* 21 July 1982:1, 25.

14. Bates and Bradford, *Financing Black Economic Development*, chap. 9.
15. Timothy Bates and Antonio Furino, "The Viability of Minority Entrepreneurship in Non-Traditional Lines of Business," unpublished manuscript.
16. Robert S. Browne, "Cash Flows in a Ghetto Community," *Review of Black Political Economy* 1, no. 3 (1971):28.
17. Myrdal, *Economic Theory and Underdeveloped Regions*, p. 28.
18. "Playing it Safe: Critics Say Lenders Hasten Urban Decay by Denying Mortgages," *Wall Street Journal* 5 Apr. 1974:1.
19. Bates and Bradford, *Financing Black Economic Development*, chap. 3.
20. Ibid., chap. 6.
21. Timothy Bates and William Bradford, "An Anlaysis of the Portfolio Behavior of Black-Owned Commercial Banks," *Journal of Finance* 35, no. 3 (1980):764–67.
22. Our description of the Bedford-Stuyvesant Restoration Project rests heavily upon a paper by Otis Troupe, assistant to the president of the Restoration Corporation "The Bedford-Stuyvesant Restoration Project," in *Community Revitalization*, ed. Gerald Whittaker (Ann Arbor: Univ. of Michigan Pr., 1979), pp. 75–83.

15. Can We Solve the Problem?

1. Thomas Sowell makes the case for individualism and achievement within the framework of an equal opportunity system, adding the further argument that economic programs such as welfare payments weaken the drive toward achievement and hinder black progress. See his *Ethnic America: A History* (New York: Basic Books, 1981); idem, *Markets and Minorities* (New York: Basic Books, 1981); idem, *Race and Economics* (New York: McKay, 1975). An earlier version of this approach, which stressed the need for education in an era of much more restricted opportunity than today, was expressed by Booker T. Washington in *Up From Slavery: An Autobiography* (Boston: Houghton Mifflin, 1901); idem, *The Future of the American Negro* (Boston: Small, Maynard and Company, 1902); idem, *The Story of the Negro: The Rise of the Race From Slavery* (1909; reprint, New York: P. Smith, 1940); idem, *The Negro in the South: His Economic Progress in Relation to His Moral and Religious Development* (Philadelphia: G. W. Jacobs, 1907).
2. See Charles Brown, Curtis Gilroy, and Andrew Kohen, "The Effect of the Minimum Wage on Employment and Unemployment," *Journal of Economic Literature* 20, no. 2 (1982):487–528 for an extended and detailed review of the attempts to study the relationship between the minimum wage and unemployment.
3. For a more extended discussion of the proposal to raise the minimum wage as suggested here, see Daniel R. Fusfeld, "A Living Wage," *Annals of the American Academy of Political and Social Science* 409 (Sep. 1973): 34–41.

4. Dunbar S. McLaurin, "GHEDIPLAN, An Economic Development Plan Prepared for the Human Resources Administration of the City of New York," (New York: Human Resources Administration, 1968); Dunbar S. McLaurin and Cyril D. Tyson, "The GHEDIPLAN for Economic Development" in *Black Economic Development*, ed. William F. Haddad and G. Douglas Pugh (Englewood Cliffs, N.J.: Prentice-Hall, 1969), pp. 126–37.

5. Frank G. Davis, *The Economics of Black Community Development: An Analysis and Program for Autonomous Growth and Development* (Chicago: Markham, 1972).

6. The idea of a bank as a sheltering organization for a group of enterprises, providing expert planning and business services, is taken from the Mondragon group of producer cooperatives in Spain. The Caja Laboral (Worker's Bank) finances production by the cooperatives, using funds obtained from local depositors, and contracts with the cooperatives to provide business services, market studies, and other assistance. One of its important functions has been to organize new enterprises that supply inputs to existing cooperatives.

7. Davis, *Economics of Black Community Development*.

Index

Pages with tables appear in italics

275

New York City (continued)
Borough Park, 146–48;
Brooklyn, 232; draft riots, 17–
18; Freedom National Bank,
229; Harlem, 7, 16, 30, 34, 111,
148, 157, *158,* 166, 214; South
Bronx, 138, 166
New York State Joint Legislative
Committee on Crime, 166, 167
New York Times, 78
Nietzsche, Friedrich, 8
Nigeria, 60
1980s, 83, 112, 127–33, 134, 153,
208, 214, 223, 224, 234
1950s, 81, 109, 110, 112, 115–18,
183, 189; economics, 97, 120–
21; farm mechanization, 61, 64,
65; unions, 78, 79, 80; urban
migration, 52, 150, 153, 199;
welfare, 66
1940s, 50, 52, 61, 64, 65, 75, 78,
79, 109, 116, 119, 187, 189
1970s, 108, 112, 124–27, 153, 159,
179, 185, 192, 208, 218, 221,
223, 224, 232; blacks' incomes,
90, 104, 109, 183; education,
106; housing decay, 138;
unemployment, 132, 133, 210;
urban migration, 110; welfare,
192, 197, 200, 206
*1972 Survey of Minority-Owned
Business Enterprises,* 216
1960s, 7, 97, 108, 109, 119–24,
142, 150, 210, 211, 232, 237,
249; black capitalism, 214, 216,
224, 229, 231; civil rights, 134,
185; drugs, 167, 168; education,
106; employment, 83, 89, 125,
128, 173; housing decay, 138;
incomes, 104, 126, 183; poverty,
204, 205, 206; welfare, 153,
196, 197, 198, 207
1930s, 54, 55, 58, 61, 64, 67–68,
70, 74, 79, 80, 81, 158. *See also*
Great Depression
1920s, 8, 34, 45, 52, 54, 58, 59,
68, 86, 89, 98, 108, 124, 158,
188, 215

Nixon, Richard, 216
Norris-LaGuardia Act, 70
North, 8, 13, 25, 26, 33, 42, 74,
79, 89, 115, 116, 133, 188
North Carolina, 97, 127, 130, 132,
133, 188
Numbers racket, 166–67

Ohio, 95, 127, 130, 131, 132, 133
Oklahoma, 60, 61, 97
Omaha, Nebraska, 20
Order of Sleeping Car
Conductors, 69
Orientals, 225

Parker, Richard, 22
Parks, Rosa, 80
Pellagra, 53, 57
Pennsylvania, 95
Peoria, Illinois, 88, 141
Philadelphia, Pennsylvania, 14, 35,
38–39, 42, 48, 70, 93, 99, 111,
192, 223; Community Council,
39
Philadelphia Plan, 123
Pittsburgh, Pennsylvania, 16, 19,
20, 125, 134, 141, 146, 161
Pittsburgh Courier, 77
Piven, Frances Fox, 211
Plumbers' union, 70
Poles, 21
Politics, 5, 7, 16, 22, 60, 107, 138,
151, 152, 210, 211, 212, 216,
235, 238; blacks' role, 222, 248–
50
Pollution, 94
*Poor Pay More: Consumer Practices
of Low Income Families, The,* 214
Population, 1, 14, 25–26, 83;
black, 14, 16, 25–26, 28, *30, 49,*
50, 52, 101; farm, 65, *66;*
trends, 4, 5, 101, 152; urban, 9,
14, 25–26, *26,* 50, *66,* 84, 93,
99, 100, 101, 136–37, 140, 143,
146, 150, 153, 208
Port facilities, 4
Portland, Oregon, 50
Post Office, U.S., 34